W9-BZJ-080

Breakthrough/Прорыв

Emerging New Thinking

EDITORS - IN - CHIEF

Anatoly Gromyko • Martin Hellman

EXECUTIVE EDITORS

Craig Barnes • Alexander Nikitin

SENIOR EDITORS

Donald Fitton • Sergei Kapitza

Elena Loshchenkova • William McGlashan

Andrei Melville • Harold Sandler

Breakthrough/Прорыв

Emerging New Thinking

**Soviet and Western Scholars
Issue a Challenge to Build
a World Beyond War**

Walker and Company

720 Fifth Avenue, New York, NY 10019

134321

Breakthrough/Proriv Copyright © 1988 by Beyond War Foundation

All rights reserved. No part of this book may be reproduced or transmitted in any form or by any means, electronic or mechanical, including photocopying, recording, or by any information storage and retrieval system, without permission in writing from the publisher.

First published in the United States of America in 1988 by the Walker Publishing Company, Inc. Published simultaneously in Canada by Thomas Allen & Son, Canada, Limited, Markham, Ontario.

Designed by Albert Burkhardt, Burkhardt & Associates

Library of Congress Cataloging-in-Publication Data

Title.
Breakthrough: Emerging New Thinking

Includes references.
1. Nuclear arms control.
2. Security, International.
3. International relations.

I. Gromyko, Anatolii
Andreevich.

II. Hellman, Martin E.
JX 1974.7.B678 1988   327.1-74   87-23009

Breakthrough: Emerging New Thinking

ISBN 0-8027-1026-3

ISBN 0-8027-1015-8

Printed in the United States of America

10 9 8 7 6 5 4 3

Published simultaneously in the Soviet Union
by Progress Publishing Company, Moscow.

Dedication

To our children and grandchildren / Нашим детям и внукам

Contents

Global Thinking:

Vision for the Future

Process of Change:

Individual Action and Collective Transformation

Acknowledgements

PROJECT DIRECTORS

William Busse • Elena Loshchenkova

Without whose endless hours of dedicated assistance and direction this project could never have happened.

WESTERN TEAM

Daniel Beswick
Lyn Gardiner
Ruth Hodos
Grace Kietzmann
Richard Lagerstrom
Jackie Mathes
Joan Sandler
Wayne Smith

SOVIET TEAM

Olga Chuprina
Vladlen Kachanov
Galina Nickolopoulos
Olga Smirnova
Galina Tverskaya
Natalia Yampolskaya
Leonid Zhurnya

EDITING STAFF

Eleanor Anderson
Samuel Anderson
Ginger Ashworth
Donald Barnett
Valentina Batassova
Winston Boone
Diji Christian
Roger Colvin
William Copeland
Anna German
Roy Gordon

Gennady Gubanov
Fred Hall
David Hibbard
Michael Hodos
Lena Jakobson
Mikhail Kobrine
Olga Kurlandskaya
Heather Leitch
Sergei Levitin
Susan Levy
Alexandra Malig

Carolyn Said
Alexander Shkolnik
Jim Stanley
Len Traubman
Jerald Volpe
Amy Vossbrinck
Riley Willcox
Jeffery Zelickson
Natalia Zykova

A Message to the Scientific Community

Sergei P. Kapitza

Professor of Physics, Institute for Physical Problems, USSR Academy of Sciences and Moscow Physical-Technical Institute, working on the development and uses of electron accelerators; Vice Chairman, Committee of Soviet Scientists for Peace against the Nuclear Threat. Dr. Kapitza is a member of the World Academy of Arts and Sciences and moderator of a Soviet television program on science and society.

Martin E. Hellman

Professor of Electrical Engineering, Stanford University. Dr. Hellman is best known as the inventor of the "public key" and "trap door" cryptographic techniques. He is a Fellow of the Institute of Electrical and Electronics Engineers.

In the present state of world affairs, one of the major sources of disparity is the discrepancy between our scientific and technical progress and our level of societal and individual development. The magnitude of the forces we command today is such that mankind can alter the environment of the planet as a whole, as we are now doing. The subsequent emergence of global problems and the recognition of their importance is certainly one of the great intellectual events of our time.

Evolution

The future belongs to those with the ability to change. Those that cannot adapt to changes in the environment, die off. That simple, seemingly harsh demand has brought forth eagles and doves, elephants and sponges, humans and ants. From that evolutionary perspective, the challenge is seen not as harsh and unnatural, but as the essential driving force in realizing the human potential in the DNA of our primitive, single-celled ancestors.

Today, the evolutionary imperative applies to our species in a totally new way. A change in thinking is required for our physical survival. The magnitude of the physical forces that we command today is so great that we are altering the environment of our planet as a whole. Human damage to the ecosystem already has extinguished a large number of species and threatens all. The emergence of global problems and the recognition of their importance is perhaps the greatest accomplishment of contemporary thought. (1, 2)

Global Problems and the Nuclear Threat

Among the global issues we face are energy, natural resources, food, and water — and the threats to the planetary life-support system that occur in our attempts to meet these challenges. As important as these issues are, the nuclear threat must head any list of the global problems that threaten humanity.

Over the last forty years we have seen the world's arsenals grow to immense proportions. In destructive power, they are equivalent to 1 million Hiroshimas. Our planet itself has finally become too small for them. Apart from their sheer might, the intelligence and the deadly accuracy of these weapons have grown to an extraordinary extent. The Goliath of the bomb has joined forces with the David of microelectronics.

There is talk of expanding armaments into the realm of outer space, as if the sea and land of our globe were not enough. Detailed technical, scientific, and military analyses of this latest move have shown its fallacy. While the technical content of these analyses may be beyond the average person, the landing of a Cessna in the heart of Moscow by a lone West German pilot in May 1987 shows in common sense terms the futility of a perfect aerospace defense.

The further buildup of armaments gives no promise of increased security for any nation, much less for the world as a whole. In pursuing the outmoded concept of "a balance of power" as a guarantee of stability we have long passed the stage where the notion was applicable. The overkill of today's nuclear arsenals makes the concepts of "military parity" and balance of power meaningless. Deterrence, that dubious contraption of a balance of terror, finally shows its true colors. It no longer offers even the hope of security it might profess to provide at a lower level of armaments.

From a more general point of view, one may also consider the conflict that we are facing to originate from the conflict between the rational and irrational parts of human nature. In its most dangerous form, we see this in the supposed rationality of the scientific contributions to the arms race and the concept of deterrence, based on irrational fear and vengeance.

We have become trapped in a futile pursuit of supremacy, and the ever-increasing power of our armaments provides us with less and less security. In the looking-glass world of the arms race, the risk of an accident or an unforeseen loss of stability is growing ever more likely, both as a direct consequence of the supercharged level of our armaments and of the resultant trigger-happy frame of mind.

The Role of Thinking

We are forced to look elsewhere in seeking a way out of the race to oblivion. Not by a technological fix, nor by constructing bigger and better gadgets and rockets will we find a haven from the nuclear threat.

Making the analogy of our world to a computer, we have developed our hardware far beyond our software and, for the hardware of technology to be useful, we must now develop the software, our thinking. As with computers, the development of software now demands much greater effort than the buildup of hardware. To move from one societally sanctioned view of the world to another is not easy. An old set of "truths" gives way to a new paradigm begrudgingly.

The main feature of the new paradigm is clear: In global thinking, the interests of humankind as a whole take precedence over those of any one nation or any one group of people. None can survive without survival of the common life-support system that sustains us all. From the past, we can see how difficult it has been for the individual to recognize the need to surrender his more limited view in order for him to survive as part of a larger entity, be it his country, tribe, or class.

How to accept and respond to this challenge is in no way obvious. Which path are we to follow so as to provide a safe and secure world? How can we reach a new level of control and understanding, while at the same time preserving all that contributes to the dignity and freedom of the individual? These questions face us all and it is to these issues that we here address ourselves.

War and Nuclear War

If we keep having wars it is only a matter of time before one escalates out of control. So the real problem is not nuclear weapons and nuclear war, but all weapons and all war. Hints of this can be seen in the difficulty of fashioning an arms control agreement to eliminate nuclear-armed missiles from Europe. Fear that conventional war would break out thereafter is slowing progress on this important front. So long as we pretend that conventional war is still feasible, we will never eliminate nuclear weapons.

Do our nations still prepare for war? Do statesmen still consider war in the nuclear age to be "a continuation of politics by other means"? In spite of protestations and even beliefs to the contrary, the unfortunate truth is that both parties still do. The US and the USSR each have millions of men under arms, tens of thousands of tanks, thousands of fighter aircraft, and tens of thousands of nuclear weapons arrayed against each other. Although proclaiming the desire not to use them, each nation has plans at the ready to do precisely that. What is planned for, however contingently, can happen.

In spite of the tremendous destructive power of modern weapons, it is now more hopeless than ever to resolve social issues or those of national destiny by military means. The lesson of Vietnam is clear. Similarly, it is now recognized after seven years of a futile military effort, that the conflict in Afghanistan can only be resolved by political means.

On the positive side, the impossibility of war is beginning to be recognized in Europe. There has been no war on that continent for more time than ever before, and definitive steps have been taken toward military disengagement. This is encouraging for a region that twice in this century has been the origin of and battleground for world wars.

We recognize that ending all war is infinitely easier to say than to do and that no nation can unilaterally disarm in the current, very dangerous state of the world. So the challenge is to find an evolutionary path which brings us to that point. An important first step would be to recognize that we can no longer develop national security except as a consequence of common security.

The efforts of the leaders of our two nations, pioneered in Reykjavik, mark a significant move toward this goal. To them we owe a debt of gratitude for creating a fertile climate for cooperative projects such as this. It is our duty as scientists to take their initiative even a step further in exploring the path to a world without war.

Discovery and the Scientific Spirit

While the path is not yet clear, the method needed to discover it is well known: the scientific spirit, exemplified by a dedicated search for the truth, with a courageous disregard for commonly held beliefs when they are contradicted by observations. We have used this approach to discover the right paths into other unknowns — the design of the solar system, the structure of the atom, the makeup of our psyches.

As men and women of science, we have ventured, somewhat tentatively, into the more complex worlds of the human psyche and society. But it has been considered improper for those of us in the natural sciences to attempt to use the scientific spirit to bring about fundamental changes in the "unnatural sciences" of public opinion, politics, and international relations. But improper we must be. Science demands it of us if science, along with humanity, is to survive. This book marks an attempt to marshal some of the considerable resources of the international scientific community in the effort to build a world beyond war. Everyone has a life-and-death stake in this endeavor. So everyone has a responsibility to participate. As scientists, we cannot claim any special role other than that we earn by our involvement.

It is instructive to recall what was said by the founding fathers of modern science. (3) More than thirty years ago, Bertrand Russell wrote: "We have to learn to think in a new way. Remember your humanity and forget the rest. If you can do so, the way lies open to a new paradise; if you cannot there lies before you the risk of universal death." These passionate and wise words of the Russell-Einstein Manifesto, signed by Einstein on his deathbed and by other great scientists, have set the pattern for the thinking of many of us.

With the publication of the Russell-Einstein statement, the "Pugwash movement" of scientists came into being. For the first time, scientists from the East and the West engaged in a regular dialogue on matters of science, war, and peace. Strategic defense systems were first discussed at the Pugwash meetings of scientists before they were negotiated by statesmen and finally formulated in the 1972 ABM Treaty.

Another signpost from the early days of the nuclear era is the idea of the open world. This concept was first suggested and discussed at length by the great physicist Niels Bohr as early as 1944, and later propagated in his Open Letter to the United Nations in 1950.

Today, the very progress of science and technology has opened up the world in a remarkable way. Modern transportation has brought unprecedented mobility to people and goods — and bombs. Communication technology has produced the "global village" and much noise. Space technology has opened up the world to an extent unimagined before. The whole concept of national privacy as part of national sovereignty has gone: The sacred cow of military secrecy cannot conceal itself from the "eye in the sky." It is only a slight exaggeration that reconnaissance satellites can count the number of stars on a general's epaulets.

Unfortunately our social behavior, our mentality both on an institutional and personal level, seriously lags behind in its ability to face this new technology, this new world, this new openness. The US jealously guards its integrated circuits from the USSR, as if their possession or nonpossession would determine the winner in a war no one can win. The USSR forbids the taking of pictures from airplanes and tall buildings, as if they might affect a military outcome. Rather than adding to either nation's security, these manifestations of old thinking fuel the other side's fears that the first is preparing for war.

We often spend more effort to control information than spread it, to entertain rather than educate, to distort information to fit our worldview rather than vice versa. In spite of these human failings, information does flow increasingly freely. The latest, most dramatic, and most hopeful changes have been the Soviet Union's move, under its new policy of glasnost (openness), to a freer flow of information.

Historical Precedents

In choosing to speak out now, we act as inheritors of a proud tradition. Einstein, Bohr, and the Soviet geochemist and pioneer global thinker Vernadsky belonged to the brilliant generation that flourished during the first decades of our century, from 1900 to 1930. In that golden age, on a scale unknown since, we saw the emergence of new arts and new sciences: modern music and mathematics, literature and architecture, physics and biology. All these came into being, together with the new cosmology and the understanding of man himself.

These developments in science and the arts took place simultaneously with revolutionary developments in social conditions. While much, if not all, was arrested by the Great Depression and the advent of dictatorial regimes, the intellectual and artistic masterpieces of those years still set the pattern for our modern culture.

Scientists were not only pioneers in this century. The Renaissance in Europe five centuries ago is an example of an important change in mentality, a change in the very concept of the world in which we live. The discovery of a new world, America, enlarged the image of the planet much to its present dimensions; the ideas of Copernicus, Vesalius, and Galileo laid the foundations for the modern scientific approach; in the seventeenth century humanism and enlightenment explored new values and modes of thinking; the Protestant Reformation carried a redefinition of work and success. These are but some of the hardly coincidental changes introduced in rapid succession during that tumultuous period in European history. It was also a time marked by the Thirty Years War and by witch hunts. Discovery of new views of the world evoked, then, as now, a certain amount of fear.

To pass to times more connected to our age, the October Revolution in Russia and the thinking that then launched major social changes elsewhere should be seen as another example. The New Deal in the United States belongs to the same type of event, when new thinking was instrumental in changing the very fabric of society. Perhaps from a broader historical perspective we should view these changes in society as part of the transformation we are undergoing now under the impact of modern science and technology, as we recognize the vital importance of emerging global issues.

Historically, it has been customary to speak of the great disparities that split our world. Of these, the most noticeable is that of wealth and misery, which today divides the North and the South on a global scale. But here we would rather draw your attention to the disparity of things and ideas, between our material and cultural development. This dichotomy of "having" and "being" is fundamental to all the other dichotomies. It is in no way new. At present, however, we have reached such a state of affairs that it jeopardizes our very existence. Our world is too small, and the forces we command too large, to ensure our planet's survival into the indefinite future without our taking ultimate responsibility for our actions.

The Contribution of Scientists

We have rather impressionistically reminded you of these events and ideas because today we are at the crossroads. Our future, and the very existence of future generations, is at stake and our mettle as scientists, citizens, and human beings is put to the test.

As in the past, scientists today can contribute to improving international understanding. International collaboration of scientists helps both the progress of science and the betterment of the world. At the same time, it aids in establishing what the diplomats and military call confidence-building measures. Traveling professorships, exchange of students, postgraduate scholarships, and visiting scientists are the real traffic of scientific intercourse. However small the numbers, this is the way connections and friendships are built up, and channels of understanding are opened that can survive the drastic upheavals of modern history. Personal connections dating back to the Belle Epoque of European culture not only survived the Holocaust, but were instrumental in establishing the Pugwash meetings which deal with the nuclear threat. Similar personal friendships growing out of scientific collaboration laid the basis for this book.

Now large projects on plasma and high-energy physics, space exploration and radioastronomy, deep sea drilling, synchotron radiation, and mapping the human chromosome have added a new scale to international collaboration. We are all studying the same universe and all building a common world science. There is but one truth to be discovered, be it in Moscow or New York. Up to now, we have pooled our resources and intellect, but not in any dramatic respect changed our way of conducting research or using the universal truths discovered.

Dealing with global issues requires a qualitatively new kind of effort since these problems are not only international but interdisciplinary in their nature. From experience we know that the boundaries between scientific disciplines are often more difficult to cross than those which divide nations or separate the known from the unknown. These projects on global problems demand a new dimension for their conception, planning, execution, and implementation. Perhaps the last step is the most difficult of all, for here we are leaving the ivory tower of our professional interests as scientists and entering the real world of public relations, business, and politics. As examples of success in implementing this global approach, we may mention conventions relating to whaling, outer space, air traffic, and the law of the sea. In each of these the concept of a common heritage is emphasized. Thus we enlarge our vision and develop our thinking.

Change in the Soviet Union

While critically needed in every nation, this new thinking has special significance for the development of the Soviet Union. As a political entity the Soviet Union encompasses a variety of lands and people, and is now on a national basis experiencing many of the problems faced by the world as a whole. This modern crisis —

there is no other word to describe the situation — is to a great extent due to structural, if not political, disparities in technological and societal development.

In any nation, it is the human condition that suffers first from such disparities, be it due to a loss of economic efficiency, the degradation of the environment, or the menace of war and fear of extinction. This is fully recognized by the new leadership which now has the great task of changing the course and pattern of Soviet development. For Soviet citizens this national challenge is the most exciting and promising thing to happen over the past decades. The new openness pursued in the Soviet Union is helping to establish new values and to exercise new thinking. As with any great change, it will not be easy to achieve. The success of these fundamental changes depends on the extent to which this new way of thinking, these new ideas, can be conceived and broadcast to the public, and the degree to which they become part and parcel of the social consciousness.

Of utmost importance, and this applies to the West as well as the East, is how the mass media — those powerful instruments of social persuasion — can become instruments of positive change and serve the basic goals of society. Here an important contribution would be to destroy, rather than build up, the "image of the enemy," and to develop an atmosphere of hope and understanding. In a longer perspective, the changes and responses of the educational system, the way we teach and train the next generations, will be of even greater importance.

These changes in Soviet society will have repercussions well beyond the Soviet Union, not only because of the Soviet Union's sheer size, but because these changes are prompted by circumstances of a general nature.

The Challenge

History repeatedly shows that conspicuous consumption — be it in ancient Rome, the French monarchy, or tsarist Russia — is a precursor of revolution. Today, for the world as a whole, the arms race is conspicuous consumption in its most menacing form, and it signals that major changes are imminent.

The evolutionary imperative, once solely physical or solely intellectual, is now both. Old ideologies have once again outlived their usefulness. It has always been the role of science to explore and discover not only new machines but also to break through barriers of human thinking. It is the latter responsibility to which we now respond. Humanity will either change its thinking or it will die a physical death from misuse of its own technological genius.

As scientists, we are dedicated to the search for truth, however far from conventionally accepted beliefs it may lead us. As scientists, we are guardians of the great tradition set by Copernicus, Darwin, Einstein, Bohr, and other courageous men and women who broke with the mind-set of their day. Therefore, as scientists, we have an added responsibility to help society break with the current, dangerously inadequate mind-set.

Breakthrough/Прорыв

Emerging New Thinking

The Challenge to Change*

Editors

In this book, scholars on opposite sides in the world's two greatest armed camps have assembled evidence that war must end. The book is in three sections: the nuclear imperative, the global thinking which must replace war thinking, and the process of change. Each section contains its own "overview." While every contributor may not agree with every word which is contained here, the fact that all are willing to be published simultaneously in the Soviet Union in Russian, and in the United States in English, is itself evidence of a breakthrough in communication between these two diverse societies. The story of the project, itself, overcoming the difficulties posed by these two frames of reference, is discussed under the heading, "Writing This Book."

War is the issue.

War, and the root causes of war. War, which at any time could escalate to total holocaust, end billions of years of development of our life-support system, end all children, all culture, all love, and all life.

War is the challenge to the modern mind as the collapse of slavery and serfdom were the challenges for Americans and Russians a

---

* This section summarizes the key ideas of the articles in this volume and all of its references refer to these papers.

1

century ago. Today, the failure of war calls us to change our view of the world even more profoundly than the discovery that the Earth is round five centuries ago.

War is the issue for this generation. War, indiscriminate and brutal, which destroys the fragile civil processes it is designed to protect, wastes and ravages everything in its path, and twice in our century has decimated a generation of young men. War, which after a long evolution of its own, has come to its last chapter in human history.

War has been made obsolete by the total, suicidal, destructive power of nuclear weapons. It has been made obsolete by the gradually increasing consciousness that cannons cannot produce social justice; only justice can produce justice; only compassion can produce compassion; only brotherhood can produce brotherhood.

War is the issue for this generation, and global thinking is the challenge.

Compelled by the threat of a nuclear Armageddon, humans must now raise themselves to a new dimension, a new level of consciousness beyond war. They must move to a new and sunlit plain of human maturity. That is the challenge to change. It is a challenge to every human being to make a shift of evolutionary proportions.

The evidence is overwhelming that if we do not do this, the species will have a short tenure on this planet. Wars are raging in Central America, the Middle East, Afghanistan, Africa, and Ireland. The interests of the nuclear powers intersect in all the regions of the globe, and infect every small war with the potential to become the last, nuclear, war. No corner of this Earth is immune from great power interests, from war, or from the threat of war.

The book does not arise out of recrimination. There is no time for that. It is time to talk about mutual survival, physically, politically, and economically. Economics and politics are not off-limits here. But blame for the past is. This book is about the present and the way we can insure the future.

An effort such as this does not supplant what the leadership of the USSR and US has done at Geneva and Reykjavik, and which one hopes will continue in further meetings aimed at significant arms control negotiations. Such meetings and the proposed reductions of nuclear forces in Europe — an interim step — are a healthy sign. These writings are designed to support them and to urge those in leadership to continue and to accelerate their efforts.

The work to be done by this generation, however, is beyond arms control.

An unabashed passion for survival drove this project. It could not be summed up better than it was by the writer Ales Adamovich, of Minsk, who, as a young man of sixteen, fought with the partisans in his native Byelorussia, and who knows war from awful, personal experience: "We must change in every way. We simply have no other choice."

The Imperative

Nuclear explosives can be made with about one coffee cup of plutonium. This plutonium is being produced in the civilian power plants of thirty-six countries. By the year 2000, there will be enough plutonium in the world for at least 500,000 nuclear weapons. Someday, somewhere, a coffee cup full will be stolen, illegally sold, or taken by terrorists in a raid and made into a nuclear weapon by someone who is not bound by the treaties and customs of the civilized world. (1)

The rest is easier. The design and manufacture of nuclear weapons is not a mystery to the international scientific community. For the possessor of the material, turning it into a nuclear weapon that can be delivered by boat, train, or plane anywhere in the world would not be that difficult.

That such a detonation — in New York, London, or Moscow — would start an all-out nuclear exchange is not certain. But the risk is not negligible. This is one way that nuclear war could start.

There are numerous other ways.

As we come to the end of the twentieth century, an intricate web of security systems is tied together more tightly than was Europe on the eve of World War I. Today's complex warning and weapons systems observe and react to one another, they are intricately interconnected. In such tightly coupled systems a perturbation in one part is quickly amplified throughout the entire system. (2)

When one great power system makes a move, the other is programmed to respond with its own increase in readiness. This, in turn, is observed by the first. Whether or not the first country originally planned to prepare for war, it is programmed to respond to the new suspicious conduct of its adversary. Since nuclear missiles could arrive virtually anywhere in the world from either side within minutes of launch, the second country has no choice but to step up its readiness. A continuation of escalations is thus preprogrammed by the nuclear powers. Lack of time or opportunity for human intervention may allow the escalations to spiral within a short time, and in the end to lead to a nuclear exchange, although neither power may know the actual first cause. The system responses to each other may cause the war, independent of the original triggering event. (3)

It is a fearful parallel that at the beginning of World War I, interlocking mobilization plans developed a momentum of their own.

Today, interlocking warning systems carry the same potential, except that instead of requiring weeks to occur, they could escalate to planetary destruction within minutes.

A nuclear exchange could also be triggered by computer error. A flock of geese, a rising moon, a mismanufactured chip sets off an alarm, starts a series of computer-controlled events which humans have only minutes to intercept. False alarms happen on the average of almost three times a week in the US. It is reasonable to expect a more or less equal number in the Soviet Union. There were 1,152 "moderately serious false alarms" between 1977 and 1984, in US systems alone. (4)

To protect against unintended nuclear war, these systems have built-in redundancy. That is, there are systems to check on systems. There is also radar to check the readings of satellites, and satellites to verify the readings of radar, and if one does not confirm the other, then it is assumed there is no real attack. Nevertheless, the probability that satellite error will overlap radar error and create two wrong messages of missiles on the way cannot be at all excluded. (5) In today's nuclear systems, complexity is built upon complexity. The very complexity increases the probability of error. At some point computerized complexity does not increase security but decreases it. (6)

Computer error is so common and overlapping, computer error so within the realm of possibility, design error so untestable, and specification omissions so unknowable, that technology provides an unsafe rampart behind which to rest the future of humankind. Once missiles have been launched, or are suspected, there is no time for adequate intervention of human intuition, no deliberation time, no calling into play the values of generations of social development. The human mind which has been trained for millenia to understand the body language of physical threats is now faced with the probability of decisions about the future of civilization which must be made in minutes against no visible enemy. (7)

Minutes are not enough. But minutes are all that an incoming missile will allow. "Mr. President, Kosygin wants to talk to you . . . on the hotline," remembers former Defense Secretary Robert McNamara, about an incident that took place at seven-fifteen one morning: "What the hell do you mean?" asked President Johnson sleepily, and then, "What do you think I ought to say?" It was 1967, the Suez crisis, and Premier Kosygin was telling the president of the United States that if he wanted war, he would have it. (8)

Did Kosygin know that the president of the United States did not like to be awakened in the early morning? Did he know, whatever his purpose, whether morning or evening would be a good time to send the message? If the matter to be discussed included matters of war and peace, certainly that would be a prudent thing to know. Likewise, did President Johnson know anything of Kosygin? "Why don't we say you'll be down in twenty minutes," McNamara suggested in response to Kosygin's call. If missiles had been on the way toward the United States, twenty minutes would have been too long. There was a small chance that nuclear war had already started.

Security depends on people. People have to make the decisions. People in group situations act differently than they do individually. They very often give up their independent judgment, support a leader, go for consensus. Or, in tension, they get rigid, minds become paralyzed. Fear numbs, the mind fails to respond to new information. (9)

An example: At the time of the Bay of Pigs invasion of Cuba in 1962, the president's advisors knew that the Cuban resistance to the invasion would vastly outnumber the invaders, that the invasion had little chance. The objective reports also said that there was little to hope for in the way of a popular uprising of Cubans to support the invaders. But the president's advisors, and the president himself, ignored those reports. They were some of the best minds in the country; bright, informed, rigorous professionals. In the moment of decision, they operated as a group going for a goal with such enthusiasm that rationality was swept aside. They were acting in a way which we now know to be a natural and dangerous — and classic — group response to crisis. (10)

Neither rationality nor objective judgment is a dependable resource in crisis.

Institutional networks of military systems, one reacting to another, escalating the ante, computer error, design error, software inadequacy, redundant systems which add complexity to complexity; humans who react sleepily in the morning, or angrily in the night; all these add up to hurricane clouds on the horizon.

Terrorist attack, someone asleep at the switch, a leader reacting in frustration, none of these has by itself a very high statistical probability of causing nuclear war. But each has a probability of its own. Cumulatively, they all add up. Together, whether it be because of one cause or another, there are too many potential causes to ignore. Combined, the probability is so great that sooner or later the holocaust is certain. That is the danger. All together, there are too many causes. No matter how improbable each may be individually, the cumulative probability that one or another will lead to war is not small at all. It is absolutely certain if we continue in our present mode.

All these sources of risk stem from a single mind-set, the mind-set of war: War is possible, even acceptable, if need be. That mind-set breeds a multitude of preparations, no one of which is great in its risk, but which together make the risk overwhelming.

That is the new reality of the nuclear age.

Yet we plunge ahead, push the ships of state ever faster into a heading wind, ignore the warnings; redouble our weapons, plan weapons for the sky, radars to check radars, computers to check computers, hold the course. Steady the course, forward into the hurricane, dead ahead into the hurricane. On this course, the probability of nuclear war is what statisticians describe as "probability one." "Probability one-half" would be a 50 percent chance. Probability one is 100 percent. It is certain. (11)

That is the imperative. In the nuclear age if we do not respond to nuclear weapons by eliminating our reliance upon war, we will use them. Probability one. And if we use them, civilization — perhaps all life on this planet — will end. That is the challenge to change.

Global Thinking

. . . we ought to recognize each other's humanity, as we move to solve today's complex problems dealing with political relations, economics, and social life. (12)

The most important message is that changes in human values, modes of thinking, and visions of the future are needed for us to live more sustainably and harmoniously — indeed to survive — in an interdependent world. (13)

The nuclear imperative is the setting for modern times. It drives us to take account, to take inventory. It calls us to examine our fundamental perceptions concerning our loyalties and allegiances. It summons us to lift our sights. It provokes us to ask what we have learned in history which will put us on a safer course, and what we are learning from science which will provide for our security more surely than has war, or the mentality of war.

To get us out of the present situation, new thinking will have to be more than a slogan. It will have to take into account these new nuclear dimensions of human life as surely as did Copernicus's discovery that the Earth revolves around the sun. In the same way, new thinking will have to guide new conduct.

Global thinking begins with the beauty and the simplicity of the unity principle discovered by the cosmonauts and astronauts during their flights in space. (14)

"What strikes me, is not only the beauty of the continents . . . but their close-ness to one another . . . their essential unity." Yuri Gagarin (15)

"From where you see it, the thing is a whole, and it is so beautiful." Russell Schweickart (16)

There is one, unique, fruitful life-support system. All depend upon it. None can live without it. Men do not breathe differently in Omsk than in Omaha. If that is so, and surely it is so, then what damages the pure air for one part of the planet damages it for all. A nuclear reactor accident in one part of the world is an accident for us all. We are bound, beyond ideologies and religions, by an over-whelming number of common biological and physiological needs. (17)

In the old perspective, before one could see with the help of television and astronauts all the way around the whole globe and back into one's own soul, blame for any predicament could always be placed on the invisible enemy over the sea, or across the mountains, in some strange land. From the new perspective, from the eye of the spaceship, there is no far-off place. There are no far-off people. All war is civil war. All humans are partners in a common endeavor. (18) There is not some other place where people are responsible for ozone damage, or soil erosion, or injustice. In the new thinking, "everyone is responsible for everything." (19) "The new thinking requires a radical change . . . . It means basic altera-tions in everything we think and do. It involves assuming a feeling of personal and historical responsibility for everything on the planet." (20)

Such thinking produces a powerful change, and the promise of great improvement in the way we all treat each other.

To be "responsible," for example, means to avoid the conduct of lying. Stereotyping of another country, calling its people and lead-ers derogatory names, is deceitful and irresponsible. (21) "They" are not vicious animals who live on the other side of the ocean, they are people. Of course we are culturally and politically differ-ent. But there are limits to our differences; and we are more alike than was apparent, or was the fact, before the age of international travel and global communications.

It is simply not truthful to blame life's disadvantages, history's inequities, failures of our economic systems, or failures of our for-eign policies on any outside "enemy." It is simply not accurate to consider that all contradictions and conflicts among social groups and cultures can be explained by an evil which is found outside one's own society, but never inside. (22) The view of the planet as a whole produces a more unified, comprehensive picture, a profoundly important fundamental premise: We are all responsible. And there is a more profound opportunity. We all can help to solve any problem.

In the prenuclear world, before the global perspective, it would not have been so dangerous to be completely self-centered, or solely self-motivated. Today, that view transferred to nations has us on the brink of disaster. The view must shift to one which consistently responds to the question: What in the long run is best for everyone involved? And what are the means, consistent with that end, which I must choose? (23)

Thinking globally requires discovery of the right relationship between the individual and the global community. Neither is insignificant. There has to be a healthy relationship between the community, the social order, the whole, and the individual.

We are all different in that each human is an original. But we are tied together, in that there is one global system in which the activities of each of us affect the lives of each other. We are separate in that each of us treasures different cultural and family values. Between these two realities, the whole and the individual, there is always tension. When the right relationship exists, the tension is worked out so that both the whole and the parts are healthy. When the relationship is wrong, war and violence are efforts to resolve that tension by imposing unity, one nation imposing its view upon another.

For centuries, war has been increasingly less effective as a means to reconcile the tension between unity and diversity. At least that has been true since the Augsburg Treaty in 1555, when a long series of battles to impose religious unity in Germany failed. (24) The effort failed again during the Thirty Years War which ended in 1648. And the twentieth century has been replete with war's failure. Finally, in the nuclear age, war is utterly useless to resolve that tension. Large portions of the world have actually settled into a pattern of stable peace, a testament to the fact that war is accepted as unthinkable in those parts of the globe. (25)

The mind-set that, in a complicated world, one side can be eliminated is therefore totally obsolete. The new thinking must include, at a minimum, recognition of the reality that within global unity, diversity is a given. (26) The threat of nuclear war now backs us up against the wall and demands that we live with that paradox, because to deny it will kill us. The long-term parallel continuation of capitalist and socialist systems is a given. There will be both global unity and diversity. We are one human species. But we are also all different. Not only will there be long-term differences between capitalists and socialists, there will be differences between forms of socialism, and between forms of capitalism. (27) It is the destiny of this generation to determine how such differences will evolve by nonviolent means.

Humans don't have to like each other, or even understand one another, to cooperate. Soldiers in the trenches in World War I — who were conditioned to hate each other, and ordered by their commanders to fire at each other on sight — often stopped firing at dinner time. They just stopped. They let each other get up out of the trenches and go behind the lines and eat. Not just a few times, but regularly. When soldiers had been in one place in the lines opposite each other for a long time, they began to act differently toward each other. When they expected to be in those same trenches indefinitely into the future, it made sense for each side to ease up a little on the other, if the treatment was reciprocated. Both would live longer. Under those conditions, they evolved their own rules. They started to evolve civilization, while above and behind them commanders continued to push for noncooperation. (28)

The soldiers discovered that cooperation evolves when the parties expect to be in a relationship — even if adversarial — for some time. They are nicer to each other when they expect to meet again — as the soldiers in World War I expected to meet again the very next morning. And they are nicer when they are dependent upon each other to survive. The parallel is clear. Nations which expect to do business again will learn to cooperate. *Acceptance of long-term coexistence between capitalists and socialists is a precondition to cooperation, and an essential ingredient of global thinking.*

Faced with the expectation of a long-term future together, it is simply common sense for all sides to keep the ends and means consistent. (29) Repeated contacts will go better if that is so. Faced with a common future, it also pays to take care to preserve food and resources for future generations. (30) The vision of global thinking is therefore of people who are dependable, interested in cooperation and right conduct, and caring. They are this way not because they are exhorted to be so, or bound by duty, ideology, or religion, but because it is human nature to find that way when the necessity demands. And — threatened by nuclear extinction — necessity now demands the highest level of exertion and consciousness.

There is a discipline imposed by the goal of coexistence. There are requirements. Humankind is at the crossroads. We must choose. Something must be decided for, something left behind. (31)

If we choose mutual survival, unilateral security is a concept to be left behind. (32) From Nicaragua to the Middle East, from Grenada to Afghanistan, the military powers have sometimes acted as if they could decide independently what should be the course of Third World development. But development cannot be controlled by capitalist, socialist, rich, or poor states alone.

In a totally mixed and interdependent world, where no nation is free to take unilateral action, security can only be multilateral, universal. "Security in the nuclear age means security for all." (33) Which means that there can be no "just" war. Not of any kind, for any purpose. Not anymore. "The superpowers must take this into account as they presently engage in small wars such as those in the Persian Gulf, Afghanistan, Nicaragua, Iran-Iraq, and Africa," says resistance fighter of World War II Ales Adamovich.

It is the diversity of interests and systems which is the source of strength for the peoples and economies of the globe. The doctrines of exclusive interest, messianic doctrines that only one politico-economic system has the right to exist, are a thing of the past.

> *... it is impossible to export revolution. Revolutionary transformation cannot take place unless favorable conditions exist inside that society. Rejecting the aggressive messianic approach is consistent with this understanding. To go out with aggressive messianic fervor and try with force to impose revolution upon other societies against the will of the people won't work.* (34)

This then must be included in new thinking: Dogmatic arrogance and messianic fervor, whether capitalist or socialist, are no longer realistic. "Following the past is far from realism." (35)

The overwhelming experience of this century is that war is obsolete. It failed to solve the distribution and equity problems that preceded World War I. It failed to achieve an empire for Hitler, or for the Japanese. War in this century has not quelled the cries of the cultures, the languages, the religions of the globe for expression through democracy and economic well-being. Nor is it working now in Central America, in Afghanistan, in the Middle East, in Africa, nor in Ireland. War is a blunt and brutal tool. War thinking is the opposite of new thinking.

"New thinking," concludes Professor Anatoly Gromyko, "stands for a process where we ought to recognize each other's humanity . . . . We live on the same planet Earth, our common home . . . . it is impossible to secure a unilateral advantage for oneself to the detriment of the other side without ultimately impairing one's own interests." Gromyko quotes from Leo Tolstoy:

> *Misinterpreters of the truth usually say that reason can't be trusted because it speaks differently in different men . . . . But such a claim is quite the opposite of the truth. Reason never speaks differently. It*

always speaks alike in all men . . . . Whether God is said to have appeared in a pillar of fire, or Buddha to have ascended on sunrays, or Mohammed to have flown to the heavens, or Christ to have walked on water . . . rational men, always and everywhere answer in a similar manner: This isn't true. But, to the questions "Is it right to do unto others as you would they do unto you? Is it good to love and forgive them, do good to them?" The reason of all men throughout time has said: "Yes, it's right and worthwhile." (36)

Humankind is on the move, emerging from a chain reaction of cause and effect that stretches back for billions of years. Now this species has the power to affect its own evolution by conscious choice.

The choice is not one which can be built upon fantasy or utopian hope about war. But the choice, if it is made, can have a solid foundation. It can be built upon a confidence in the capacity of the human to be responsible, the will of the human to do right when to do so is required to survive, the experience of each human with every alternative to ending war, the love of the human for home, and the recognition — which is the hallmark of this century — that this whole planet is now home.

The Process of Change

We are at a threshold, not only because of the nuclear threat, but because our planet is circled by unprecedented new means of communication. The people know more now than ever before. Radios, televisions, computers, telephones, and copiers have spread across the globe in a century. No generation ever had these to add to newspapers, magazines, and the arts. Ours is a time of unlimited possibility for exchange, interaction between cultures, travel, and learning.

Such communication gives us an opportunity as big as the challenge. Where there are pockets of people who are not aware, we should not hide the facts from them, but begin the process of making the facts known. (37) Awareness of the need for change can be furthered by leadership, and it can be spread by the mass media. (38) Democratization in the USSR and building public support in the US are essential. Openness is crucial. (39) Most importantly, the spread of a new idea depends upon building connections among people who have the new information. People listen to their peers. (40)

Everything we know about the human tells us that the species has the capacity for change. That is why we are alive and well in Siberian cold and Arizona heat, in Moscow highrises and in Sierra high valleys. Although no two nations start in the same place, culturally or socially, the capacity for adaptation and change is present everywhere.

The Soviet Union is now engaged in one of the most intensive efforts to bring about change in its history. "Glasnost" and "perestroika," openness and restructuring, are intimately related. The movement of Soviet society toward decentralization is revolutionary. (41)

There are multicandidate elections going on at local party levels, elections of managers in factories, multicandidate elections for local soviets. There are newspapers engaging in criticisms of officials as part of the new democratization. There are plans to introduce cost and price accounting into state enterprises, to decentralize the economy, and to release new creative and competitive impulses. (42) Such moves have been deliberately made to involve the people. Without their help and widespread democratization there is no hope for the next step forward in growth and modernization of Soviet society. Without strong support by the people, there can be no hope of economic rebirth. (43)

In the US the challenge is the reverse of that in the USSR. It is to form consensus, to convince millions to come to a common view, and to act upon it. In the US, innovators who are the first to take on a new idea, are often not opinion leaders. But, as a strategy to build consensus, the innovators must find a way to reach the opinion leaders and through them, the majority. The idea of a world beyond war must be broadly publicized, networks of working volunteers must be assembled, personal relationships built with new people who have not thought about the subject before. (44)

For Americans, the problem is to consolidate a constituency from 250 million separate, independent-minded building blocks. When that can be done, as it was done in support of the ABM treaty, for example, changes in US–USSR relations have been possible. (45)

There is, therefore, a constant challenge to the people of the US to exercise the democratic rights they have. There is an important and revolutionary effort being made in the USSR today to learn democracy. In each case, change depends upon engagement of people. (46)

What will cause people to decide about war? What will cause them to fix on the highest goal of all, the goal of survival of life?

"Activity and talking," says Academician Natalia Bekhtereva, of Leningrad, quite simply. "The social process," meaning the conversation between peers or networks of friends, says Professor Everett Rogers of Los Angeles.

In inactivity, we can be numbed into accepting the probability of nuclear war and continue to do nothing. Depression can under-stimulate or fear can overstimulate the mind; in either case it will function less well. It can settle into a pattern of low function, which is ineffective, tolerant of impending trouble. The cure? Talking about the problem.

It seems too simple a place to start. The process of change, of course, depends upon thinking. Obviously, the mind needs information, must distill and weigh facts, cannot decide on intuition alone. But the studies of the human mind in the USSR and the subsequent study of the social process done in the US reinforce one startling conclusion: merely having the information and dwelling upon nuclear facts in silence can be a depressing trap. To engage the discouraged mind, it helps to start talking. Talking is itself action. Talking heals the mind. Talking is taking the initiative. (47)

Activity directed toward the source of negative emotion can be especially effective. Large numbers of people engaged in discussions and actions to prevent the extension of the arms race and the extinction of humanity would help assure the creativity and the goodwill to achieve a world where humanity's survival is assured. (48)

It may be of profound significance to realize that it is the activity, the talking, or the discussion, which accomplishes the change of mind.

Mass media channels are more effective in creating knowledge of innovations, while interpersonal channels are more effective in forming and changing attitudes toward an innovation and thus in influencing the individual's decision to adopt or reject the innovation . . . . Diffusion [of an idea] is essentially a social process, involving social relationships among individuals in a system. (49)

It is not so clear therefore, as one might have imagined, that the change of mind precedes the talking. Rather, the engagement in the issue is itself a factor in the change of mind. Knowledge, awareness, must precede the change of mind. But the knowledge, by itself, is insufficient. Even with the knowledge, the brain may achieve a stable pathological state, may decline into psychic numbing. To break out requires more than a minor perturbation. We must take the knowledge to the step of action and verbalization if it is to become an idea which is held with conviction. (50)

Nothing is as important, therefore, to the psyche of the individual as participation. Participation is required not only for good government, but also to preserve one's own sense of well-being. And the sense of well-being overcomes the feeling that an individual is powerless to make a difference. (51)

The challenge in both countries is to find citizens who will move the world across a phase boundary from unstable to stable peace. (52) It can be done. The requirement to make it happen is to act:

Act, by getting the information, making a decision about war. Act, by making the ends and means in personal and national conduct consistent. (53) Act, out of moral commitment, in excess of what even law requires. (54)

Act, by talking about the problem, engaging it, vigorously embracing it. (55) Act, by talking to one's neighbors, peers, friends, building networks of discussion. (56)

Act, by battling stereotypes and resisting the temptation to form images of the enemy. (57) Act, by telling the truth to children. (58) Act, through a love of our fellow man. (59) Act, by accepting strangers and diversity between systems and cultures as a given, a benefit, a strength of life on planet Earth. (60) Act, by insisting that the psychology of the nuclear age be reoriented, changed, faced about to become a psychology of survival. (61)

Act, by proposing and encouraging new standards of conduct, building security "regimes," as they are called, customs of civility between nations. (62) Act, by insisting upon reality as the basis for security calculations, calling truth to bear on the spiraling arms race. (63)

Act, by breaking through the temptation to hide behind old ideals, as an excuse for inaction. Think, as if in the moment of death, about the seriousness of the human condition, and do not be satisfied with any separation between the real and the ideal in one's own life. Act, to put our ideas for the future into practice today. (64) Act, as if in the moment of death, with a passion and fire in the belly. Act, because all of life depends upon overtaking and halting the momentum of war, and all the generations to come and all the generations we remember, all literature, all love, all art, all humor depend upon men and women of passion speaking truthfully and forcefully. (65)

Act, by building an arms control constituency, an informed, constructive, politically aware public to be reckoned with by all governments, everywhere. (66)

Act, in any of these ways. But act. Acting will change the mind. And changing the mind is the key to more action, and more action is necessary to end war. An aroused public, firmly possessed of a new idea, is itself a material force. (67)

The challenge to change is to act. The dream, bigger than any other, is to act as individuals who have chosen a new and higher level of human consciousness. Prevention of war is the imperative. Global thinking is the response. The individual is the engine of change. And survival can be the outcome.

— The Editors

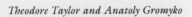
Boris Raushenbakh and Martin Hellman   *Stanislav Roshchin*

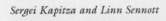
Theodore Taylor and Anatoly Gromyko   *Sergei Kapitza and Linn Sennott*

Inevitability
Collision Course with Disaster

OVERVIEW

Institutional Collapse

World War I was a disaster waiting to happen. An intricate network of interlocking alerts and mobilization plans required only a minor incident to trigger an uncontrollable political and military chain reaction. Today, the construction of fantastically complex nuclear command organizations in the US and the USSR parallels the interlocking military institutions built in the decade before 1914. Today's systems are sophisticated, tightly coupled, and quick reacting, so that the effect of a small perturbation can be amplified throughout the entire nuclear force system. The US and the USSR have thus institutionalized a system with a propensity for rapid escalation toward nuclear war. ("Instabilities in the Control of Nuclear Forces," Paul Bracken)

Computer Error

Today's nuclear forces could not function without high-speed computers to automate the warning process, control communications, and should it be deemed necessary, guide missiles to their targets. But computer systems can and do fail. Hardware, software, and design failures are common. Computers used in nuclear command and control are not only exceptionally complex but cannot be tested under conditions of actual use.

Reasonable attempts to protect against failure by adding redundancy and backup actually add complexity on top of complexity, compounding the probability of malfunction. ("Computer System Reliability and Nuclear War," Alan Borning)

Overlapping Errors

With three nuclear false alarms in an average week, it is unlikely that a single false alarm will cause a nuclear war. They are too routine. But their high rate of occurrence creates a significant chance for overlapping false alarms which can be much more dangerous. To protect against a single system failure, both the US and the USSR require independent verification of an attack by satellite and radar systems. The probability, however, of overlapping false alarms in these two systems, triggering a nuclear war, is surprisingly high. ("Overlapping False Alarms: Reason for Concern?" Linn I. Sennott)

Instabilities in Systems without Error

There is a dangerous instability in computerized defense systems even if they are working perfectly. One can assume that all the nuclear warning software works without error, and that the hardware is fail-safe. Nevertheless, the combination of two such correctly functioning systems together is unstable. This is because secrecy prevents either system from knowing exactly what the other is doing, which means that any input which could be interpreted as a danger signal must be responded to by an increase in readiness on the receiving side. That readiness change, in turn, is monitored by the opposing side which then steps up its readiness, and so on. This feedback loop triggers an escalating spiral. There is therefore the possibility of an entirely unprovoked attack triggered by the interaction of two perfectly operating computer-based systems. ("Computer War," Boris V. Raushenbakh)

Human Error

To err is human in the best of times, but in times of crisis, it is quite likely. The evolution of our species has not prepared us for making extreme-risk decisions in ultra-short time frames, yet this is precisely what must be done when indication is received, right or wrong, of a nuclear attack. The brain functions poorly when understimulated, as in constant, repetitive monitoring at a missile silo or on a submarine which has been months at sea. On the other hand, high tension, which in the event of a sudden alert can follow immediately on the heels of boredom, can produce temporary mental paralysis. Further, group thinking is also highly unreliable when the stakes are high and the time pressure intense. Illusions of invulnerability and moral superiority promote irrational decision making. ("To Err Is Human: Nuclear War by Mistake?" Marianne Frankenhaeuser)

Rationality in Crisis?

When the chips are down and the pressure is intense, groups tend to act with increasing conformity. Independent judgment is forfeited for the sake of consensus, and the role of the leader is exaggerated for the sake of loyalty. The need for speed compromises the search for objective facts. These factors operated when President Kennedy and his normally brilliant advisors decided to support the disastrous 1961 Bay of Pigs invasion of Cuba. The risk of accidental nuclear war also depends on over 100,000 people who have contact with nuclear weapons, a surprising number of whom have been found to be dependent on alcohol or drugs. Human beings, whose rational behavior is counted on to provide the final and decisive check to prevent an unintended nuclear war, are — especially in that moment of profound tension — often irrational. ("The Myth of Rationality in Situations of Crisis," Einar Kringlen)

Denial of Threat

Surveys of young people in the US show that a significant number fear nuclear war. In the USSR the proportion is not quite as high, but still significant. Dreams, marriage, family, and career plans, all can be colored by this fear. Perhaps an even more serious danger is the denial among those who do not register the threat. ("Young People and Nuclear War," Stanislav K. Roshchin and Tatiana S. Kabachenko)

Proliferation

It is not hard to learn how to make nuclear weapons, nor are they difficult to manufacture and assemble. The knowledge is widespread. The most difficult part of the process is making, or obtaining, the nuclear material. Safeguards are designed to keep such materials from spreading, being sold on the international market, being stolen, or being taken in terrorist raids. The worldwide spread of civilian nuclear power reactors, however, has produced "latent proliferation," the ability to produce nuclear weapons in short order, in over thirty countries. By the year 2000, there will be enough plutonium from such reactors for at least 500,000 nuclear weapons. The spread of such material and the low level of security which is possible in multiple locations substantially increases the probability that the materials will be accessible by states or individuals who do not agree to be bound by nonproliferation treaties or any other international guarantees. ("Proliferation of Nuclear Weapons," Theodore B. Taylor)

The Cumulative Probability

There is only a small likelihood that any one of the causes of nuclear war which have been described in these chapters will trigger nuclear war. The probability can be compared to risks associated with "pistol roulette" in which one chamber of a many-chambered gun is loaded, the cylinder spun, the gun put to the head, and the trigger pulled. Each time the trigger is pulled, there is only a small chance that the gun will go off. But if the trigger is pulled often enough, the probability approaches certainty that the gun will eventually fire. Whether from the escalation of interlocking war mobilization plans; whether from human error, or group dynamics and the lack of independent judgment in time of crisis; whether from computer error, or computers functioning correctly but in an escalating feedback loop; or whether because of nuclear proliferation by states or by terrorists who have obtained the materials illegally, if we do not change our course it is inevitable that nuclear weapons will eventually be used. The only way to alter the inevitability is to change the mentality which is the source of all these factors, that is, to eliminate the mentality of war. ("Nuclear War: Inevitable or Preventable?" Martin E. Hellman)

Instabilities in the Control of Nuclear Forces*

Paul Bracken

Professor of Public Policy and Political Science, Yale University. Author of the highly popular book, *The Command and Control of Nuclear Forces*, Dr. Bracken specializes in international security issues. He is a member of the editorial boards of the *Journal of Conflict Resolution*, *Orbis*, and *Defense Analysis*.

No single dictator, no single event pushed Europe into war in 1914. But during the preceding decade, motivated by various political and economic self-interests, the nations of Europe had institutionalized the potential for catastrophe. They had built interlocking alerts and mobilization plans that, once triggered, swamped and outran the political control process. It was a disaster waiting to happen.

The lesson from the outbreak of World War I is that a nation's actions in a crisis are profoundly influenced by the defense institutions built years before the crisis occurs. The construction of fantastically complex nuclear command organizations in the US and the USSR has created an extremely volatile situation, but on a far more spectacular and quick-reacting scale. A review of today's nuclear command organizations, and their governance, is clearly in order.

---

* This article is adapted from Paul Bracken's book, *The Command and Control of Nuclear Forces*, copyright 1983 by Yale University, New Haven. The reader is referred to the book for further reading and for documentation on specific facts. Reprinted by permission.

Warning System Reliability

Warning systems are an important part of the command and control of nuclear forces. They help protect vulnerable strategic weapons, such as bombers and missiles, against surprise attack. If one country knows that the other has an effective warning system, it is less likely to attack in the first place and the world is more stable as a result.

More sophisticated warning may therefore mean better security — but not always. During the past twenty-five years, both the US and the USSR have made immense investments to build highly complex warning systems. The sophistication of these systems, and their interconnection, have advanced in a manner that defies comprehension. And that may be the heart of the problem. With these systems tightly coupling the nuclear arsenals of each side, the effect of small perturbations is amplified throughout the entire nuclear force system.

"During the past twenty-five years, both the US and the USSR have made immense investments to build highly complex warning systems. The sophistication of these systems, and their interconnection, have advanced in a manner that defies comprehension."

The average person seems to realize, or at least intuit, the possible danger. Since the early 1950s, the specter of nuclear war by technical accident has been a pervasive theme of popular novels and movies. The story from the 1950s, of a flock of Canadian geese that triggered the Distant Early Warning Line radar system into mistakenly interpreting the event as an attack by Soviet bombers has been enshrined in the lore of the nuclear age. As warning systems became more sophisticated, variants of the episode inevitably followed. In 1960, meteor showers and lunar radar reflections, rather than Canadian geese, excited the new Ballistic Missile Early Warning System (BMEWS) radar, temporarily leading the North American Aerospace Defense Command (NORAD) to believe that a Soviet missile attack was en route. In 1980, a 46¢ computer chip failed in the computer warning system, producing an image of a Soviet submarine-launched ballistic missile (SLBM) attack on the US. While information is not available on Soviet false alarms, it is reasonable to assume that they have had similar experiences.

Official reaction to these false alarms tends to be defensive: Corrective actions are taken to prevent repeated accidents; nobody, including the military, wants accidental war; the system has been designed to make sure that the decision to go to war is not driven by a flock of geese or a defective computer chip. These arguments seem persuasive. Man is always in the decision loop; positive control is exercised at every point. I am convinced of the validity of these propositions at the intellectual level at which they are offered.

Yet, there is a latent fear. Intuition and common sense tell us that all is not well. Broadly speaking, people believe in Murphy's law: "If anything can go wrong it will." They believe it because it applies to the world of experience, and it applies with special force to large, technically complex systems. In the world in which people live, power grids fail, trains derail, bridges and dams fall down, DC-10 engines fall off, and nuclear power plants come close to meltdown. These things don't happen often, but they do occur.

A 1965 power failure in the American Northeast was traced to a single inexpensive switch. It was said repeatedly after 1965 that such a cascading power blackout could never occur again, since the freak accident had been carefully considered in new designs based on the lessons of 1965. But it did happen again, in 1977, in New York.

Engines fell off an inspected DC-10 airplane, leading to public outcry, high-level attention, and lawsuits. Even after repeated warnings, the same type of engine fell off the same type of plane two months later. Similarly, the cargo doors of the DC-10 blew out, not once but three times. Ultimately, the blown-out cargo doors caused a plane crash with major loss of lives.

The nuclear power plant failures at Three Mile Island in 1979 and Chernobyl in 1986 came after innumerable engineering studies had been made on the safety of these plants. Nuclear power experts had claimed that getting hit by a meteor was far more likely than a major nuclear plant accident, in retrospect clearly an invalid analogy.

"In the world in which people live, power grids fail, trains derail, bridges and dams fall down, DC-10 engines fall off, and nuclear power plants come close to meltdown. These things don't happen often, but they do occur."

When an expert states that a flock of geese or a lunar radar reflection will not trigger the automatic launch of a nuclear weapon, he or she is making a particular remark about a single system, a particular possibility. Our intuition, on the other hand, takes the flock of geese triggering World War III as an example of a wider concern. In the world of experience, we feel complex systems are bound to go awry precisely because they are complex.

Power blackouts, DC-10 failures, and nuclear power station accidents reinforce our intuitive concerns. In each of these examples, it was not the isolated accident that led to trouble, but a series of compound, and highly correlated events, which triggered a sequence of human, bureaucratic, and technical reactions. These reactions resulted in incorrect diagnoses of what was going wrong, which led to the initiation of actions that either had nothing to do with the problem or, even worse, exacerbated it.

Multiple Errors

Discrete accidents are easy to design against. The flight of geese, the lunar radar reflection, and the imperfect computer chip are all isolated events. With so many checks and balances overlaid onto the control system for strategic weapons, the likelihood of accidental or inadvertent war from a single failure is very, very low in peacetime. Each layer of the warning and intelligence system inspires new checks, new balances, and new authentication procedures. Against the discrete accident, malfunction, or operator error, the total system is massively redundant. I believe the likelihood of nuclear war due to a single failure is much lower today than it was twenty-five years ago precisely because of today's more complex warning and control system.

Multiple errors or malfunctions are a different matter altogether. The problem with compound accidents, especially those involving human behavior, is that the number of possible reactions is enormous and no design can protect against all of them. The likelihood that multiple events will lead to trouble increases when there is increased military activity. Thus, when forces are placed on alert, the complexity of the warning system may not only cease to provide redundancy; it may also amplify the mistakes.

What set off the interlocking alerts of the European armies in 1914 was not the isolated assassination of the archduke in Sarajevo but the decision to mobilize. The effect of the thousands of orders issued was to create an unstoppable chain reaction of reinforcing alerts. The alerts acted like ratchets, step-by-step moving Europe into war but unable to function in reverse toward peace.

"In the world of experience, we feel complex systems are bound to go awry precisely because they are complex."

In the summer of 1914, everything functioned the way it was supposed to. There were no accidents in the usual sense of the term. Political leaders lost control of the tremendous momentum built up when their armies went on alert. The institutions designed to protect the peace moved the nations of Europe into war. It pays to examine some implications of this theme for the nuclear forces of today.

Tight Coupling

A major element in the evolution of both American and Soviet warning systems has been their thoroughgoing integration with the command and control of nuclear weapons themselves. The result is a tightly coupled system in which a perturbation in one part can, in short order, be amplified throughout the entire system. The greatest single change in nuclear forces during the past twenty-five years is this shift from loose to tight coupling. (See Raushenbakh's paper in this volume for an analysis of the danger from a control theory point of view.)

Two false alerts, in 1979 and 1980, illustrate the strong interconnectedness between warning and weapons systems. In the first, an operator mistake led to the transmission of an erroneous message that the US was under nuclear attack. This information was sent to NORAD fighter bases, and ultimately ten fighters from three separate bases in the US and Canada were scrambled and sent airborne. American missile and submarine bases across the nation automatically switched to a higher level of alert.

"In the summer of 1914, everything functioned the way it was supposed to. There were no accidents in the usual sense of the term."

Several months later, in 1980, a failed chip in a minicomputer led to the transmission of a similar message to American forces. This time about a hundred B-52 bombers were readied for takeoff, as was the president's emergency aircraft. The airborne command post of the American commander in the Pacific took off from its base in Hawaii.

These incidents suggest some of the problems of a tightly coupled nuclear force and also illustrate how different nuclear forces are from conventional armies, navies, and air forces. For conventional armies, the key to survival was loose coupling. A part of the force could be sacrificed to save the whole. For nuclear forces, however, everything affects everything else. A seemingly small threat in one area, say one submarine, could wipe out much of the opponent's bomber force, or it could try to totally paralyze the opponent by destroying his national leadership and command centers — a "decapitation" strike. To protect itself, a nuclear force does the opposite of what a conventional army does. It tries to "manage" every small threat in detail by centralized direction, reliance on immediate warning, and dependence on prearranged reactions. The result is a system in which relatively small stimuli in one part produce vast reverberations throughout the rest of the system.

Such tightly coupled systems are notorious for producing overcompensation effects. A malfunctioning 46¢ computer chip initiated a chain of events thousands of miles away in Washington and Hawaii. Had the accident proceeded a bit longer, the president of the US would have had to be awakened to be told he had fourteen minutes to get out of the White House and to decide on a retaliatory plan in the event that the attack was real, and even less time to get on the Hot Line to Moscow. Nearly a hundred B-52s would have been launched to airborne positions over the Arctic, alert messages sent to ICBM crews, and warning messages sent to American military units from Korea to Germany.

The missile alert in question did not lead to such actions. But to argue that the major lesson of the NORAD missile alerts of 1979 and 1980 is that the warning system proved successful is to miss the point. They revealed a deeper, more fundamental truth about nuclear forces: They have developed into highly interdependent systems. Under peacetime conditions, the system's massive complexity does prevent isolated accidents from leading to catastrophe. This is why NORAD and other commands were able to deal safely with some fifteen hundred false alarms in 1979 through 1982. But during heightened military activity, the system is likely to become even more tightly coupled than it ordinarily is.

On a full alert, with worldwide warning and intelligence sensors flooding the headquarters with information, it is safe to say that much stronger reactive dynamics would drive the system this way and that. The institutional checks and balances that ordinarily dampen the internal overcompensation dynamics would be removed, either totally or partially, depending on the level of the alert. That, after all, is what it means to go on alert. At the highest levels of alert, the coupling might become so tight, and the checks and balances so removed, that the stability of the command system itself would be in doubt.

The Global Warning System

Sophisticated warning and intelligence systems have produced a tight, interactive coupling of American with Soviet forces. In certain respects, American and Soviet strategic forces have combined into a single gigantic nuclear system. A threatening military action or alert is detected almost immediately by the other side's warning and intelligence systems and conveyed to force commanders. The detected action may not have a clear meaning, but because of its possible dire consequences, protective measures must be taken against it. The action-reaction process can spiral, extending from sea-based forces to air- and land-based forces.

In addition to observing opposing forces, the American and Soviet intelligence systems now have the ability to monitor the other side's warning and intelligence systems themselves. The possibility exists that each side's warning and intelligence system could interact with the other's in unusual or complicated ways that are unanticipated, to produce a mutually reinforcing alert. This last possibility is not a new phenomenon; it is precisely what happened in Europe in 1914. What is new is the technology and the speed with which it could happen.

An example of mutually interacting strategic moves occurred in April 1978 when two Soviet submarines moved unusually close to the eastern coastline of the US. In such close-in positions these nuclear missile equipped submarines had the capability of launching attacks with minimal warning on bomber bases, command and control centers, submarine bases — and on Washington itself. Their movements were tracked by the underwater acoustic detection network operated by the US Navy.

"On a full alert . . . the institutional checks and balances . . . would be removed . . . That, after all, is what it means to go on alert . . . the stability of the command system itself would be in doubt."

The American response was to "let the Soviets know that we know" how close in they had moved. This was done by raising the alert level at several SAC bomber bases and ultimately by dispersing the aircraft to other bases. Such an action in a crisis might suggest that the bomber force was preparing to launch against the USSR. These actions were apparently detected almost immediately by Soviet electronic reconnaissance satellites or by other technical means. The Soviet submarines soon moved from their close-in positions to their usual deployments farther out in the Atlantic.

In peacetime nonalert conditions, the response to a single discrete threat can be to take a small number of precautionary moves. If Soviet nuclear submarines move unusually close to the Eastern coast, then SAC bombers can be removed to different airfields. Similarly, the Soviets observe that only American bombers are active, and that American nuclear submarines in port, for example, are inactive.

But once warning and intelligence systems are stimulated beyond a certain threshold, or once a certain level of alert has been ordered by political or military authorities, the situation may alter dramatically. Tight coupling of the forces increases, information begins to inundate headquarters, and human, preprogrammed-computer, and organizational responses are invoked. Although each side might well believe it was taking necessary precautionary moves, the other side might see a precaution as a threat. This would in turn ratchet the alert level upward another notch.

Whether or not such a chain-reaction alert could lead to nuclear war is difficult to imagine, stated in these terms. Unfortunately, it is not that difficult to envision a political crisis leading to an alert, and the alerting process escalating until one side felt forced to disperse its nuclear weapons from their storage positions, or until conventional attacks were authorized against Soviet or American submarines patrolling near each other's coasts. It is also possible to imagine a mutual alerting process reaching the point where interference or direct attack of satellites was undertaken, or where spontaneous evacuation of Soviet and American cities would occur for civil defense reasons.

"Instead of war versus peace, the decision would be seen as either striking first or striking second — precisely the dilemma faced at the outbreak of World War I."

Few people would disagree that operating nuclear forces at such high states of alert in this environment could easily tip over into preemptive attacks and all-out war. Each nation might not want war but might feel driven to hit first rather than second. Instead of war versus peace, the decision would be seen as either striking first or striking second — precisely the dilemma faced at the outbreak of World War I.

Reactions to Compound Stimuli

A 1956 example illustrates how compound warning stimuli can contribute to the false perception of danger. In early November, at the same time as the British and French attack on Suez, the Hungarian uprising was taking place. TASS, the Soviet press agency, was describing fears of worldwide nuclear war. Moscow issued a strong warning to London and Paris, and suggested to Washington that joint American-Soviet military action should be taken in Suez. This last message was received at the White House in the late afternoon of November 5.

Against this context, on the same night, the following fourfold coincidence took place. The headquarters of the US military command in Europe received a flash message that unidentified jet aircraft were flying over Turkey and that the Turkish air force had gone on alert in response. There were additional reports of a hundred Soviet MiG-15s over Syria and further reports that a British Canberra bomber had been shot down, also over Syria. (In the mid-1950s, only the Soviet MiGs had the ability to shoot down the high-flying Canberras.) Finally, there were reports that a Russian fleet was moving through the Dardanelles. This has long been considered an indicator of hostilities, because of the Soviet need to get its fleet out of the

Black Sea, where it was bottled up in both world wars. The White House reaction to these events is not fully known, but reportedly General Andrew Goodpaster was afraid that the events "might trigger off all the NATO operations plan." At this time, the NATO operations plan called for all-out nuclear strikes on the USSR.

As it turned out, the "jets" over Turkey were actually a flock of swans picked up on radar and incorrectly identified, and the hundred Soviet MiGs over Syria were really a much smaller routine escort returning the president of Syria from a state visit to Moscow. The British Canberra bomber was downed by mechanical difficulty, and the Soviet fleet was engaging in long-scheduled exercises. The detection and misinterpretation of these events, against the context of world tensions from Hungary and Suez, was the first major example of how the size and complexity of worldwide electronic warning systems could, at certain critical times, create momentum of its own.

While the fourfold compound events in the Suez incident did not lead to war, they demonstrate a dangerous feature of warning systems that cover a multiplicity of phenomena over a widespread geographic area. Turkish radars, a listening post in the Dardanelles, and communications intelligence from Syria and the USSR each contributed to a false overall picture. The simultaneity of the events, an arbitrary accident, was interpreted as evidence that they were all related.

"In broadest terms, the danger facing the world is that the superpowers have institutionalized a major nuclear showdown."

Once again, in retrospect, it is easy to see that each warning was not a sign of attack. But in November 1956, at the time they were happening, the compound events did not seem benign. There has been a tendency for the US and the USSR to be suspicious of each other and expect the worst. When warning incidents appear simultaneously, the simultaneity itself will contribute to the belief that the situation really might be dangerous.

The warning and intelligence systems of 1956 were primitive compared with those built over the next thirty years. The warning systems improved technically. More important, both in the number of phenomena covered and their geographic spread, the American coverage of the USSR — and the Soviet coverage of the US — has increased immensely. This trend would seem to make it more likely that simultaneous events will be picked up by warning and intelligence sensors and will, by the very reason of their simultaneity, be interpreted at headquarters as related.

Conclusions

The massive redundancy inherent in a system as complex as the world's nuclear forces reduces the danger of war resulting from a single technical accident. It very likely mitigates the danger of war from even a handful of such isolated stresses. When the stresses occur close together in time, the situation is a bit more dangerous. The situation becomes very dangerous, however, when the stresses occur in the midst of an international crisis. The real danger during Suez occurred because the simultaneous incidents took place during a political crisis. In a future crisis, one in which nuclear forces are placed on increased alert as a demonstration of political resolve, the warning system may have to contend with a strong random input of simultaneously threatening events. Some of the events will be part of the directed alert and some won't, but the system will not be able to discern the difference. In such a future crisis, going to high levels of alert could be a much more dangerous game than it was in the 1950s or 1960s.

In broadest terms, the danger facing the world is that the superpowers have institutionalized a major nuclear showdown. Today's complex nuclear defense system is strongly reminiscent of the institutionalized conflict mechanisms of the early twentieth century. World War I was a war waiting to happen at any time in the decade before 1914. Remarkably enough, during the very time when the general staffs of Europe were working out the interlocking mobilization programs, a feeling of security and complacency dominated popular and elite opinion. Although the war was waiting to happen, the fact that it hadn't happened was taken as a sign that all was well. Bertrand Russell tells how the absence of conflict during the Victorian era lulled people into confidently projecting peace into the indefinite future. Skirmish wars aside, they felt that no one would be so irrational as to initiate a major war.

The abrupt suddenness of World War I surprised everyone. Yet, in retrospect, almost nothing else could have occurred, given the institutionalized mobilization plans and firepower developed in the preceding decade. The same is true today.

LIBRARY
BRYAN COLLEGE
DAYTON. TN 37321

Computer System Reliability and Nuclear War

Alan Borning

Associate Professor of Computer Science, University of Washington, Seattle. Dr. Borning's work with Computer Professionals for Social Responsibility resulted in a definitive analysis of the role of computer failure in accidental nuclear war.

False Alerts

On Tuesday, June 3, 1980, at 1:26 A.M., the display system at the command post of the Strategic Air Command (SAC) near Omaha, Nebraska, indicated that two submarine-launched ballistic missiles (SLBMs) were headed toward the United States. (1) Eighteen seconds later, the system showed an increased number of SLBM launches. SAC personnel called the North American Aerospace Defense Command (NORAD), who stated that they had no indication of attack.

After a brief period, the SAC screens cleared. But, shortly thereafter, the warning display at SAC indicated that Soviet ICBMs had been launched toward the United States. Then the display at the National Military Command Center in the Pentagon showed that SLBMs had been launched. The SAC duty controller directed all alert crews to move to their B-52 bombers and to start their engines, so that the planes could take off quickly and not be destroyed on the ground by a nuclear attack. Land-based missile crews were put on a higher state of alert, and battle-control aircraft prepared for flight. In Hawaii, the airborne command post of the Pacific Command took off, ready to pass messages to US warships if necessary.

31

Fortunately, there were a number of factors which made those involved in the assessment doubt that an actual attack was underway. Three minutes and twelve seconds into the alert, it was canceled. It was a false alert.

NORAD left the system in the same configuration in the hope that the error would repeat itself. The mistake recurred three days later, on June 6 at 3:38 P.M., with SAC again receiving indications of an ICBM attack. Again, SAC crews were sent to their aircraft and ordered to start their engines.

The cause of these incidents was eventually traced to the failure of a single integrated circuit chip in a computer which was part of a communication system. To ensure that the communication system was working, it was constantly tested by sending filler messages which had the same form as attack messages, but with a zero filled in for the number of missiles detected. When the chip failed, the system started filling in random numbers for the "missiles detected" field. (1)

The Question

Due to the short warning times involved — measured at best in minutes — today's nuclear forces could not function without high-speed computers to automate the warning process, control communications, and, should it be deemed necessary, guide missiles to their targets. How reliable are the computers used in the command and control of nuclear weapons? Can they be made adequately reliable? These are the questions addressed in this paper.

The concept of "reliability" extends beyond merely keeping a system running. It invades the realm of system intention or even of what we should have intended, had we only known. To what extent are we able to state and codify our intentions in computer systems so that all circumstances are covered?

"The SAC duty controller directed all alert crews to move to their B-52 bombers and to start their engines ... Three minutes and twelve seconds into the alert, it was canceled."

Is it responsible for the USSR or the US to adopt policies which could result in an accidental nuclear war, should a computer system fail? As outlined below, I argue that it is not. The standard of reliability required of military computer systems whose failure could precipitate a thermonuclear war must be higher than that of any other computer system, since the magnitude of possible disaster is so great.

Sources of Failures

Computer systems can fail because of incorrect or incomplete system specifications, hardware failure, hardware design errors, software coding errors, software design errors, and human error such as incorrect equipment operation or maintenance. Particularly with complex, normally highly reliable systems, a failure may be caused by some unusual combination of problems from several of these categories.

Hardware failures are perhaps the most familiar cause of system failures, as in the June 1980 NORAD false alerts. Individual components can be made very reliable by strict quality control and testing, but in a large system it is unreasonable to expect that no component will ever fail, and other techniques that allow for individual component failures must be used. However, when one builds very complex systems — and a command and control system in its entirety is certainly an example of a complex system — one becomes less certain that one has anticipated all the possible failure modes, that all the assumptions about independence are correct. (2, 3, 4) A serious complicating factor is that the redundancy techniques that allow for individual component failures themselves add additional complexity and possible sources of error to the system.

Another potential cause of failure is a hardware design error. Again, the main source of problems is not the operation of the system under the usual, expected set of events, but its operation when unexpected events occur. For example, timing problems due to an unanticipated set of asynchronous events that seldom occur are particularly hard to find.

"We can have confidence in complex systems only after they have been tested for a considerable time under conditions of actual use ... The untestability of the [nuclear] warning and control systems under highly stressed conditions is grounds for considerable concern."

It is in the nature of computer systems that much of the system design is embodied in the computer's software. The cost and complexity of the software typically dominate that of the hardware. It is generally accepted that reliability cannot be "tested into" a software system; it is necessary to plan for reliability at all points in the development process. As with high-reliability hardware, there are codified standards for how critical software is to be specified, designed, written, and tested. Even so, errors may be introduced at any of the steps in software production: requirements specification, design, implementation, testing and debugging, or maintenance. (5, 6, 7)

Errors in the system requirements specification, for both hardware and software, are perhaps the most pernicious. We must anticipate all the circumstances under which the system might be used and describe what action it should take in each situation. For a complex system, one cannot foresee all of these circumstances. We can have confidence in complex systems only after they have been tested for a considerable time under conditions of actual use. Short of having many periods of great international tension and high military alert — clearly an unacceptably dangerous proposition — the nuclear weapons command and control systems cannot be tested under conditions of actual use. Testing under the most extreme conditions in which these systems are expected to function — that of limited or protracted nuclear war — is an impossibility. The untestability of the warning and control systems under highly stressed conditions is grounds for considerable concern.

Errors may also be introduced when the requirements are translated into a system design, as well as when the design is translated into an actual computer program. Again, the sheer complexity of the system is a basic cause of problems. Anyone who has worked on a large computer system knows how difficult it is to manage the development process. Usually, no one person understands the entire system completely.

Program maintenance, either to fix bugs or to satisfy new system requirements, has itself a high probability (typically from 20 to 50 percent) of introducing a new error into the program.

Another source of failure is human operator error. People do make mistakes, despite elaborate training and precautions, especially in time of stress and crisis. On November 9, 1979, a test tape containing simulated attack data, used to test the missile warning system, was fed into a NORAD computer, which through human error was connected to the operational missile alert system. During the ensuing six-minute alert, ten tactical fighter aircraft were launched from bases in the northern United States and Canada. (1)

"On October 5, 1960, the warning system at NORAD indicated that the United States was under massive attack by Soviet missiles with a certainty of 99.9 percent. It . . . had spotted the rising moon."

Human error becomes more likely under the influence of alcohol or drugs. Dumas cites some worrying statistics about alcohol, drug abuse, and aberrant behavior among American military personnel with access to nuclear weapons. (8) Alcoholism is a health problem in the Soviet Union and may be a problem among Soviet military personnel as well.

Some Instructive Failures

It is instructive to look at a few of the impressive failures of systems designed to be highly reliable. Most examples concern US systems, since this is the data available to the author. One would expect similar failures in the USSR or any other industrialized nation.

The June 1980 NORAD false alert described in the opening of this paper is an example of a hardware failure. However, this false alert also illustrates hardware design error. It was a grave oversight that such critical data, reporting a nuclear attack, was sent without using standard, well-known error-detection techniques. (1)

"Incidents such as Three Mile Island and Chernobyl, the tragic explosion of the space shuttle Challenger in 1986, and the 1965 Northeast power blackout are sobering reminders of the limitations of technology."

Another example of hardware failure was the total collapse of a Department of Defense computer communications network in October 1980. This failure was due to an unusual hardware malfunction that caused a high-priority process to run wild and devour resources needed by other processes. This communications network was designed to be highly available — the intent being that it should prevent a single hardware malfunction from being able to bring down the whole network. It was only after several years of operation that this problem manifested itself.

The launch of the first space shuttle was delayed at the last minute by a software problem. For reliability, the shuttle used four redundant primary avionics computers, each running the same software, along with a fifth backup computer running a different system. A patch to correct a previous timing bug created a 1 in 67 chance that, when the system was turned on, the computers would not be properly synchronized. There are a number of noteworthy features of this incident. First, despite great attention to reliability in the shuttle avionics, there was still a software failure. Second, this failure arose from the additional complexity introduced by redundancy in an attempt to achieve reliability. And third, the bug was introduced during maintenance to fix a previous problem.

There are many examples of errors arising from incorrect or incomplete specifications. On October 5, 1960, the warning system at NORAD indicated that the United States was under massive attack by Soviet missiles with a certainty of 99.9 percent. It turned out that the Ballistic Missile Early Warning System radar in Thule, Greenland, had spotted the rising moon. Nobody had thought about the moon when specifying how the system should act. Gemini V splashed down one hundred miles from its intended landing point because a programmer had implicitly ignored the motion of the earth around the sun — in other words, he had used an incorrect model. In 1979, five nuclear reactors were shut down after the discovery of an error in the program used to predict how well the reactors would survive in earthquakes. One subroutine, instead of taking the sum of the absolute values of a set of numbers, took their arithmetic sum instead.

In hindsight, the blame for each of the above incidents can be assigned to individual component failures, faulty design, or specific human errors, as is almost always the case with such incidents. But the real culprit is simply the complexity of the systems, and our inability to anticipate and plan for all of the things that can go wrong.

What about similar failures in the Soviet warning systems? I have been unable to ascertain whether or not such failures have occurred, and to date the Soviet government has not revealed them if they existed. However, the Korean Airlines Flight 007 incident, in which a civilian aircraft was shot down by the Soviet Union more than two hours after it had entered Soviet airspace and just before it was back over international waters, would seem to indicate that the Soviet command and control system has problems. The fatality rates for American astronauts and Soviet cosmonauts and the nuclear power plant failures at Three Mile Island and Chernobyl also indicate comparable failure rates of high reliability systems in both countries.

Incidents such as Three Mile Island (7) and Chernobyl, the tragic explosion of the space shuttle Challenger in 1986, and the 1965 Northeast power blackout are sobering reminders of the limitations of technology.

Prospects for Future Improvements

What are the prospects for improving the reliability of military computer systems in the future? Substantial progress is possible simply by using state-of-the-art hardware and software engineering techniques. (5, 6, 9) A system, like NORAD's, that in 1980 used 1960s vintage computers or transmitted critical data without error detection is not state-of-the-art.

State-of-the-art techniques can help, but what are the practical and theoretical limits of reliability, now and in the next decade? The Department of Defense is engaged in several efforts to develop new technology for software production and to make it widely available to military contractors. The Software Technology for Adaptable, Reliable Systems program, and the Software Engineering Institute at Carnegie-Mellon University are examples. Use of these techniques should decrease, but not eliminate, errors in moving from the specification to the program.

In the long term, formal techniques such as proofs of program correctness (program verification), automatic programming, and proofs of design consistency have been advocated as tools for improving computer system reliability. (5) In a proof of program correctness, either a human or a computer proves mathematically that a program meets a formal specification of what it should do. In automatic programming, the program is written automatically from the specification. In a proof of design consistency, the proof must show that a formal specification satisfies a set of requirements, for example, for security or fault tolerance.

But program verification and automatic programming techniques can offer no help with the hardest and most intractable problem in the construction of software for complex tasks, such as command and control systems: specifying what the system should do. How does one know that the specification itself is correct, that it describes what one intends? Are there events that may occur that were simply not anticipated when the specification was written?

"Both the practical and theoretical limits of reliability bump up against this problem of specification. It constitutes the major long-term practical barrier to constructing reliable complex systems."

A proof of correctness, for example, only shows that one formal description (the specification) is equivalent to another formal description (the program). It does not say that the specification meets the perhaps unarticulated desires of the user, nor does it say anything about how well the system will perform in situations never imagined when the specification was written.

For example, in the 1960 false alert, proving that the system met its specifications would not have helped since no one thought about the rising moon when writing the specifications. The term "proof of correctness" is thus a misnomer — a better term might be "proof of relative consistency."

Both the practical and theoretical limits of reliability bump up against this problem of specification. It constitutes the major long-term practical barrier to constructing reliable complex systems. The answers to such critical questions as, "Will the system do what we reasonably expect it to do?" or "Are there external events that we just didn't think of?" lie inherently outside the realm of formal systems. Computer systems (including current artificial intelligence systems) are notoriously lacking in common sense: The system itself will typically not indicate that something has gone amiss and that the limits of its capabilities have been exceeded.

Conclusions

How much reliance is it safe to place on life-critical computer systems, in particular, on nuclear weapons command and control systems? At present, a nuclear war caused by an isolated computer or operator error is probably not a significant risk, at least in comparison with other dangers. The most significant risk of nuclear war at present seems to come from the possibility of a combination of such events as international crises, mutually reinforcing alerts, computer system misdesign, computer failure, or human error.

A continuing trend in the arms race has been the deployment of missiles with greater and greater accuracies. This trend is creating increasing pressure to consider a launch-on-warning strategy. Such a strategy would leave very little time to evaluate the warning and determine whether it was real or due to a computer or human error. We would be forced to put still greater reliance on the correct operation of the warning and command systems of the US and the USSR. Deployment of very accurate missiles close to an opponent's territory exacerbates the problem.

More exotic weapons systems, such as envisioned in the Strategic Defense Initiative, equipped with extremely fast computers and using artificial intelligence techniques may result in battles (including nuclear ones) that must be largely controlled by computer. (9)

Where then does that leave us? There is clearly room for technical improvements in nuclear weapons computer systems. I have argued, however, that adding more and more such improvements cannot ensure that they will always function correctly. The problems are fundamental ones due to untestability, limits of human decision making during high tension and crisis, and our inability to think through all the things that might happen in a complex and unfamiliar situation. We must recognize the limits of technology. The threat of nuclear war is a political problem, and it is in the political, human realm that solutions must be sought.

Overlapping False Alarms: Reason for Concern?

Linn I. Sennott

Professor of Mathematics, Illinois State University, Normal, Illinois. Dr. Sennott is a member of the Mathematical Association of America, the Operations Research Society of America, and the Association for Women in Mathematics.

Overlapping False Alarms

The brief history of the nuclear era is replete with nuclear false alarms, including a flock of geese being mistaken by radar for a flight of missiles, a flock of swans being mistaken for a squadron of MiGs, the rising moon being mistaken for a massive ICBM attack, and a war games tape being accidentally left on a computer and mistaken for the real thing. False alarms are so frequent that no one, by itself, is likely to start an accidental nuclear war. Yet there is reason for concern.

Data made available by the American government under its Freedom of Information Act show that a total of 1,152 moderately serious false alarms occurred during the period 1977 to 1984, an average of almost three false alarms per week. (1) Officially known as "Missile Display Conferences to Evaluate Possible Threats" (MDCs), these are called as soon as a possible launch is detected or unusual information appears from warning sensors. The issue of false alarms is considered so sensitive that data are no longer being released by the American government and data on the Soviet system have never been available. But one may assume fairly stable rates of occurrence over time and similar rates of occurrence from one nation to the other.

A nuclear false alarm does not usually cause much concern. With three occurring in an average week, they are too routine. However, a new and potentially dangerous situation arises if a second false alarm occurs before the previous one has been resolved. Two such simultaneous false alarms tend to corroborate each other and could lead to disastrous actions. Bracken's paper in this volume provides a detailed explanation of the danger inherent in such multiple failures.

The high frequency of false alarms makes overlap a significant possibility. I have therefore analyzed the probability distributions involved, using the available data on failure rates in the North American Aerospace Defense Command (NORAD) Early Warning System. The complete mathematical analysis can be found in my other work; this paper restricts itself to summarizing the results. (2, 3)

"A nuclear false alarm does not usually cause much concern. With three occurring in an average week, they are too routine. However, a new and potentially dangerous situation arises if a second false alarm occurs before the previous one has been resolved."

The problem of overlapping false alarms can be analyzed using the mathematics of queueing theory. We have all had the annoying experience of waiting in a long line or queue, be it waiting for service in a store or waiting for an open telephone line. Queueing theory was developed to analyze these situations and to tell the store or the phone company the trade-offs that are possible between waiting time for customers and waiting time for servers. Having more servers means that customers wait less, but servers are idle more often, waiting for a customer.

In our model, the "customers" are false alarms and there is just one server, the command and control apparatus that deals with false alarms. An overlapping false alarm corresponds to a new "customer" having to "wait" when it seeks "service." That is, a new false alarm arrives and finds that the previous one has not yet been cleared ("served") by the command and control system.

While the average resolution time of false alarms (MDCs) is not public information, there have been reports that they typically take a minimum of one minute for resolution. It is also known that at least one such alarm lasted six minutes. In my model, I use the average of these two numbers, 3.5 minutes, as the assumed resolution time. The average time until two false alarms overlap is then derived, with the results shown in Table 1 for various rates of individual false alarms. (While there is some sensitivity to

False alarms per year	Expected time until two alarms overlap (years)
5	6,000
10	1,500
50	60
100	15
150	6.7
200	3.8
300	1.7

Table 1: *Expected Time until Overlapping False Alarms*

the assumed resolution time, my general conclusions are not affected if a different resolution time in the range one to six minutes is used.) (2)

Using the figure of 144 false alarms per year (NORAD's MDC rate for 1977 through 1984), overlapping false alarms should occur about once every seven years. If less serious false alarms than MDCs are counted, overlaps occur much more frequently for two reasons. First, there are literally thousands of less serious alarms per year. Second, doubling the number of false alarms quadruples the rate of occurrence of overlaps. The mathematics behind this statement is beyond the scope of this paper, but the principle is evident from Table 1. For example, doubling the false alarm rate from 150 to 300 per year quadruples the rate of overlaps from one every 6.7 years to one every 1.7 years.

"The more frequent false alarms are usually regarded as less serious. But . . . these may be the most dangerous . . . of all."

The more frequent false alarms are usually regarded as less serious. But, given the quadrupling phenomenon and the instabilities in military command and control systems (see Bracken and Raushenbakh's papers in this volume), these may be the most dangerous false alarms of all.

Failure of Dual Phenomenology

Another failure mode of warning systems can also be modeled by queueing theory. Warning systems consist basically of two components: satellite systems to detect the infrared trail of a burning missile motor and radars to detect and track incoming ICBMs.

Because of the severe consequences of incorrectly declaring that we are under attack, a requirement has evolved for "dual phenomenology" — the requirement that an indication of attack picked up by satellite sensors be independently verified by radar. (4) Satellites orbiting the earth see the missile at the time of launch while radar installations around the defending country see it a short time later as it comes within range. In our model, dual phenomenology fails if a radar false alarm occurs before the last satellite false alarm has been resolved. We require this order of events because satellite detection must precede radar detection to simulate an attack.

"With each nation aware that the other might consider a decapitation strike, there is tremendous pressure to strike first."

Again thinking of false alarms as customers and their resolution as service times, we now have two kinds of customers: satellite customers and radar customers. Dual phenomenology fails if a new radar customer finds the last satellite customer still being served (resolved). Our model assumes that false alarms in the satellite and radar systems are independent (totally random), but is conservative because correlation (a tendency of false alarms to cluster together) would increase the chance for overlap and failure.

Again using a resolution time of 3.5 minutes for each satellite false alarm, the expected time until a failure of dual phenomenology is given in Table 2. (2)

False alarms per year		Expected time until failure of dual phenomenology (years)
Satellites	Radars	
5	5	6,000
10	10	1,500
50	50	60
100	50	30
50	100	30
100	100	15
200	200	3.8

Table 2: *Expected Time until Failure of Dual Phenomenology*

Note that doubling the rate of either type of false alarm halves the expected time until failure of dual phenomenology, and that doubling the rate of both types cuts the expected time by a factor of four, similar to Table 1.

Significance of Launch on Warning

The short flight time of today's ICBMs (approximately thirty minutes) and the even shorter flight time of some submarine launched and intermediate range ballistic missiles (less than ten minutes) has reduced warning times to virtually zero. One possible response to this threat is to move to launch on warning (LOW) or launch under attack (LUA). Consideration of such policies is motivated by fear that, without them, a surprise attack could prove crippling, for example, by a "decapitation strike."

"While there is general recognition that human control of the decision process is absolutely necessary, we are rapidly approaching a situation in which the 'man in the loop' is obsolete."

"Decapitation" is a strategy in which one nation, fearing an imminent attack by the other, strikes at the opponent's national leaders and command centers. (5) The hope is to paralyze the opponent's ability to attack before he exercises that option. With each nation aware that the other might consider a decapitation strike, there is tremendous pressure to strike first. As Bracken notes in this volume: "Each nation might not want war but might feel driven to hit first rather than second. Instead of war versus peace, the decision would be seen as either striking first or striking second."

To counter decapitation and similar strategies, LOW or LUA would initiate a counterattack as soon as reliable evidence is received that a nuclear attack is under way, before the enemy missiles arrive. Such reliable evidence consists essentially of satellite-sensor indication of attack, corroborated by radar a few minutes later. This is the requirement of dual phenomenology analyzed above.

There is much speculation about, and disagreement over, whether the US follows an LOW or LUA strategy. In a recent article, Bruce Blair and Robert McNamara urged that the US should publicly disavow such a policy immediately. (6) The official response has been neither to confirm nor deny the adoption of such a strategy. The USSR has warned that it might move to launch on warning as a response to the deployment of short-flight-time Pershing missiles by NATO. (7) Table 2 shows that the expected time until failure of dual phenomenology is an uncomfortable fifteen years if the false alarm rates are one hundred per year for both satellites and radars.

Conclusions

Borning, Bracken, and Raushenbakh's papers document the destabilizing effect that technological escalation of the arms race has had to date. The future promises more of the same.

As stealth technology decreases the ability of radar to detect bombers and missiles, the quality of the evidence required to say that an attack is underway will have to be lowered and the number of false alarms will increase.

The presence of Soviet missile-carrying submarines near the coast of the US, the presence of similar short-flight-time American missiles in Europe and off the coast of the USSR, coupled with a fear that a decapitation strike would be the likely precursor to a full-scale nuclear attack, is dramatically shortening decision times and making the system increasingly unstable.

While there is general recognition that human control of the decision process is absolutely necessary, we are rapidly approaching a situation in which the "man in the loop" is obsolete. Launch on warning and launch under attack are discussed as if they were serious options.

These factors, coupled with the significant chance for overlapping false alarms or failure of dual phenomenology, have created an extremely volatile and hazardous situation.

Computer War

Boris V. Raushenbakh

Professor of Theoretical Mechanics and Control, Moscow Physical-Technical
Institute; Member, Committee of Soviet Scientists for Peace against the Nuclear
Threat. Dr. Raushenbakh is a member of the Academy of Sciences of the USSR
and the International Academy of Astronautics. His work has been awarded the
Lenin Prize.

The need for a new way of thinking in our nuclear age has been lately affirmed by many. Man has become all too powerful; so great is his might that he can annihilate all life on the Earth, his own kind included, a situation that was deemed unthinkable early in this century. Under these new conditions, man cannot afford to think and act solely in terms of the welfare of his own kin, his own community, or his own country. Nowadays man must also heed the global consequences of his actions.

The global nature of human activities is discernable in various ways and makes itself felt in the exhaustion of our resources, in ecological problems and, unquestionably, in the arms race.

When humanity meets the challenge of ecological problems, "to err is human" may be an acceptable rationale. The ecological processes are sufficiently slow that they can be observed and studied with a certain measure of detachment so that necessary adjustments can be made to change the human course. If these adjustments prove ineffective, new measures can be taken and the problem would ultimately be solved by trial and error.

In the event of a nuclear war, errors would produce entirely different consequences. There would be no time to correct mistakes. The first mistake is likely to become the last. The time of a ballistic missile flight is

45

measured in minutes and hence the duration of a nuclear conflict is very short.

Computers in War

Due to the short duration of battle operations and the extreme complexity of military equipment and its control, computers have become an indispensable element of weapons systems. As a rule they are man's helpers and are capable of helping to control sophisticated weaponry. However, with more complex equipment and shorter duration battles, humans could be forced out of the decision loop and crucial decisions left to computers.

"In the event of a nuclear war . . . the first mistake is likely to become the last."

The possibility of triggering this kind of "computer war" is a reality if launch on warning strategies are adopted or if current plans to militarize space are carried out. Total computerization of any battle system is fraught with grave danger. This paper will use space-based weapons for illustrative purposes. This example helps concretize the analysis and is extremely relevant to current defense planning. Some space-based weapons would require complete computerization due to their virtually instantaneous propagation of destructive energy, literally a fraction of a second.

The conventional three-component formula of military action control consisting of a warning as to the emerging situation, waiting for a decision to be made by the authority, and execution of the order issued, is rendered invalid by this kind of "computer war." No person can appraise the situation and make a correct decision in a matter of seconds, nor is it feasible to wait until the decision is made by the political or military authority. The decision, therefore, will be made by suitably programmed computers.

People thus become hostages of computers. In terms of potential nuclear war, the very existence of mankind is becoming dependent on hardware and software. In a situation like this, the discussion of the possibility of an accidental triggering of an attack by one of the sides, an attack by mistake or chance coincidence, ceases to be academic.

The Effect of Secrecy

The issue of accidental and unprovoked triggering of a nuclear conflict is now being increasingly perceived as one of the most grave dangers threatening humanity. Such a course of events may be set off by various causes. Here we shall confine ourselves to the discussion of those causes that involve computers.

Two such causes that are normally mentioned meet the eye. The first cause consists in a hardware failure. Malfunctioning of some element of the system may not only cripple its effectiveness but also result in triggering an unprovoked attack. The second cause lies in errors that may creep into software.

"The decision . . . will be made by suitably programmed computers. People thus become hostages of computers."

There also exists a third source of danger that has so far been largely disregarded. It involves neither malfunctioning hardware, nor errors in software and is, therefore, unremovable. This cause is associated with a lack of concordance in the software of two counteropposed systems. Computers in these systems will be fed data representing a model of the potential enemy's system attributes, rather than factual data on these attributes. Because each side maintains secrecy concerning its design, aspects of the model may be imprecise and, occasionally, downright false. It is this substitution of an unavoidably imprecise model for the actual properties of the potential enemy's system that we call a lack of concordance in the software of the two systems.

To simplify the ensuing examination of this problem, let us make the improbable assumption that the software of the two counteropposed systems is error-free and that the hardware is fail-safe. The only errors that will be allowed for are the errors in planning, i.e. mistakes stemming from insufficient information on the opposing system.

Stability

Space-based multifunctional systems will make up a certain strike capability complex. To retain effectiveness against surprise attack, a fair share of resources will be spent on prompt detection of ballistic missile launchings as well as on detection of preparations for launching, preparations for activating space-based weaponry, and other support operations.

Let us now proceed from two all but obvious assumptions: that detection of operations immediately preceding the use of space-based weaponry is feasible, and that both sides refrain from plunging into a nuclear conflict on early detection of signs that may be interpreted as preparations to attack.

If system A has detected the preliminary operations of system B, it must proceed with similar preparations, but refrain from immediate attack since the actions of system B may have been misinterpreted. System A will be provoked to attack only after detection of a sufficiently large number of danger signs. Even then, there may be an alternative to a nuclear attack among the system's capabilities. Thus there is a certain gradualness of countermeasures aimed at ruling out the possibility of triggering a nuclear conflict by accident.

To make these rather general observations more graphic, the following pattern of system A's response to system B's behavior may be suggested. Suppose system A's designers constructed a sequence of actions based on the assumption that simultaneous appearance of six danger signals is critical. Then the actions of system A may be represented in the following manner:

Observation	*Response*
The first emergence of one sign	Enhanced observation such as activation of supplementary tracking systems
Simultaneous emergence of two signs	Relatively time-consuming support operations to put the system into the ready-for-action mode
Simultaneous emergence of three signs	Intermediate readiness
Simultaneous emergence of four signs	Full readiness
Simultaneous emergence of five signs	Nonnuclear military action (e.g. destruction of some satellites in system B)
Simultaneous emergence of six signs	Nuclear war

The above scheme is but an illustration. The critical number of danger signals may be different depending on the nature of the signs. Also, countermeasure patterns are far from being this elementary. Yet whatever the actual programs are, they will always proceed from the need to gradually step up the response so as to make it adequate to the potential threat. It is equally obvious that disappearance of danger signals (reduction in their number) will entail the corresponding annulment of countermeasures. Given that the system B behavior was simply misinterpreted, the disappearance of danger signals or their modified interpretation (e.g. they might be generated by some rare natural phenomena) will bring system A back into the initial state.

The described sequence of actions, their gradualness, and reversibility make system A stable. That is, slight perturbations (a small number of danger signals) cause the system to act "proportionately," adding or subtracting countermeasures according to the above plan. This mechanism appears to have a safety valve to prevent explosive development of the process culminating in a nuclear conflict on marginal grounds. This "proportionality" seems to rule out accidental triggering of a nuclear conflict.

System B is most likely to be designed along the same lines and will also be stable and have the same built-in "proportionality" discussed above. The stability of systems A and B taken separately, however, does not imply the stability of the large system A+B.

Instability

Examination of the large system A+B, i.e. of the interacting systems A and B, shows that conventional techniques used in designing, modeling, processing, and testing of large systems to ensure stability of their concurrent operation cannot be fully implemented. Since systems A and B belong to adversaries, the design and debugging of each system will go on independently and under tight security cover. Their "marriage" will take place only when they are deployed and put on round-the-clock duty. It is in the first conflict situation that they will start functioning together, and a military action may be their first test.

Modern control theory holds that integration of two stable systems into one large system frequently entails instability of the latter. (1) The point is illustrated in Figure 1.

Rectangles A and B designate the corresponding systems, while lines X and Y which end in arrows stand for information flows which systems A and B exchange after they have been integrated into the large system A+B. These "information flows" represent danger signs detected by one system in the other.

Let us examine the problem by turning to the "open loop" system, obtained by assuming that at point C the communication between A and B is broken and the transfer of the information Y into system B does not take place. That is system B is not capable of detecting the processes going on in system A.

Suppose also that under peacetime operation of system B, some processes occur in this system that are registered by system A. (The figure shows it as the information X input.) Let us assume that these processes are not associated with preparations for attack, but stem from some minor

Figure 1. Computer War

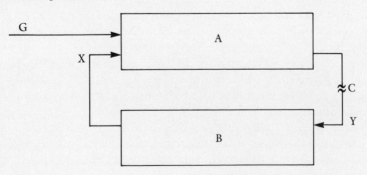

malfunction, testing, or other similar procedures. Let us now assume that system A perceives these operations as signals indicating preparation of system B to attack. (Since system A does not have complete information on system B, mutual suspicion is not only understandable, but also warranted.) Having received the information X, system A will switch to the operational mode appropriate to that information. If after some time interval the malfunctioning in system B is corrected or testing is completed, information X ceases to carry the danger signs and system A returns to the observational mode. Here the occasional emergence of danger signs produces no tragic consequences.

". . . integration of two stable systems into one large system frequently entails instability . . ."

The above process indicating the "stability" of system A proved possible because information Y on the action of system A was not transferred to system B. Let us now consider the behavior of the two systems when the feedback is closed at point C and they turn into a single system A+B.

Suppose both systems are "stable" in the described sense, and function perfectly. System A receives signal G which is not relevant to the operation of system B but stems from an unusual phenomenon, some chance occurrence in space, or anything that may be interpreted as a danger signal by system A. Let us assume that the signal is not too alarming and that system A will only go through the initial stages of response. As soon as information Y on these measures is received by system B it will reciprocate and the system A input will deal with two simultaneous signals G and X, the latter being due to sytem B's actions.

The appearance of two danger signals instead of one will cause system A to take another step toward attack, which will immediately change the information Y input into system B, causing further alarm. The appropriate response in system B will change the content of information X, which will become progressively more alarming, producing further action by system A. Eventually this will trigger off an explosive process of measures and countermeasures, leading to a nuclear conflict.

The above example is instructive in that it indicates the possibility of an entirely "unprovoked" nuclear attack triggered by the interaction of two perfectly operating computer-based systems, each of which taken separately is "stable."

Control theory readily explains the instability of the system A+B as generated by positive feedback. (System A responds to system B's actions in such a way that the latter is further activated.) (1)

All-or-Nothing Control

It may appear that designing either system to disregard minor danger signs would solve the problem and remove the instability of system A+B. The limiting case would be to block the response of one system to perceived preparations of the other, but have a hair-trigger that would execute a nuclear attack as soon as an attack was launched by the other side.

The problem arising in the development of such a system with an all-or-nothing response (termed "bang-bang control") is pinpointing the threshold value of the danger signs which would imply imminence of an attack and would give sufficient grounds for a preemptive response. Analysis shows that there is more to this issue than meets the eye.

"Where man might stop, the computer goes on, for computers know no moral code."

Suppose system A's designers know that a certain attack scenario may be reliably identified on the emergence of five known danger signs. Considering the lack of complete concordance of their software with the factual properties of their adversary's system, it is touch-and-go when three or four signs out of five are registered. Should they attack or shouldn't they? They should attack if the lack of some signs is a "feint" or a result of differences between the factual properties of system B and the model of these properties stored in system A's computer. The attack should by no means be launched if this lack of signs signifies any occurrence other than the attack, or system A's response would trigger a war by mistake. To compound the problem, this decision should be built into the software long (probably years) before the decision must be made by system A's computer. This uncertainty can bring about a fatal lack of the retaliative response or an even more fatal overreaction, an accidental nuclear war.

The task that software designers on both sides have to face is compounded by the possibility of false target launchings. The side that launches false targets tries to overstate the corresponding signs rather than to disguise them, in an attempt to undermine the deterrent potential of the other side. Software designers will thus have to seek additional signs which would help differentiate between false and real targets. Uncertainty in the interpretation of the incoming information will be greatly magnified, further "destabilizing" the software, with a consequent increase in the probability of an inadequate or dangerous response, including a nuclear attack.

Software is likely to include parts based on the proportionate response concept and parts of the bang-bang design or other modes of response known in control theory. Analysis shows that this in no way invalidates the conclusions. When the mutually uncoordinated systems A and B are integrated into combined system A+B, they will obey the laws that are pertinent to system A+B and are unknown to designers of respective software.

The above example shows that the cardinal properties of a large system and of its components may be qualitatively different. (Systems A and B are separately stable, while system A+B is unstable.) It follows that neither party can guarantee a "reasonable" behavior of system A+B. It should be emphasized that political and military authorities will have no time to interfere with the instantaneous hostilities triggered by mistake.

Conclusion

Humanity thus entrusts its fate to computer systems that, even if they function perfectly (no malfunctioning occurs, there are no errors in software design and execution), follow logic known to no man. Given some entirely unknown circumstances, this logic can lead to war and hence to death of humankind. Where man might stop, the computer goes on, for computers know no moral code.

To avert such a course of events, a new way of thinking is required today. The viewpoint of the separate systems A or B must give way to the viewpoint of the large system A+B, that is the viewpoint of the entire human family. And from this vantage point, any military strategy which would force the use of computers to override human reaction time is seen as an irresponsibly dangerous act.

To Err Is Human:
Nuclear War by Mistake?*

Marianne Frankenhaeuser

Professor and Head of Psychology Division, Karolinska Institutet, Stockholm.
Author of 200 papers, Dr. Frankenhaeuser has been President of the European
Brain and Behaviour Society, and an advisor to government, the World Health
Organization, and the Institute of Medicine, National Academy of Sciences.

War has often broken out by mistake — a consequence of misunderstandings and misinterpretations. When misunderstandings can result in mass destruction, it is vitally important to analyze the nature of human fallibility.

The Evolutionary Perspective

In order to understand how difficult it can be for people to cope with the demands of the modern world, it is necessary to view human capability and human constraints in an evolutionary perspective. (1) Our ancestors evolved into the present species over millions of years, when conditions for survival were entirely different from today. They adapted gradually to an environment which changed very slowly, and it was the slowness of the change that made adaptation possible. Then the rate of change began to increase. The history of humankind tells us that the human species spent 3 million years in the forest, 3,000 years on the fields, 300 years in the factories, and now — barely — 30 years at the computer terminal.

In striking contrast to this accelerating pace of social evolution, the human brain has remained essentially the same over thousands of years.

---

* This paper is based on an invited address presented by the author at the First Congress of Psychologists for Peace, held in Helsinki, August 1986. Congress Proceedings, K. Helkama Editor, Helsinki, 1987.

For our ancestors, ability to adapt to heat, cold, and starvation was a pre-requisite for survival. Thanks to the body's ingenious mechanisms of adaptation, our ancestors survived the hardships which were part of their everyday existence. Today's demands, while generally more psychological than physical in nature, trigger the same bodily stress responses which served our ancestors by making them "fit for fight." These bodily responses may, of course, be totally inappropriate for coping with the pressures of life today.

Thus, there is nothing in the history of humankind to prepare us for coping with the high-technology environment that we have so rapidly created for ourselves. Neither have we used the new technology to adapt environments to people's abilities and constraints. In fact, we have today a very poor fit between the ancient humans and their modern environment. This poor person-environment fit induces stress and prevents people from functioning at the peak of their ability, thereby increasing the risk for performance errors and irrational decisions.

Human Failure

Human errors are often blamed on so-called accident-prone individuals, but there is no one special category of people who commit errors. It happens to all of us, including the well-trained, the highly skilled, and the so-called stress-tolerant people. All of us from time to time make mistakes, such as flashing the wrong signal, taking the wrong turn, or pushing the wrong button. Human beings are inherently nonfoolproof: To err is human.

"Fallibility, lack of perfection, is the key characteristic of human behavior and is built into each system that we create."

The risk of committing errors increases under emotional stress, and people involved in complex defense systems are commonly exposed to emotionally arousing conditions characterized by high time pressure. Think of people faced with incidents such as nuclear false alarms, accidental nuclear explosions, or unintentional firing of missiles. (2) Judgment and decision-making ability could be greatly impaired under such conditions.

In incidents of this kind, technical and human failures tend to interact. However, threats are generally discussed in purely technical terms, with the implication that improved technology would more or less abolish the risk. This is an illusion.

Fallibility, lack of perfection, is the key characteristic of human behavior and is built into each system that we create. Computers make mistakes. They are no more foolproof than the people who constructed them. And most importantly, computers cannot cope with the unpredicted, the unexpected. Computers cannot be programmed for events that cannot be foreseen. When something unforeseeable happens, it takes human initiative to put things right.

"This sudden switch from understimulation to overstimulation when something goes wrong, combined with emotional pressure, may cause temporary mental paralysis . . . The consequences . . . may be disastrous because of the narrow time margins."

But it also is very difficult for humans to cope with the unexpected, particularly when under severe time pressure. And high-technology defense systems operate with ever narrower time margins. The time that one has for correcting a false alarm has shrunk to a few minutes. And, the more weapons we deploy, the more people will be interacting with them, and the greater will be the likelihood of disaster resulting from human error.

History is full of incidents showing how temporary indisposition or irrational behavior of people in leadership positions has caused catastrophic failures. Much less attention has been paid to the danger of temporary incapacity — due to either fatigue or overexcitement — of all the other people in the chain, who receive and transmit the information on which the leader at the top has to act. There is a considerable risk that messages will be misinterpreted and distorted before reaching the decision maker at the top of the hierarchy.

Underload and Overload

Brain research and behavioral research have taught us the conditions under which people perform well and when performance breaks down. The inverted U-curve of Figure 1 illustrates the relation between level of stimulation and performance efficiency. There is a biological basis for this relationship. In order to function adequately, the human brain needs to be fed a moderate amount of impressions from the outside world. If the total inflow to the brain falls below a critical level, disturbances occur in brain function and mental performance deteriorates. Under the opposite condition, when the stimulus flow exceeds a certain level, brain function is likewise disturbed. (3)

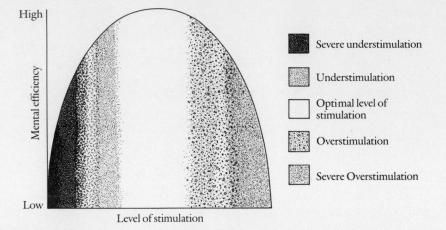

Figure 1. Stimulation versus efficiency.

The optimal level of human functioning is located at the midpoint of a scale ranging from sleep to overexcitation. In between these extremes the brain is moderately aroused, we are alert, and perform to the best of our abilities. Mental efficiency declines both when the inflow decreases and when it increases from the optimal point.

An early sign of understimulation is difficulty concentrating, accompanied by feelings of boredom, distress, and loss of initiative. One becomes passive and apathetic. Against this background, consider the demands put on those whose task it is to monitor processes in monotonous work situations. The brain is likely to be undernourished because nothing happens. One is not allowed to act, only to control and monitor. At the same time, the situation demands unfailing attention and preparedness to intervene.

Work demands of this kind are unavoidable in modern, complex defense systems, for example, people isolated in silos underground and people serving aboard submarines for long periods in tedious, unchanging routines. Hence, there is a great risk that signals will be overlooked, messages misinterpreted, and information distorted. Studies show an increasing tendency to commit errors during monotonous monitoring even during the first half hour. (4)

Now, consider what happens when a monotonous situation suddenly becomes critical. When something goes wrong, the person on duty must switch, instantaneously, from passive, routine monitoring to active problem solving. His task then is to quickly form a picture of the alarm signals, interpret their overall message, decide which measures to take, and carry them out.

This sudden switch from understimulation to overstimulation when something goes wrong, combined with emotional pressure, may cause temporary mental paralysis. During this brief but critical time interval, the person in charge may be incapable of making use of the available information. The consequences of such a mental paralysis — however brief — may be disastrous because of the narrow time margins. And the time margins for decision making in a crisis situation are steadily shrinking as the sophistication of nuclear weapons increases and the warning times become shorter. (5)

Performance during Crisis

Let us take a brief look at what is known about factors affecting skilled performance in crisis situations.

1. Attention narrowing: When our stress level rises, we develop tunnel vision. Important dimensions of the situation may be completely blocked out from conscious awareness.

2. Perceptual distortion: Messages tend to become distorted in the direction of our expectations. Such distortions occur, in particular, when stimuli are ambiguous, when past experience influences interpretations, and when wishful fantasies color what is perceived.

3. Mental rigidity: A related psychological phenomenon is loss of mental flexibility. Coping with the unfamiliar and the unexpected becomes even more difficult in a crisis. When people are under strong emotional pressure, their cognitive processes become rigid. Their ability to take in new information is reduced, particularly information which is not consistent with established beliefs. The ability to weigh alternative courses of action is impaired, as is the capacity to reevaluate conclusions. We know from the accident at Three Mile Island that the operators adhered rigidly to a picture of the system that did not tally with the facts.

4. Vigilance fluctuation: It is also significant that the accident at Three Mile Island took place about 4:00 A.M. It is well known that mental alertness is associated with the diurnal rhythm which characterizes most physiological processes. This rhythm adapts slowly to shifts in the pattern of sleeping and waking hours. For example, when a worker changes to the night shift, his adrenalin secretion — highly important for alertness — is at the bottom of its daily rhythm during working hours. Safety is seriously threatened when an operator on the graveyard shift is out of step with his daily rhythm. He cannot be expected to function at peak level during a crisis.

In summary, errors are perfectly normal during crises because of the built-in limitations of human beings. The narrowing of attention, perceptual distortions, mental inflexibility, and vigilance fluctuations discussed above are not psychological disorders in disturbed individuals. They are the normal human responses to severe strain. They are components of how we function and are not defects which can be remedied by training.

Decision Making in Groups

Let us shift from the psychology of accidents to the psychology of group processes, for example, in so-called "war cabinets." Yale University social psychologist Irving Janis uses the concept "group-think" to account for a way of thinking which easily takes hold of people who are deeply involved in decision making in closed and cohesive groups. (6)

The group-think phenomenon is likely to develop when the stakes are high and the time pressure intense, in short, when the pressure to reach rapid consensus becomes the overriding goal. To achieve unity in a crisis situation, members of a decision-making group often abandon their own critical judgment. This group process may lead to actions and decisions which the members would never have accepted as individuals. Six characteristics can be distinguished:

1. Illusion of invulnerability: The group starts viewing itself as perfect and immune from external dangers.

2. Ignoring and rationalizing information: This state is achieved by collective efforts to ignore information which challenges already accepted assumptions, and to rationalize away any indication that these assumptions might go wrong.

3. Moral superiority: One adopts an unquestioned belief in the group's inherent moral superiority.

4. Stereotyping: The enemy is stereotyped as either too stupid to be a threat or too evil for negotiations.

5. Illusion of unanimity: An illusion of unanimity is built, which fosters feelings of immunity from outside pressures. Thinking becomes oversimplified with a tendency to see everything in black-and-white terms.

6. Mind guards: Self-appointed "mind guards" protect the group from information that does not tally with the prevailing picture. These mind guards suppress any sign of latent disagreement among the group members.

In a group-think situation, there is a deep uncertainty about the opponent's intentions, a basic lack of trust. This is true of several political fiascoes of our time which can be understood in terms of the group-think syndrome. For an example, see Kringlen's discussion of the Bay of Pigs in this volume.

Concluding Comments

Technical systems are designed on the assumption that human performance remains intact during crises. Likewise, decision-making bodies operate on the assumption that their ability to make rational decisions is maintained under conditions of crisis. Contrary to both these assumptions, psychological evidence shows that emotional stress and time urgency impair performance and endanger the rationality of decision making in both individuals and groups. These psychological facts, combined with the decreasing time margins imposed by modern weapon systems, make the risk of nuclear war by mistake a very real one.

How is it possible that human beings, with their unequaled ability to plan and to predict, to choose and to control, have placed themselves in a predicament so hazardous that perfectly normal human errors can destroy the whole globe? Part of the answer is to be found in psychological defense mechanisms. The nuclear threat is collectively denied, because to face it would force us to face some aspects of the world's situation which we do not want to recognize.

---

*"What is called for now is not more pseudo adaptation.
On the contrary, we need people who respond by a 'healthy
maladaptation' to the nuclear threat, strong enough to
cause a revolt against the present course of development."*

By denying the threat, one achieves a state of "pseudo adaptation," which kills our tendency to rebel. Pseudo adaptation is facilitated because the nuclear threat has grown through gradual escalation, a successive increase of weapons over decades. This has led to an emotional blunting. Feelings of distress and anxiety have faded away without eliciting corrective responses.

Yet another aspect of pseudo adaptation, closely related to emotional blunting, is the decrease of emotional involvement with increased distance in time and space. People show a lack of ability to become emotionally involved in problems which are not perceived as part of the present — problems perceived as belonging to the future. One of the strategies that we use for coping with our fear of nuclear war is to push it into the "non-involving future time zone," where its emotionally arousing quality is lost. We may acknowledge the risk, but we shut our eyes to its imminence.

What is called for now is not more pseudo adaptation. On the contrary, we need people who respond by a "healthy maladaptation" to the nuclear threat, strong enough to cause a revolt against the present course of development.

The nuclear era calls for a psychological reorientation, a change in human motivation with a new emphasis on involvement in future human welfare on a worldwide basis. Instead of resorting to a very dangerous coping strategy, we must learn to cultivate the greatest human resource:

people's capacity for attachment and love. Human attachment is a strong force, capable of assuming mountain-moving proportions.

The challenge now is to help people extend their attachments, their loyalties, and their engagement, to include people outside their own narrow circle, their own country, their own imminent future. This global reorientation is a prerequisite for changing the present fatal course of development.

The Myth of Rationality in Situations of Crisis

Einar Kringlen

Professor and Head of the Department of Psychiatry, University of Oslo, Norway.
Dr. Kringlen has authored several books on psychiatry and the behavioral sciences
in medicine, and was a Fellow at Stanford University's Center for Advanced Study
in the Behavioral Sciences.

How do people behave under severe pressure, when they have only minutes to make major decisions? That is a question of profound significance in the nuclear age.

Stimulation, a small amount of stress, increases an individual's ability to react rationally. However, once the tension passes a certain threshold, fear and anxiety set in and have an adverse effect. Individuals regress to conventional reaction patterns not suitable in the new situation, rather than becoming engaged in finding creative solutions. Fear of the enemy is intensified by propaganda and political pressure. Tension increases. "All or nothing" solutions become the focus. Any action begins to seem better than no action at all. The urge to act can be so strong that actions are taken even if the consequences could be disastrous.

Conflict and Group Dynamics

The danger is enhanced by certain group dynamics. In crisis situations, lower level groups tend to report information that they believe high-level groups want to hear. Under strong pressure, groups tend to react with increasing conformity. They become more open to suggestion, allowing a domineering leader to be the deciding force. A group's perception of reality is often distorted by a misreading of relevant data. Sometimes information is even screened and tailored to fit the group's preconception of reality. Pressure to reach internal agreement, to be a member of the team, pushes individuals to join the majority view.

An American social psychologist, Irving Janis, has analyzed President Kennedy's decision to support the Bay of Pigs invasion of Cuba in 1961. (1) How could a president with such normally brilliant advisors be so mistaken? Why was the decision made to invade in spite of intelligence reports which indicated that Castro's army was 140 times stronger than the potential invasion force? Part of the answer, according to Janis, is that the close assistants of the president mutually influenced each other in a direction which they thought was expected of them, without protesting.

"He said, 'Mr. Secretary, Kosygin wants to talk to the president.' . . . And I said, 'Why the hell did you call me?'"

Let us look at some of the factors that explain why the president took the fatal step. Kennedy had just gained power. In his administration, one could observe an elation similar to what one might observe in a battle unit that had gone from victory to victory. Nobody around the president argued strongly against the invasion, and in an atmosphere of apparent agreement, no one revealed his personal doubts. Although strong objections to the invasion were stated in three written reports, one report was kept away from the president and the other two were kept from internal circulation by the president himself. One member was asked to hold back his skepticism in order to support the president, and the secretary of state did not allow experts on Cuba in his department to review the invasion plans. At the final meeting, the president invited the members to an open trial voting — a situation which puts pressure on individuals to agree with the majority.

This episode shows that even groups and leaders who have the best of intentions can go wrong under the influence of group dynamics. Human beings are not infallible. They can and do act irrationally under pressure, even if self-created.

Human Fallibility

A statement by former US Secretary of Defense Robert McNamara illustrates the critical importance of human frailty and the time needed for decision making:

> Are you so certain we'll never again, in the whole history of the human race, have another conflict? I'm not. Read history . . . Look at Berlin in 1961 or Cuba in 1962, or the events since that time. We damn near had war in 1967. I'll

never forget, I went to the Pentagon, as I always did at seven in the morning, and at seven-fifteen the duty officer called.

He said, "Mr. Secretary, Kosygin wants to talk to the president. What should I say?" And I said, "Why the hell did you call me?" And he said, "Well, the hotline ends in the Pentagon." Now, I'd been secretary seven years and . . . I didn't even know it ended in the Pentagon. This was the first time the hotline had ever been used, except for exercises. And he said (as you know, it is not a telephone, it's a teletype), "The teletype station, or the end of the hotline is in the Pentagon." Damned if I knew it. But I said, "Look, we're spending $80 billion a year for defense. You better get a few of those damn dollars and get that hotline patched over to the White House immediately. And I'll call the president and tell him Kosygin wants to talk."

So I called him, and I knew Johnson never was up at seven o'clock in the morning . . . Johnson came on the line and, you know, he's groggy and sleepy, and he says, "God damn it, Bob. Why'd you call me at this time?" I said, "Mr. President, Kosygin wants to talk to you." "What the hell do you mean?" "Well," I said, "he's on the hotline; the hotline ends in the Pentagon." "Well, what do you think I ought to say?" "Why don't we say you'll be down in twenty minutes. In the meantime, I'll get Dean Rusk and we'll meet you down there in the Situation Room."

So we got over there and it was one of those dreary, tough messages. I don't know whether it's ever been declassified but the essence of it was: "If you want war, you'll have war." You know, Nasser was saying our aircraft were bombing (which they absolutely were not) the Jordanian forces. We had turned a carrier around in the world to go from west to east. It had been going west, we turned it around to go east toward Israel, and that's what led to this thing.

"At the time we had that false alarm . . . it seemed like hours to us — panic broke out."

But the point of the story is simply that: Are any of you prepared to say that we won't bungle into conflict? I'm not. I don't know when it's going to occur, how it's going to occur, but the risk of deterrence failing, the risk of bungling into a confrontation that nobody intended, and nobody wants, and nobody planned, is very high. (2)

US Senator Charles Percy has described the panic surrounding another real-life experience, a false alarm at NORAD command headquarters:

At the time we had that false alarm — that must have been a six-minute period, because it seemed like hours to us — panic broke out. It was a very frightening and disconcerting thing. You wonder what recommendation they would have made at the end of those minutes, until they discovered that it was just an electronic problem. (3)

Who Holds the Trigger?

Ultimately, the risk of accidental nuclear war involves everyone who has contact with nuclear weapons. Who are these people? In the US, congressional testimony has demonstrated a surprisingly wide use of drugs and alcohol among military personnel who monitor radars for signs of a nuclear attack. While such information is not available from the USSR, it is known that alcohol is a serious social problem, and it would be unreasonable to believe that the problem is absent among Soviet military forces.

Many people, whether from isolation, boredom, or stress, seek refuge in alcohol and drugs. All reports seem to indicate that the consumption of alcohol is high in the military forces, both in the East and the West. The Burt study from the United States revealed that 27 percent of military personnel were reported to function less well in their work because of alcohol. (4) The same study also reported a high prevalence of drug abuse.

"Many people, whether from isolation, boredom, or stress, seek refuge in alcohol and drugs. All reports seem to indicate that the consumption of alcohol is high in the military forces, both in the East and the West."

To illustrate the size of the problem, during the years 1975 through 1977, 120,000 people in the US military forces had direct contact with nuclear weapons. In this politically quiet period, 5,000 people were removed from service each year because of alcohol, drug abuse, delinquency, or extremely deviant behavior. (5) Persons with acute psychoses are usually removed swiftly, but an alcoholic might remain in service a long time before action is taken.

Hope for Sanity?

While the danger of intended nuclear war is decreasing as world leaders realize that it would be suicide, the risk of an unintended war is growing. Because of the effects of group dynamics, because of simple human frailties, and because of the decreasing time for decision making in a crisis, the opportunity for a war to start by misjudgment is increasing.

The situation is, as I have tried to show, gloomy. But, when people were fighting slavery, the situation was also dismal — many thought that slavery could not be abolished. Even so, laws against slavery were instituted. In fact, little more than a hundred years ago slavery was legal in the United States and serfdom was legal in Russia. In the progress made since that time lies hope for the future.

Young People
and Nuclear War

Stanislav K. Roshchin

Deputy Head of Social Psychology Laboratory, Institute of Psychology, USSR
Academy of Sciences. Specializing in the field of political psychology, Dr.
Roshchin is the author of a book and seventy papers on the problems of political
and social psychology.

Tatiana S. Kabachenko

Senior Research Fellow of the Faculty of Psychology, Moscow State University.
Author of more than twenty papers on psychology, Dr. Kabachenko is a specialist
in the study of psychology, organization, and management in the field of attitudes
which can lead to a nuclear war.

Although no bombs have yet exploded in World War III, there are
already victims — not physically, but psychologically. Worse yet, these
victims are often those most precious to us, our children. This paper ex-
amines the impact of the nuclear threat on the human psyche with particular emphasis on the mental state of young people and children.

While a few farsighted individuals from the psychological commmunity,
notably D. Krech, E. Hilgard, R. Lifton, and J. Frank, took the threat to
heart early in the nuclear era, it took almost forty years for the community
in general to realize the danger. Now we may have very little time left.
Hence the need to understand and overcome the psychological barriers
that prevent people from responding adequately to this life-and-death
struggle.

Nuclear Victims

In an American study of the 1960s, M. Schwebel surveyed 3,000 children and adolescents of school age. The survey showed that even then
nuclear war figured prominently in the thoughts and feelings of the
younger generation. Of those asked, 95 percent expressed a serious concern about the danger of war and 44 percent lived in fear, waiting for war.
(1) In similar work, S. Escalona surveyed more than 300 subjects, from

age four to teenagers. (2) When asked how they saw the world in the time of their adulthood, over 70 percent spontaneously mentioned the possibility of nuclear war.

Large scale research into the reactions of children and adolescents to the threat of war was initiated in the United States in 1978, when the American Association of Psychiatrists set up a special task force. In the course of two years, from 1978 to 1980, J. Mack and W. Beardslee surveyed 1,151 secondary school students, including both boys and girls. The questionnaires asked about the subjects' attitudes to the future; how the threat of war affected their plans, including family planning; chances for survival in the event of war, among other topics.

". . . an American study of the 1960s . . . surveyed 3,000 children and adolescents . . . 95 percent expressed a serious concern about the danger of war and 44 percent lived in fear, waiting for war."

Writing about the results of their survey, Mack stated: "The questionnaires showed that these adolescents are deeply disturbed by the threat of nuclear war, have doubt about the future, and about their own survival ...There is also cynicism, sadness, bitterness, and a sense of helplessness. They feel unprotected. Some have doubts about planning families or are unable to think ahead in any long-term sense." (3)

Here are some illustrative answers to the question: "Have thermonuclear advances affected your way of thinking (about the future, your view of the world, time)?":

> I am constantly aware that at any second the world might blow up in my face.
>
> I think that a nuclear war which could break out in a relatively short period of time in the far future could nearly destroy the world.
>
> I think that unless we do something about nuclear weapons, the world and the human race may not have much time left. Corny, huh?

Even the more neutral question, "What does the word 'nuclear' bring to mind?" produced the following responses:

> Danger, death, sadness, corruption, explosion, cancer, children, waste, bombs, pollution, terror, terrible devaluing of human life.

In psychology, this method of questioning is called association technique. It helps bring out people's emotional experiences and their fears without asking them too directly. That typical answers to such a neutral question produced few associations with peaceful uses of nuclear power reflects how strongly the emotional experiences associated with the threat of nuclear war suppresses all other ideas. Most of the answers were of the kind described.

The data collected by American psychiatrists show that deep anxiety stemming from the fear of war can appear in children at an early age and that often they are unaware of it. In answer to the question: "When did you first begin to be aware of the threat of nuclear war?" a seventeen-year-old boy from Boston wrote:

> When I was very young, seven or eight. It was in a dream. I didn't know what the dream was at the time. I first felt intense fear, then complete and utter destruction. This dream came back throughout my childhood, and it wasn't until five or six years ago that I figured out that this dream was a nuclear holocaust. The idea of this scares me more than anything I've known yet." (4)

An eleven-year-old girl complained to her psychiatrist that she was afraid of not having enough time to commit suicide if war started. (5) A ten-year-old boy was taken to a doctor to be cured of insomnia and nightmares caused by fear of nuclear war. Similar symptoms were found in the fifth-grade students of a private school. Many children treated by psychiatrists and psychotherapists have dreams of being lost after their parents and family have been killed. Scientists who have studied the problem are almost unanimous in their opinion that doubts about the future, fear, and helplessness have a severely adverse effect. Escalona refers to the effect as "malignant," Schwebel as "corrosive," and Mack as "terrifying."

"An eleven-year-old girl complained to her psychiatrist that she was afraid of not having enough time to commit suicide if war started."

The authors of the present article have conducted a related study of Soviet youth. Our study, conducted from 1984 through 1986, covered over nine hundred high school and college students. Particular attention was given to the techniques employed. Many people are reticent to talk about their thoughts and innermost feelings, especially when part of a public opinion poll. In addition, some emotions or the reasons behind them are not always perceived and, therefore, may not be properly articulated.

Our American colleagues have used mostly direct questioning. Since our study was intended to identify the respondents' feelings, their depth, and even hidden thoughts, we also used projective and semiprojective methods. In such methods, the subject is given a stimulus that is neutral and specifically designed not to "lead" the answers. Our choice of this

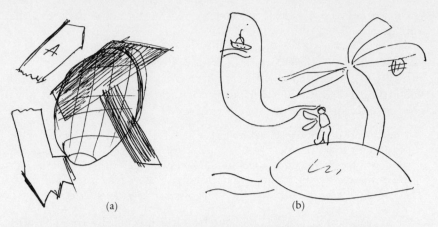

(a)   (b)

Figure 1. The subjects were asked to make simple drawings in response to certain words. The drawings reflect an emotional association of the word with something which was personally important to the subject. a) A drawing in response to the word "Hope," reflecting emotional concern about the nuclear danger. (A boy age 13). b) A drawing to the same word, manifesting the absense of any concern about war. (Also a boy age 13).

technique coincides with empirical conclusions reached by some American researchers who pointed out that direct questions about the nuclear threat can be "leading" and create a mental set which can affect the respondents' answers. Our study used both direct and projective questions, but the projective were asked prior to the direct in order not to bias the subjects' answers to the projective questions.

Our projective questions asked subjects about their appraisal of the present and future, their plans, and things that might interfere with their intention to start a family. The use of such level-of-optimism and attitude-to-the-future indicators helps avoid the leading nature of direct questions.

In our 1984 series of tests, 37 percent of the respondents thought nuclear war to be "probable" or "highly probable," 48 percent thought it "hardly probable," 12 percent "improbable," and 3 percent thought it "inevitable." Averaged over the entire set of tests, there were 5 percent in this last group.

As to the consequences of nuclear war, 46 percent of our subjects believed that it would result in the complete annihilation of humankind, 41 percent thought that 10 percent of the Earth's population would survive, and the remaining subjects estimated possible survival rates at 20 percent to 50 percent.

Optimism

In spite of their awareness of the danger, our subjects held a predominantly optimistic attitude concerning the future. This was demonstrated

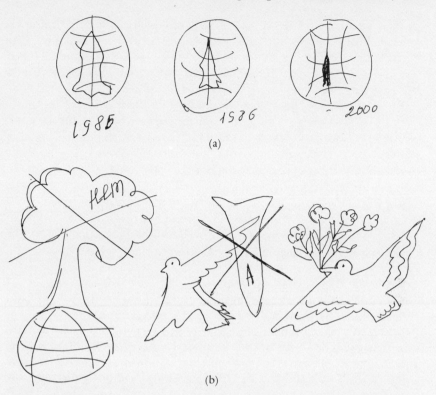

Figure 2. Examples of consistent reactions of the subjects. a) An unusual image of the "Future" reflecting gradual elimination of the nuclear threat. War was "improbable" in the opinion of this subject. (A boy age 13). b) Reflection of a serious doubt about the future. From left to right, the pictures were in response to the words "Fear," "Peace," and "Hope." The subject believed war to be inevitable." (A girl age 14).

not only in their answers to direct questions, but also in their drawings (the "pictogram" technique), and in their assessments of the future elicited by the technique of semantic differentials.

In answer to the question, "How do you see yourself in the year 2000?" more than 95 percent of the subjects made projections without any reference to the threat of nuclear war. Some pictured themselves as actively involved in public life, others banked on professional excellence, some hoped to achieve high moral standards, and some dreamed of love and family happiness. Only a very few answered that they had no personal plans because those plans were useless considering the threat of nuclear catastrophe.

We also included a "control" question in which the subjects were asked how many children they thought that a modern family should have and what might interfere with starting a family. In most cases, the reasons given as possible obstacles for starting a family were of the most common kind: lack of financial independence, unsatisfactory housing, and poor health. However, 12 percent of the respondents mentioned the threat of war as one of the reasons interfering with family planning. But, it turned out that some of these young adults were already married and had children, which raises a question about the depth of their personal concern.

In their views of the future, 46 percent believed that the threat of war would be eradicated by the year 2000; 10 percent described the world of the year 2000 as "bright," "joyous," or "cloudless"; 4 percent forecast moral improvement of society as a whole; 13 percent viewed the future in terms of the scientific and technological advances; 10 percent thought the world will change little; 8 percent predicted complications in world development and in the life of society; and 5 percent associated these complications with the threat of war (most of these also thought nuclear war to be "inevitable," showing a consistency of concern).

Effect of World Events

Our study found a correlation between the mood of the subjects and the state of Soviet-American relations. The first series of tests was completed before the summit meeting between General Secretary Mikhail Gorbachev and President Ronald Reagan in November 1985. The second was conducted after that summit meeting, the third in the tense international atmosphere following the US raid on Libya, and the fourth after the summit in Reykjavik.

In the two series of tests conducted twelve months and one month prior to the Geneva Summit, about 40 percent of our subjects thought nulcear war to be "probable" or "highly probable," while after the summit only 29 percent held that view. Similarly, after the summit, 68 percent thought nuclear war to be "hardly probable" or "improbable," as contrasted to 60 percent recorded earlier.

In the tests conducted after the raid on Libya, the number who thought nuclear war to be "probable" or "highly probable" increased to 53 percent and the share who thought it "hardly probable" or "improbable" decreased to 41 percent. After the Reykjavik summit there also was a shift toward pessimism.

Questions about the possibility of accidental nuclear war also were telling. The share of those who thought that chance might have a fatal role to play rose after the Geneva summit from 66 to 84 percent. While this may at first seem paradoxical, the result may be interpreted in the following way: When people have confidence in the goodwill of political leaders in matters of war and peace, their apprehension concerning intentional nuclear war decreases, but their fear of an accident becomes more pronounced. This hypothesis is supported by the fact that, after the military action against Libya, the importance of accidental nuclear war decreased to 70 percent, while the perceived probability of an intentional war increased.

Children

Our study was based mostly on youth aged from 16 to 22. But children have not been without attention. Based on work with American children, a US team headed by Dr. Eric Chivian, worked cooperatively with Soviet researchers over the past eight years to obtain similar data on Soviet youth. Findings confirmed previous studies which demonstrated that fewer youths in the Soviet Union fear nuclear war. In the most recent study conducted in October and November 1986, responses to questionnaires from 3,372 Maryland teenagers (average age 14.5 years) were compared to 2,263 similarly aged (average age 13 years) Russian children from the Tambov and Rostov provinces. About three-quarters of those interviewed from each nation agreed: "There can be no winners in a nuclear war since most countries would be totally destroyed." But 56 percent of Russian teenagers thought a nuclear war would never happen, while only 14 percent of Americans thought so.

"In a number of cases, the drawings contained the figures of children who seemed to try to stop a rocket with their hands, or to cover themselves from a nuclear explosion."

In June 1987, we conducted another series of interviews of teenagers from eleven to fifteen years old, employing our previously described techniques. One hundred and ten boys and girls from three Soviet republics — the Ukraine, Uzbekistan, and Armenia — were surveyed. Our results turned out to be somewhat different in comparison with the above described data of the Soviet-American cooperative research. To the direct question about the probability of nuclear war, only 26 percent stated that they believed it to be "improbable" and 7 percent considered it "inevitable."

However, if we take into account only the answers of those children to the question about the probability of nuclear war that were consistent with answers to the projective questions and tests, then the general results would be approximately the same as with the older youth of our previous tests (5 percent thought nuclear war to be "inevitable," and 14 to 16 percent thought it to be "impossible").

But, in general, this sort of consistency in the answers of children was significantly lower than with the older youth. In our opinion, this might be a manifestation of some peculiarities of the child's mental processes as well as (and more importantly) a demonstration of their more sensitive

Figure 3. Examples of inconsistent reactions of the subjects. The children who made these drawings said that nuclear war was "improbable." But these drawings were their responses to the words "Fear." (Drawings by girls age 14).

emotional reactions to the threat of nuclear war. For example, in making a drawing in response to the word "fear," asked before the questions about war, 41 percent of the teenagers drew something including images connected with nuclear war (nuclear explosions, rockets) and 6 percent used different symbols of death. In a number of cases, the drawings contained the figures of children who seemed to try to stop a rocket with their hands, or to cover themselves from a nuclear explosion (see Figure 3).

Conclusions

The variations in the data from different studies indicate the need to use some caution in interpreting the results. Naturally, we cannot rely absolutely on the obtained percentages. They vary depending on the state of world events during the period of the study, and possibly on other factors as well — for example, films recently seen or books recently read which discuss the consequences of nuclear war. This is the first major psychological study of the problem in the Soviet Union and it should be continued under different conditions and with different groups of the population so that, in the end, we might have a range of more reliable data. Nevertheless, these first results might be considered as a manifestation of some very important facts.

Soviet as well as American children and youth are aware of the magnitude of the nuclear threat and this awareness has a negative impact on their feelings, their emotions, their perception of life, and their plans for the future. In short, a significant fraction of the younger generation constantly lives with consciousness of the tremendous danger and perceives it more acutely than adults. We agree with our American colleagues that fear, anxiety, helplessness, and lack of confidence in the future leave an ominous imprint on the personality of the youth in both our countries. One may say that many are already victims of a war which has not yet started.

". . . fear, anxiety, helplessness, and lack of confidence in the future leave an ominous imprint on the personality of the youth in both our countries. One may say that many are already victims of a war which has not yet started."

Comparing the Soviet and American data, it might seem that Soviet youth are somewhat more optimistic about the problem of war and that the number of people who thought nuclear war "inevitable" is somewhat less in the Soviet Union. But the most important point is not the difference in the percentages, which as we have pointed out already, are rather changeable. The most important fact is that behind each percentage point in both countries, and in the world as a whole, there are millions of living people who are deeply disturbed by the threat of nuclear war.

There is a significant percentage (14 percent to 16 percent depending on the particular study) of people who think nuclear war to be "impossible" (we termed these "extreme optimists"), and even more who might be called "moderate optimists." But we should acknowledge that the time for real and complete optimism will come only when the nuclear threat has been eliminated.

Proliferation of Nuclear Weapons

Theodore B. Taylor

Chairman, Nova, Damascus, Maryland. Dr. Taylor, a former nuclear weapons designer, received the US Atomic Energy Commission's 1965 Lawrence Memorial Award and was Deputy Director of the Defense Nuclear Agency. He is a Fellow of the American Physical Society.

Nuclear proliferation is greatly enhancing the likelihood of nuclear war. It dramatically increases the number of scenarios for small-scale nuclear wars or nuclear terrorism, that could escalate to nuclear war between the superpowers. Deterrence, the cornerstone of national security in present strategies, fails against nuclear terrorism simply because there are no well-defined targets against which to retaliate.

Proliferation among Nations

Any determined nation could develop and start stockpiling reasonably efficient and reliable nuclear weapons within ten years and, in many cases, in a much shorter time. The knowledge, nonnuclear materials, and components needed for the production of nuclear weapons are accessible worldwide. (1) The main technical barrier is obtaining the required nuclear material (highly enriched uranium or plutonium), but even that is not much of a barrier today.

Detailed information needed to design facilities for producing nuclear weapon materials is public. Key components of such facilities can be purchased through international markets. Using plutonium extracted from spent fuel from nuclear reactors is also open to any country that has a civilian reactor or high-power research reactor. Another alternative, applicable to at least a dozen nations, is the diversion of highly enriched uranium or plutonium from other types of research facilities. These often contain enough material for at least several nuclear weapons.

There are several ways that present safeguards against diversion of nuclear material from nonmilitary reactors and their supporting facilities could be defeated. These facilities produce nuclear material suitable for use in weapons and many, allegedly used for peaceful purposes, are not subject to proliferation safeguards of the International Atomic Energy Agency (IAEA). Further, even where IAEA safeguards do apply, they cannot detect diversion of small amounts of nuclear material and, at many facilities, the annual threshold of detection is significantly greater than the amount of material needed for a nuclear explosive. In addition, even nations currently adhering to international safeguards can break the agreement at a later date if the nation decides its vital interests so dictate, for example if the nation is losing a conventional war.

"By the year 2000, there will be more than 3 million kilograms of plutonium in the world, enough for at least 500,000 nuclear weapons."

Even where there is no current diversion of nuclear materials, the worldwide spread of plutonium produced in civilian nuclear power reactors has produced "latent proliferation" — the ability to produce nuclear weapons in short order — in every country with a nuclear power plant. Nuclear explosives can be made with less than 6 kilograms of plutonium (1), in size about enough to fill a coffee cup. The world's present inventory of plutonium produced in civilian reactors is roughly 700,000 kilograms, greater than the total amount in the world's nuclear arsenals. This plutonium is being produced in thirty-six countries. By the year 2000, there will be more than 3 million kilograms of plutonium in the world, enough for at least 500,000 nuclear weapons. (2)

The plutonium produced in a reactor must be separated before it can be used in a weapon. While commercial facilities are more complex, a separation plant suitable for military purposes can be built for less than $50 million in several months time. (3) Every nation with a commercial nuclear power plant has such resources, since they are small compared with those needed for acquiring the power plant itself. Each year, the reprocessing plant can extract approximately 250 kilograms of plutonium from a single commercial reactor, enough for forty nuclear weapons at the very least.

To summarize the point: The most difficult technical barrier for the production of nuclear weapons is access to the required nuclear material. But thirty-six countries with nuclear power plants produce at least enough plutonium for forty nuclear weapons per year from each such plant.

It is also possible that international illegal markets in nuclear weapon materials or, conceivably, in complete nuclear weapons, may develop in the future, as they have for a wide variety of other weapons in the past. As with other weapons, the illegal suppliers of such materials could be criminals who steal the materials or act as middlemen between illegal suppliers and the buyer.

The Psychology of National Proliferation

As long as nations possessing nuclear weapons continue to behave as though they feel more secure with than without them, more nonnuclear states can be expected to join "the nuclear club." The danger of proliferation to the Indian subcontinent illustrates the psychology behind the phenomenon and how proliferation spreads like an epidemic. In 1945, near the end of World War II, the United States exploded its first nuclear weapon. In the tense East-West relations of the postwar period, the Soviet Union detonated its first weapon in 1949. As relations between the Soviet Union and China chilled in the 1960s, China conducted its first nuclear test in 1964. In its turn, India, which had fought a border war with China in 1962, then conducted a nuclear test in 1974.

Although India's nuclear test was claimed to be for peaceful purposes, and it has repeatedly denied having any nuclear weapons, there is no question that India could quickly produce deliverable nuclear weapons at any time it so desired. In response, India's traditional enemy, Pakistan, has pushed its own nuclear program to the point where, probably, it too can make nuclear weapons any time it desires. (4) Proliferation enters a new, ironic phase with India now considering production of nuclear weapons in response to their possible acquisition by Pakistan.

The Middle East is another area with high danger of proliferation. There have been strong indications that, in spite of official denials, Israel has been producing nuclear weapons since the late 1960s. Convincing public revelations by a former employee of the Israeli nuclear establishment in the fall of 1986 leave little doubt that Israel has a substantial stockpile of nuclear weapons, credibly more than a hundred. (5) This creates an atmosphere in which the Arab nations can easily justify their own attempts at developing nuclear weapons. In fact, the 1981 Israeli air raid on the Iraqi research reactor at Osirak (Tammuz) was motivated by fear it would be used as a source of materials for nuclear weapons.

Proliferation is also encouraged by the fact that nearly fifty nations — including Argentina, Brazil, Chile, China, France, India, Israel, Pakistan,

Portugal, Saudi Arabia, South Africa, Spain, and Vietnam — have not signed the Non-Proliferation Treaty. The US and the USSR were required by Article VI of the treaty "to pursue negotiations in good faith on effective measures relating to cessation of the nuclear arms race at an early date and to nuclear disarmament." Yet since the treaty went into effect in 1970, the American strategic nuclear arsenal has grown from 4,000 warheads to 12,000 and the Soviet arsenal has increased from 2,000 to 10,000. (6,7)

". . . as long as we believe nuclear weapons are an important part of our security, we cannot expect the rest of the world to think or act differently."

We, in the US and the USSR, may feel powerless to stop proliferation since the parties involved are not under our direct control. But, as long as we believe nuclear weapons are an important part of our security, we cannot expect the rest of the world to think or act differently. If we succeed in changing our own behavior, there is hope for the rest of the world. If we do not, we have no one to blame but ourselves as nuclear weapons proliferate.

Nuclear Terrorism

Proliferation of nuclear weapons among nations is terrifying enough. But, starting in the mid-1960s, there has been a steadily increasing concern that nonnational organizations might acquire nuclear weapons. Such organizations include established terrorist organizations; new terrorist groups, possibly including criminals planning to use the weapons for extortion; and desperate factions of an established government during a coup. An extensive and detailed expression of this concern and possible ways for alleviating it has recently been published by the International Task Force on Prevention of Nuclear Terrorism. (1)

The most straightforward way for terrorists to acquire nuclear weapons would be to steal complete weapons from military facilities or transport vehicles. The terrorist's job is complicated somewhat because many weapons are protected by Permissive Action Links (PALs). PALs are like combination locks which prevent the weapon from being detonated until the correct secret access code ("combination") has been entered. Some PALs go further and are designed to make the nuclear weapon inoperable after any unsuccessful attempt to bypass the PAL.

While detailed assessment of the effectiveness of PALs is classified information, they are not an insurmountable obstacle. Organizations with access to skilled technicians (internal or hired) could disassemble the stolen weapon and build a new one detonated in a different way. And smart terrorists would focus on weapons that are not protected.

Terrorist organizations could also construct a nuclear weapon from scratch. As with nations, the main technical barrier is the acquisition of the required plutonium or highly enriched uranium. This material could be obtained by theft, by "donation" from a nation sympathetic to the terrorists, or by purchasing it on a black market.

The problem of theft brings out an important difference in protecting against national versus terrorist diversion of nuclear materials. In the case of national diversion, only detection is required. But in the case of terrorist diversion, strong physical security is also needed since terrorists or criminals might obtain material through a physical attack. While the details of the physical security mechanisms to counteract such threats are classified, what has been publicly revealed tends not to inspire confidence. It is highly doubtful that the physical security afforded to plutonium and highly enriched uranium would be effective against thefts involving the sophistication displayed in many modern thefts of money or other materials less valuable than a nuclear weapon; the value of stolen nuclear materials would be measured in millions of dollars and a complete weapon would be worth many times more.

"The most straightforward way for terrorists to acquire nuclear weapons would be to steal complete weapons from military facilities or transport vehicles."

Whether they obtain nuclear material by theft, diversion, or purchase on a black market, nuclear terrorists would require less material if they could obtain metallic plutonium or highly enriched uranium rather than the more commonly available plutonium oxide or uranium oxide. Even if an organization only had access to the oxides, weapons in the kiloton range could still be made. While they would require several times as much material and would be less reliable than weapons made from metallic material, with proper design they still would present an awesome threat. (1)

Although, to date, there has been no reported evidence of nuclear weapons possession by terrorist organizations, the likelihood of nuclear terrorism is increasing for several reasons. The incidence, sophistication, and lethality of acts of "conventional" terrorism have increased dramatically in recent years. There is growing evidence of state support, or even sponsorship, of terrorist groups (one nation's "freedom fighters" are often another's terrorists). Nuclear weapons are often stored and deployed in areas of increasing terrorist activity. The number of places where nuclear weapon materials or assembled military nuclear weapons are in storage or in transport are increasing. Several hundred threats of nuclear terrorism based on claimed possession of at least one nuclear explosive have been investigated by authorities and found to be hoaxes. Some of these threats have been credible enough to cause serious concern.

Conclusion

Nuclear proliferation — be it among nations or terrorists — greatly increases the chance of nuclear violence on a scale that would be intolerable. Proliferation increases the chance that nuclear weapons will fall into the hands of irrational people, either suicidal or with no concern for the fate of the world. Irrational or outright psychotic leaders of military factions or terrorist groups might decide to use a few nuclear weapons under their control to stimulate a global nuclear war, as an act of vengeance against humanity as a whole. Countless scenarios of this type can be constructed.

". . . a nation in an advanced stage of 'latent proliferation,' finding itself losing a nonnuclear war, might complete the transition to deliverable nuclear weapons and, in desperation, use them."

Limited nuclear wars between countries with small numbers of nuclear weapons could escalate into major nuclear wars between superpowers. For example, a nation in an advanced stage of "latent proliferation," finding itself losing a nonnuclear war, might complete the transition to deliverable nuclear weapons and, in desperation, use them. If that should happen in a region, such as the Middle East, where major superpower interests are at stake, the small nuclear war could easily escalate into a global nuclear war.

A sudden rush of nuclear proliferation among nations may be triggered by small nuclear wars that are won by a country with more effective nuclear forces than its adversary, or by success of nuclear terrorists in forcing adherence to their demands. Proliferation of nuclear weapons among nations could spread at an awesome rate in such circumstances, since "latent proliferation" is far along in at least several dozen nations, and is increasing rapidly as more nuclear power plants and supporting facilities are built in more countries.

In summary, much more serious international attention than is now evident needs to be given to the consequences of nuclear proliferation among nations, terrorists, or criminals. Continuing to neglect this menace is a recipe for disaster.

Nuclear War:
Inevitable or Preventable?

Martin E. Hellman

Professor of Electrical Engineering, Stanford University. Dr. Hellman is best
known as the inventor of the "public key" and "trap door" cryptographic
techniques. He is a Fellow of the Institute of Electrical and Electronics Engineers.

The Nuclear Gamble

Almost everyone agrees that nuclear weapons cannot be used to advantage because to do so would be suicide. But the policy of nuclear deterrence requires that those weapons always be ready for use. Deterrence is therefore a gamble that what we are always ready to do, we will not ever do. The gamble has worked for the last forty years but, in the long run, is it a good bet?

Probability theory is a natural approach for evaluating the nuclear gamble. The early contributions of Blaise Pascal, Pierre de Fermat, and Christiaan Huygens all had as their main consideration the expected winnings in games of chance. (1) From there it was a short leap to expected losses, as in insurance or medicine, and finally to diverse applications from communications satellites to quality control. This paper expands the area of application to the most serious issue of all time — preventing a nuclear holocaust. But, as in the early days, the stage is best laid with a surprising result from gambling.

Coin Tossing. Coin tossing is the archetypal game of chance. Two players, A and B, bet a dollar on whether tossing a fair coin will show heads or tails. A tosses and B calls. If B guesses correctly, A must pay him a dollar and vice versa. A very simple, not too interesting game.

The game becomes more interesting — positively intriguing to some, judging by the sums that have been lost — if B not only guesses the outcome, but also gets to decide the size of the wager on successive tosses. This is the situation in casinos that offer roulette. The gambler chooses red or black and also the size of his bet.

Returning to the fair coin toss, A reasons that there is no harm in letting B vary the size of his bet. A fair game is a fair game whatever the size of the wager. But B thinks differently.

B bets a dollar on the first toss and calls heads or tails at random — neither is more likely to win than the other. If he wins, he stops and is a dollar ahead. If he loses, he bets two dollars on the second toss. If he wins the second time, he stops and is a dollar ahead, having lost $1 on the first toss and having won $2 on the second. If he loses on the first two tosses, he doubles his bet again, betting $4 on the third toss, etc.

This doubling approach, known as the Martingale Strategy, is one of the oldest "sure win" gambling strategies around: B keeps doubling his bet until he wins. (2) When he does, he is a dollar ahead. And he is bound to win eventually. He cannot keep guessing wrong forever, even if he wants to! Try it and see. With high probability, no one will have to wait more than thirty tosses before he wins. Only one in 1 billion should be that unlucky.

While this strategy guarantees that B will inevitably win, there is a flaw: The strategy only works if he has unlimited funds at his disposal. (3) With any finite amount of money, there is a small chance of losing the whole sum. This small chance of a large loss exactly offsets the large chance of a small ($1) win, keeping the game fair. But that is not the point of this paper. Now we come to the serious part.

Pistol Roulette. Consider a new game in which A repeatedly tosses the coin and B calls heads or tails each time. The game continues until B guesses incorrectly, at which point he is shot. Just as B was sure to win in the doubling strategy, he is sure to die at this game. Try it — without the gun. Before, no one was likely to go beyond thirty tosses to win a dollar; now, no one is likely to go beyond thirty tosses before he will be shot. The chance of surviving thirty tosses is roughly one in 1 billion!

This suicidal game is like loading one chamber of a two-chambered revolver, spinning the cylinder, putting the gun to your head, and pulling the trigger — a game we will call "pistol roulette." If we change the game to the usual version, with a six-chambered revolver, the probability of being killed with each pull of the trigger is one-sixth instead of one-half. The lower probability changes the time scale until you expect to be killed, but does not change the inevitability of that result. Because the probability per trial is one-third what it was before, you expect to live three times as long. But, if you play this game day in and day out, your death is merely delayed.

In the same way, playing with one bullet in a 600-chambered revolver prolongs the process — you expect to live one hundred times as long as with a six-chambered revolver. But that does not change the inevitability of your death. If you play once each day, you might be lucky enough to live several years. Or you might be unlucky enough to go in the first month — there is roughly a 5 percent chance of that.

Nuclear Roulette. What does pistol roulette have to do with nuclear war? During the Cuban missile crisis, President Kennedy estimated the odds of nuclear war as being "somewhere between one out of three and even." So the Cuban missile crisis was equivalent to nuclear roulette — a version of pistol roulette in which the entire world is at stake — with a two- or three-chambered revolver.

> *"During the Cuban missile crisis, President Kennedy estimated the odds of nuclear war as being 'somewhere between one out of three and even.' "*

The events support Kennedy's view: Early in the crisis, most advisors recommended military action to remove the missiles, a so-called "surgical strike." Later assessments by these same advisors concluded that, far from being "surgery," such action almost certainly would have meant a catastrophic war with the Soviet Union. (4,5)

George Ball, one of Kennedy's senior advisors, wrote that when he met with the other advisors many years after the crisis, "much to our own surprise, we reached the unanimous conclusion that, had we determined our course of action within the first forty-eight hours after the missiles were discovered, we would almost certainly have made the wrong decision, responding to the missiles in such a way as to require a forceful Soviet response and thus setting in train a series of reactions and counter-reactions with horrendous consequences."

In his chronicle of the event, Robert Kennedy reports that one of the members of the Joint Chiefs of Staff "argued that we could use nuclear weapons on the basis that our adversaries would use theirs against us," and that "the B-52 bomber force was ordered into the air fully loaded with atomic weapons. As one came down to land, another immediately took its place in the air." The air of tension that this created was almost ignited when, at the height of the crisis, an American reconnaissance plane accidentally strayed into Soviet airspace. Khrushchev challenged Kennedy, "What is this? . . . an intruding American plane could easily be mistaken for a nuclear bomber." (4)

These events justify Kennedy's estimate that the Cuban missile crisis created a high probability of nuclear war and was equivalent to a game of nuclear roulette with very few unloaded chambers in the gun. Crises of lesser magnitude also threaten the world, and on a much more constant basis. There are more chambers in the gun — the probability of disaster is smaller for each pull of the trigger — but that does not change the inevitability of the gun going off.

Paul Bracken in this volume describes how a minor crisis ignited World War I in just this way. There was only a small probability that the assassination of Archduke Ferdinand in 1914 would lead to general war in Europe. But with sufficient pulls of the trigger, even such a limited terrorist attack in an out-of-the-way place can be the act which ushers in catastrophe.

Every "small" war pulls the trigger in nuclear roulette. Because the US and the USSR back different sides, the conflict in Nicaragua has the potential for disaster. The Iran-Iraq war is another. Because Saudi Arabia provides Iraq with vital financial aid, Iran has threatened to cut off the flow of Saudi oil. Such action would be likely to bring American military action against Iran. This would be as unacceptable to the Soviets as it would be for America if the Soviets attacked Mexico. The USSR and Iran share a border.

"Every 'small' war pulls the trigger in nuclear roulette."

Every day in which a missile or computer system can fail also pulls the trigger in nuclear roulette. It has been established that on December 28, 1984, a Soviet cruise missile went off course and flew over Finland and Norway. The results of such an accident can be horrendous, particularly if it happens in a more populated part of Western Europe, in the Mideast, or during a time of tension.

In 1979 and the first half of 1980, there were 3,703 low-level false alerts in the United States alone. A few were sufficiently serious to come within minutes of launching nuclear war. One false alert lasted for a full six minutes before the error was discovered — a dangerously long time considering that the flight time for some submarine-launched ballistic missiles is less than ten minutes. (6) Because it takes time to detect a launch and orders must be given some minutes before retaliation can take place, the decision time is even shorter or nonexistent.

Even events as dangerous as the Cuban missile crisis could be repeated. General Edward Meyer, former army Chief of Staff, reported that during his tenure, "a naval quarantine or blockade of both Nicaragua and Cuba" had been considered. (7)

Inevitability

Every day, the United States depends on 30,000 nuclear weapons for its security. Every day, the Soviet Union depends on 20,000 nuclear weapons for its security. These weapons are ready for use. There are plans for how to use them, so every day there is a small probability they will be used. In the metaphor of nuclear roulette, every day, we pull the trigger of the many-chambered nuclear gun pointed at the head of civilization.

Every day, there is a small chance that one of the forty conflicts going on in the world will escalate. With many of these wars touching upon the perceived vital interests of the major powers, with the experience of the past forty years in the Middle East, with the experience of the 1962 Cuban crisis, there is ample evidence that every war pulls the trigger.

"Each of these probabilities, by itself, is small. But taken together over a year's time, they add up to a cumulative probability which is no longer small . . . Taken together over a century, they make nuclear war virtually inevitable."

Every day, there is a small chance that a Third World hot spot will escalate and push the interlocking command and control systems of the US and the USSR into instability. There is an unhealthy parallel between today's military plans and those which catapulted Europe into World War I. Each time the far-flung military forces of the two great powers go on alert, the trigger is pulled in nuclear roulette.

Every day, there is a small chance that failures in high technology military equipment will start an accidental nuclear war. Every computer error, every false alert, every test missile that goes off course, pulls the trigger.

Every day, there is a small chance that a governmental or military group high up in either nation will succumb to group dynamics to such a degree that individual judgment will be lost and rash decisions made. Each time a team is called upon to decide how to respond to a provocative incident, each time warriors gather to decide what steps to take, the trigger is pulled.

Each of the hundreds of thousands of people with responsibility for nuclear weapons who drinks or uses drugs adds a small increment to the chance for nuclear war. Each time a custodian of nuclear materials, or nuclear plans, or keys to a nuclear facility, uses alcohol or other drugs, the trigger is pulled.

Every day, there is a small chance that terrorists or renegade governments will construct a nuclear weapon. The know-how, the materials, and the places where such construction can occur are scattered all over the globe. Fissionable material suitable for use in weapons is produced as an unwanted by-product at every civilian nuclear power plant in the world. More than 100,000 nuclear weapons could be built from the world's current nuclear wastes. Every coffee cup of fissionable material that a terrorist might obtain pulls the trigger in nuclear roulette. (8)

Each of these probabilities, by itself, is small. But taken together over a year's time, they add up to a cumulative probability which is no longer small. Taken together over a decade, the probability is significant. Taken together over a century, they make nuclear war virtually inevitable. We cannot continue on our present course forever.

What Is Enough?

Freezing nuclear arsenals at their current levels would help, but would not change the inevitability. Nor would cutting the number of nuclear weapons in half from 50,000 to 25,000. Twenty-five thousand nuclear weapons is still 25,000 potential accidents, each far more destructive than Chernobyl. Even eliminating all existing nuclear weapons would not alter the logic. We will always know how to build new ones and, during war, there would be tremendous pressure to do so. So what can we do? What is enough?

The only thing that will work is to address each of the small probabilities that together add up to inevitability. We have to change the thinking that drives us to stockpile tens of thousands of nuclear weapons, place them in depots that are increasingly vulnerable to terrorist attack, and guard them with people subject to the influence of alcohol or other drugs. We can no longer allow the survival of civilization to be dependent on the error-free operation of high technology defense systems — or on the rational functioning of sometimes irrational human beings. We have to stop threatening military force. We have to stop engaging in small wars.

While we must change each of these, there is a common source. It is the mentality of war which spawns each of these individually small, but collectively disastrous, risks. It is the mentality of war which is the conceptual umbrella. It is the mentality of war which drives us every time we pull the trigger in nuclear roulette.

The only way to survive pistol roulette is to put down the gun. The only way to survive nuclear roulette is to move from the mentality of war to a totally new way of thinking.

Anatoly Gromyko   *Elena Loshchenkova, Richard Roney, Harold*
Sandler, and Anatoly Gromyko

Ales Adamovich   *Natalia Yampolskaya, Donald Fitton, and Andrei Kortunov*

SECTION TWO

Global Thinking
Vision for the Future

OVERVIEW

A Call to This Generation

Life is at the crossroads. At the end of one road lies survival, at the end of the other is extinction. Our history and experience tell us that we have the capacity to change. Our evolution as a species demonstrates that we have repeatedly done so. No past change was ever bigger than the one we are called upon to make now, which is to move consciously from a limited self-identification to identification with all of life. This generation must reestablish the correct relation between the individual and the whole, between unity and diversity. To make that relationship right is the central demand of our time. We will come to collective or societal change as the result of individual change. The individual is the starting place for transformation of the mentality of the species as a whole. ("Beyond War: A New Way of Thinking," edited for the Beyond War Foundation by Richard Roney)

The Reality of Interdependence

A transnational, global perspective is more than an intuition or an imagination of things to come. Interdependence is the reality of today and can be measured, evaluated, and tested in computer models. Since the

1970s, these calculations have produced results which previously have been confined to literary or religious exhortation: The world is a single system; decisions which are made with the whole system in mind are more likely to lead to human survival. Cooperative approaches are more beneficial in the long run than competitive approaches. The system can be exploited, or it can be sustained. If we choose to sustain the global system, the greatest leverage will come from working in the area of values, goals, and the political will to develop understanding of human interdependence. ("Messages from Global Models about an Interdependent World," John M. Richardson, Jr.)

Our Common Home, Our Mutual Survival

That the Earth is our home is now common knowledge. But do we always remember that it is home for more than just two, or several, of the largest nations? Genuine security can only be universal, international. Therefore, no matter how much we differ or disagree over what is just and unjust, we will have to learn to express our opinions in ways that do not excite fear and hatred of those who think differently. In a nuclear world, the use of force to resolve conflicts is no longer possible even in small regional disputes. The long-term existence of both capitalism and socialism is now a given. We must now begin to explore what mutual survival means. ("Security for All in the Nuclear Age," Anatoly A. Gromyko)

There Is No Just War in the Nuclear Age

We like to think that there could be some kind of "just war." But no more. All wars, including just wars, are a thing of the past. Now, our literature must express this new reality and the urgency of change. Who are better equipped for this task than literary figures who in the past have always led the way? Do we remember Dostoyevsky and Tolstoy? We must write with a passion about the obsolescence of war and a love for life and our fellow man in a way that is so fiery, so full of conviction, so relentless that we once again wake the world up to the overwhelming reality of our time. We must write as if our lives depended upon it, as if we had no time at all, as if these were the last words we ever might utter. We can no longer do anything less. ("Problems with the New Way of Thinking," Ales Adamovich)

Individual Is Responsible for Everything

It is not realistic to follow dogmas of the past. New times shed a whole new light on what is real or realistic. And as Einstein's physics was not merely an extension of Newton's, neither can a new global view be merely an extension of something past. It must be a whole quantum leap up. Something at a new level. What was good yesterday may be totally useless today. If one were to think new, there could be enormous, until-now-undiscovered economic relationships between the East and West. There is no necessary structural limitation. Similarly, there is no logical extension of the old balance of power diplomacy to the new world. War, acceptable before, romanticized, is no longer working. Is someone else responsible to make this change in thinking? No. Morality, unlike law, is always the result of individual action. And the imperative of this age is that everyone see that he or she is responsible for everything. ("Realism and Morality in Politics," Andrei V. Kortunov)

Beyond War:
A New Way of Thinking

Richard T. Roney

Editor of this article for the Beyond War Foundation; Director, National
Strategy Planning, Beyond War Foundation, Palo Alto, Ca. In 1980 Mr. Roney
was a Rotary International Study Exchange Fellow. Formerly an executive with
ROLM Corporation, he works now as a full-time volunteer for Beyond War, an
international, non-partisan educational foundation. Beyond War is dedicated to
building a world where war is no longer used to resolve conflict.

Life is at a crossroads. One direction leads to death, destruction, and
possibly the extinction of life on earth. The other direction opens new
possibilities for the human species; a world where all people have the
opportunity to satisfy their basic human needs, where life has meaning and
purpose.

In the past forty years, the human species has accumulated more knowledge of our physical world, more understanding of the inner dimension of
the human mind, more ability to effect change than we have gained
through all our previous history. But that knowledge has not created the
utopia we might have hoped for.

Instead, we find the survival of everything we value at risk. Given the
enormity of this challenge, piecemeal solutions, reactions to symptoms,
limited perspectives will no longer suffice. The preservation of life now
requires an enormous leap in human functioning.

The transformation needed now is of greater magnitude than any
change since the dawn of consciousness. The renowned historian Arnold
Toynbee chronicled the rise and fall of all the world's major civilizations.
He concluded from his lifetime of study that there have been two nodal
points in human history. (1) The first was when we crossed the threshold

91

from instinct to self-consciousness nearly 100,000 years ago. The second is occurring now, when our survival requires we cross a threshold equally large. This change cannot wait for thousands, or even hundreds, of years. It must be completed in this generation.

Possibility

Is it possible for us to change? Our experience tells us it is. Our ability to change has made us the dominant species on the planet.

Physically we are very ordinary. We are not the strongest or the fastest species; we cannot fly, we cannot breathe underwater; our offspring are quite incapable of fending for themselves for many years.

But the capacity of the human mind has enabled us to overcome these physical limitations. We have used our minds to probe the secrets of nature. With knowledge, we have accomplished what once seemed impossible. We have learned to fly, to live underwater. We can create artificial environments that enable us to see at night, be warm in the cold, be cool in the heat.

We inherit the lifetimes of experimentation and learning of those who went before us. We accumulate knowledge and pass it on to others. We communicate through time and space. We deal with abstract concepts. We think about the past and the future.

In accordance with the laws of nature, we have changed the world we live in. How have we done this? It has always been the same process: commitment to a goal and the process of discovering how to achieve that goal. In 1950, Jonas Salk committed himself to find a cure for polio. In 1961, John Kennedy committed his nation to put a man on the moon and bring him home safely by the end of the decade. Neither could "prove" at the time that their goal was possible. But their commitment, and their willingness to be open, to discover, enabled them to accomplish these goals.

Discovery requires that we adopt a unique relationship with reality: one where nature "tells" us how it works. Salk did not decide that his vaccine would be effective against polio, he discovered it. He developed possibilities, tested them experimentally, validated or rejected them. The Apollo scientists did not decide what effect the moon's gravity would have on the lunar landing module; they, too, discovered what would and would not work.

By applying this same process, we can work together, East and West, North and South, to build a world beyond war. We can commit ourselves to this most essential goal. We can dedicate ourselves to a search for the truth of how to accomplish it. We can discipline ourselves to disregard our preconceptions in the face of conflicting evidence. We can find the way. We can move to a new level of human functioning.

Knowledge

In the last century, we have often used the process of discovery to pursue incorrect goals. We discovered the laws of nature that enabled us to make nuclear, chemical, and biological weapons. We have discovered new technologies and implemented them without regard for their by-products — the hazardous wastes, the pollution of the atmosphere and the oceans, the acid rain. (2) We have created the tools of our own extinction.

Over the same time period, by applying this process of discovery to understand the fundamental purpose and direction of life, we have also learned the principles that can ensure our survival.

Our Journey through Time

We know that we are products of a distant past, a past that stretches beyond the twentieth century, beyond even human history. Each of us is connected to the beginnings of time and space, energy and matter, to the beginnings of life itself. We are the end points of a living process. By examining that process, we have discovered the principles that govern survival.

---

*"We have created the tools of our own extinction.
. . . we have also learned the principles that can ensure
our survival."*

Our story begins 10 billion to 15 billion years ago. (3) The beginning of the universe — all matter, all energy compacted into one finite place at one finite time. How? No one knows. Ultimate mystery. But begin it did. And through billions of years a process unfolded: energy condensing into hydrogen, hydrogen atoms collecting to form stars, nuclear fusion building new elements. Stars being born, dying, exploding, scattering their products through space. New stars, nuclear fission producing the higher elements, molecules, and eventually our sun and the earth.

Enormous changes shaped the Earth, the formation of the oceans, the atmosphere, the continents. The beginning of life! How? Again, mystery. The growth and development of life from sophisticated molecules, to cells, to organized colonies of cells. Specialization: organs, nervous systems, primitive brains. The acceleration of change: fish, reptiles, amphibians, mammals, and humans.

With the human came self-consciousness; the search began to understand the universe of which we are part. Language, tools, and communication became the foundation for agriculture, cities, and civilizations. More and more knowledge: religion, science, music, poetry. More and more change: no longer solely geological and biological, but now initiated by the creativity, the energy, the power of the human mind. (4,5)

We stand at the end of a chain of indescribable length and enormous complexity. We are not the creators of this system; we are a finite, limited part in an infinite web of relationships. Our continued existence depends upon the same principles that have governed life for billions of years. Survival has always been the goal of life. No creature, no species, could have been aware of the role it was playing in the development of life. But, driven by an instinctual will to live, each played a critical part in the unfolding process.

Success or failure was always measured by the same objective standard: an ability to meet the changes in the external environment. If a creature or a species was able to do so, it survived. If not, it became extinct. (6) For the human species in the nuclear age, the standard is the same. We changed our own environment; we unlocked the power to destroy all life. To survive we must respond to that change.

It has been the response to change that has propelled life forward. As when plant life was in danger of poisoning its environment with oxygen, life evolved to animal form and began to breathe that oxygen. As the seas, lakes, and rivers were drying up, life moved onto the land. As when the forests were disappearing and the savannahs were expanding, life moved out of the trees and walked erect. Without these environmental pressures, there would have been no movement, no dynamism, no change. Each change, in turn, created new possibilities for the future. (4,5)

We are the inheritors of billions of years of successful adaptation to changes in the environment. We are unique in our ability to fulfill or deny our heritage. No other species has ever had the power to end the process of evolution. No other species has ever had the ability to consciously participate in its unfolding. This generation will decide if that magnificent process is to continue. We owe a debt to the past; we have a responsibility to the future.

Stages in the Journey

As we look back upon that enormous sweep of time, we can see there have been distinct stages in our journey.

From the beginning of time, until the advent of self-consciousness, there was a fundamental unity in the universe. There was constant differentiation, from pure energy, to energy and mass, to elements and combinations of elements, but always the relationships were defined by the fundamental laws of physics. With life came more variety, which also functioned in an unconscious, instinctive way that maintained the intrinsic unity of the whole system.

With the human being and self-consciousness came the idea of separation from the system. The human mind became the only thing we know of in the universe that could violate the principle of unity. We could choose. We could view ourselves as separate from each other and from the rest of the universe.

We could no longer depend solely upon instinct to survive. We needed to understand the system in which we lived and we began the process of reductionistic thinking. With our minds, we divided, isolated, and categorized pieces of reality in order to discover cause and effect relationships. Our discoveries enabled us to develop tools, shelter, agriculture, and transportation.

"With the human being and self-consciousness came the idea of separation from the system."

For most of our history, there were relatively few of us scattered around the planet, and we had little impact on the whole system. We were able to ignore the by-products of our material progress. We could deforest the land, deplete the soil, pollute the rivers, and go to war with each other. Individually and as groups of individuals we paid a price for those actions, but the system as a whole was able to replenish itself.

There are now 5 billion human beings with extraordinary technological power. Everything we do has a significant effect on everything else. We can no longer "do" and "develop" what we please. We can no longer ask ourselves "What can we do?" or "What do we want to do?" and ignore the consequences for the whole system.

Modern technology has given us a magnificent symbol of that system — a view of the Earth from space. Virtually every human being who has flown in space, whatever his or her nationality, has been deeply touched and changed by that perspective of our home.

Yuri Gagarin, the first Soviet cosmonaut, the first human in outer space, reported: "Circling the Earth . . . I marvelled at the beauty of our planet . . . Looking at our Earth from space, what strikes me is not only the beauty of the continents . . . but their closeness to one another . . . their essential unity. The different parts that make up the world all merge into one whole . . . How worthwhile life would be on our planet, if the people of all the continents were to really become aware of their closeness . . . their common interests . . . Let us safeguard and enhance this beauty — not destroy it!" (7)

An American astronaut, Russell Schweickart, lunar module pilot on Apollo 9, had similar feelings. "You look down there and you can't imagine how many borders and boundaries you cross again and again . . . and you don't even see them. From where you see it the thing is a whole and it is so beautiful . . . And there you are — hundreds of people killing each other over some imaginary line that you're not even aware of, that you can't even see . . . You realize that on that small spot, that little blue-and-white thing is everything that means anything to you — all history, and music, and poetry, and art, and birth, and death, love, tears, joy, games." (8)

All of humanity now shares that picture of the earth from space. We are one human species; we live on one tiny, fragile planet suspended in the darkness of space; there is one life-support system that maintains us all. The borders and boundaries that separate us are artificial. Whatever our differences — however emotional they are, however intractable they have become, however inevitable they may seem — they are insignificant compared to what we share.

"The ultimate sign of our autonomy is the choice we make as individuals; to contribute to the well-being of our whole species."

The guiding principle of all human thought, all human activity in the nuclear age, must reflect this fundamental unity. We must realign ourselves with the direction that has carried life forward for billions of years, we must unify at a whole new level of consciousness. This is the leap that must be made by this generation.

Action

The transformation of the human species will occur one person at a time. No one can make this change for us. No one can force us. The ultimate sign of our autonomy is the choice we make as individuals; to contribute to the well-being of our whole species.

There are implications of this change in our own personal lives which will have a powerful impact on our institutions and nations.

Individual Change

Every individual has a very basic definition of who he or she is. This definition contains a set of values, standards, and loyalties which are the product of one's own life experience and the interpretations that have been made about that experience. (9) This is the individual's identity and it determines how he/she interacts with life and responds to any given situation.

To understand the nature of the shift our individual identity must undergo, it is important to set forth the two basic relationships we can have with life.

The first relationship is limited in its perception. It only sees and acts upon what is useful to maintain an existing point of view, thought, or attitude. Decisions are based on a limited self-interest: "What is best for 'me or mine'?", "How do 'I' want it to be?" The assumption is that "I can choose both the goal and employ any means I want to use in order to achieve it."

The "I," the "we," that is considered in this "limited self-interest" will vary. Sometimes it will be just one person. Other times it might include family and close friends, at times the nation, or perhaps those who hold the same religious or ideological beliefs, or racial identification.

But the "me and mine" is limited; there are always many outside my definition. This limited view of the world, this artificial division of reality, is in conflict with the underlying unity of the whole system. From the perspective of the whole system, responses based upon this limited self-interest are inconsistent, inadequate, undependable, and "unrealistic." (10) It is this limited perspective, this limited identity, that is the root cause of the many varied problems the human species faces. The long-term outcome of collective thinking of this type will be the inevitable catastrophe of nuclear war.

"In a unified system, violation of another damages the whole system and therefore oneself."

The second basic relationship is inclusive and global in its perception. This relationship acknowledges that we are all part of one system. It is aligned with the value and direction of life. (10) It makes an empathetic connection to other human beings. Decisions are based upon global self-interest with longtime horizons: "What, in the long run, is best for everyone involved?" The basic assumption is that "If I choose a goal, the means must be consistent with it." In which case, the individual's responses are dependable, responsible, and directional. This global mode of thinking will lead to survival of life into the future.

This change to a global identification and a commitment to act accordingly has enormous implications. The individual then takes total responsibility for his/her own attitude. He/she is not preoccupied with defending existing ideas and opinions, but instead is continually engaged in a sincere search for the truth.

Violence can no longer be an optional response to even the most difficult of human situations. In a unified system, violation of another damages the whole system and therefore oneself. Those with different views cannot be seen as enemies. Diversity is viewed not as something to be eliminated, but as a source of creativity and resourcefulness.

When this change in identification occurs, there is a constancy to this attitude; it does not vary from day to day or situation to situation. The individual is truly mature, dependable, and reliable.

The process of mastering the unitive principle requires working together in real life situations with real people. This mastery does not occur overnight. It requires openness, courage, motivation, perseverance, and time. Working with others — whether in small teams, neighborhoods, communities, nations, or the world — is the transforming process. The outcome of this mastery is a profound sense of goodwill for our fellow human beings and our whole life system.

Collective Change

Nations must also change. We can no longer allow our nation-states to be exempt from the moral principles that guide our personal lives. The actions of our institutions must be congruent with our individual standards.

"Significant reduction or elimination of nuclear weapons will not occur as long as one nation thinks another will go to war in a crisis."

This change can only occur when enough individuals and enough leaders pledge themselves to build a world beyond war. There will need to be a critical mass of people in the US, the USSR, and throughout the world who have the commitment and dedication to persevere.

Some of the beginning steps are obvious. All nation-states, including the US and the USSR, must eliminate the use of violence in their foreign policies. Significant reduction or elimination of nuclear weapons will not occur as long as one nation thinks another will go to war in a crisis. All nuclear nations, especially the US and USSR, must model to each other and to the world a consistent commitment to resolve conflict without war and violence. (11,12)

The US and the USSR must begin to use the technology and resources of the arms race to help solve some of the basic problems of the Third World — the hunger, the disease, the violations of human dignity. They must work together with all nations to address the global crisis of the degradation of our life-support system.

Both nations must focus on fulfilling the aspirations of their own citizenry. This means developing a sustainable economic system that allows all people to participate productively. It means building a society where people are able to freely express ideas and opinions, to fully participate in the forging of their own destiny.

We will discover other steps as we proceed along this path toward a sustainable future. There is no valid reason that the future of all life must be in danger. There is no need for hunger and starvation on the planet; there is no need for the disease, the poverty, the ignorance. The root causes of war, of injustice, of alienation can be eliminated.

The human species has been on a journey for tens of thousands of years. We have discovered the secrets of nature. We have reaped a tremendous reward from the ability to think and to choose. But we now see the enormous price we will pay if we continue to remain separate from the direction of life. It is time for us to return home again, to the basic unity from which we came.

". . . we shall not cease from exploration . . . and the end of all our exploration will be to arrive where we started and know the place for the first time."

—*T. S. Eliot*
Four Quartets

Building a world beyond war: It can be done. It is the destiny of this generation to do it.

Messages from Global Models about an Interdependent World

John M. Richardson, Jr.

Professor of International Affairs and Applied Systems Analysis, American University, Washington, D.C. Dr. Richardson is an internationally recognized leader in the field of global modeling. He is the principal author of the book *Ending Hunger* and has written numerous works on global interdependence.

Global Interdependence: A Fact of Life

Most human beings have never heard of global models, let alone seen one. But periodically, major catastrophes, made vivid by media attention, remind us that we are small, fragile elements in a tightly linked, interdependent system — 1986 provided two examples. A chemical fire and spill in Basel, Switzerland poisoned 185 miles of the Rhine River, destroyed ten years of ecological restorative work, and threatened public water supplies. The long-term consequences are a matter of debate and speculation. A nuclear reactor explosion at Chernobyl produced measurable increases in radiation in far distant places. In the immediate region of the reactor, agricultural fields were contaminated. In some European countries, crops were contaminated and precautionary measures were initiated. The long-term consequences of this event are also a matter of debate and speculation.

Most examples of global interdependence lack this vivid quality. But their impact may be no less important in both ecological and human terms. Consider the following cases:

Cassava Farmers in Thailand. Fifteen years ago, cassava farmers in Thailand belonged to the lowest-income farm families. Protectionist agricultural policies in the European Economic Community (EEC) that set high support prices for grains and restricted imports have improved their lot

100

considerably. Cassava, in the form of tapioca, is not covered by EEC import restrictions and has proved to be a highly competitive substitute for feed grains.

In 1985, Thailand shipped 7.5 million metric tons of tapioca to Western Europe. This export has boosted foreign-exchange revenues considerably. Competition from tapioca, coupled with high import duties, have reduced grain imports to Western Europe resulting in considerable surpluses and also causing fiscal and financial problems in the American farm economy. But the story may not have a happy ending in Thailand. Continuous growing of cassava in poor soils heavily reduces soil fertility if nutrients are not replaced.

Cuisse de Grenouilles (Frog's Legs) from India. Frog's legs constitute more than 10 percent of India's marine exports and provide a substantial source of foreign exchange. Indians kill an estimated 100 million frogs each year to satisfy foreign palates. Western Europe is a major importer, but frog's legs are also shipped to Canada, Saudi Arabia, the United Arab Emirates, and Japan.

Unfortunately, frogs serve a useful function in the Indian ecosystem. The Indian bullfrog (Rana tigrina) eats its own weight in insect pests every day. Thus, thousands of tons of mosquitoes and other pests are surviving in India that would otherwise be consumed by frogs. This has resulted in a substantially greater local market for insecticides. Two of the most effective and widely used insecticides for mosquito eradication and crop pest control are Sevin and Temik. Before it was shut down, the Union Carbide plant in Bhopal, India, produced 2,500 tons of these substances each year. (1)

Common Messages from Global Models

Work with global models was initiated nearly twenty years ago, in April 1968, when a small group of Western European industrialists and scientists created the Club of Rome. This "invisible college," as it is termed by its members, became a forum for ideas concerning the syndrome of problems facing humankind, or the problematique, as termed by its charismatic first president, Aurelio Peccei. (2)

The syndrome of problems had a common cause: the unrecognized, unplanned, and unanticipated consequences of global interdependence. Population growth, economic expansion, and technological innovation had, within a few decades, transformed our world into one, tightly coupled system. In this system, problems were interrelated; apparent solutions to one problem aggravated or interfered with others. Addressing the problematique would require a global perspective and radically new analytical, planning, and decision-making tools that incorporated a planetary view. Global computer simulation models were chosen as the tools that could meet this requirement.

Thirteen major global models were developed during the period from 1970 through 1984. They were built in many parts of the world, and for varied purposes. They differed in level of aggregation, methodology, key variables, time horizon, and output. The smallest model treated the world as a single, aggregated unit. The largest disaggregated the world into more than one hundred nations.

Modeling groups made different choices about what to put in and what to leave out. Only three models contain any mention of resources and environment. Only one says anything about war or politics. Some models were specifically built to refute others. One model was built for the purpose of emulating other models and contrasting their worldviews.

"Population growth, economic expansion, and technological innovation had, within a few decades, transformed our world into one, tightly coupled system."

After a major global modeling conference held in 1978, Donella Meadows, Gerhart Bruckmann, and I compiled a list of important conclusions from the seven models that were presented. Surprisingly, we discovered in each model similar qualitative conclusions about the current state of the world and possible scenarios for the future. Of course the modelers did not agree on everything and their numerical projections were quite different. But on the broadest level, there were consistent messages. Subsequent global modeling work has affirmed these messages and none has contradicted them.

The basic messages are:

1. There is no known physical or technical reason why basic needs cannot be supplied for all the world's people into the foreseeable future. These needs are not being met now because of social and political structures, values, norms, and world views; not because of absolute physical scarcities.

2. Population and physical (material) capital cannot grow forever on a finite planet.

3. There is no reliable, complete information about the degree to which the Earth's physical environment can absorb and meet the needs of further growth in population and capital. There is a great deal of partial information, which optimists read optimistically and pessimists read pessimistically.

4. Continuing "business as usual" policies through the next few decades will not lead to a desirable future — or even to meeting basic human needs. It will result in an increasing gap between the rich and the poor, problems with resource availability, environmental destruction, and worsening economic conditions for most people.

5. Because of these difficulties, continuing current trends is not a likely future course. Over the next three decades the world socioeconomic system will be in a period of transition to some state that will be, not only quantitatively but also qualitatively, different from the present.

6. The exact nature of this future state, and whether it will be better or worse than the present, is not predetermined, but is a function of decisions and changes being made now.

7. Owing to the momentum inherent in the world's physical and social processes, policy changes made soon are likely to have more impact with less effort than the same set of changes made later. By the time a problem is obvious to everyone, it is often too far advanced to be solved.

8. Although technical changes are expected and needed, no set of purely technical changes tested in any of the models was sufficient in itself to bring about a desirable future. Restructuring social, economic, and political systems was much more effective.

"There is no known physical or technical reason why basic needs cannot be supplied for all the world's people into the foreseeable future."

9. The interdependencies among peoples and nations over time and space are greater than commonly imagined. Actions taken at one time and on one part of the globe have far-reaching consequences that are impossible to predict intuitively, and probably also impossible to predict with computer models.

10. Because of these interdependencies, single, simple measures intended to reach narrowly defined goals are likely to be counterproductive. Decisions should be made within the broadest possible context, across space, time, and areas of knowledge.

11. Cooperative approaches in achieving individual or national goals often turn out to be more beneficial in the long run to all parties than competitive approaches.

12. Many plans, programs, and agreements, particularly complex international ones, are based upon assumptions about the world that are either mutually inconsistent or inconsistent with physical reality. Much time and effort is spent designing and debating policies that are, in fact, simply impossible. (1)

Following the Ninth International Institute for Applied Systems Analysis (IIASA) global modeling conference, and after listening to the presentations from twenty projects (including the original seven), Donella Meadows identified eight additional areas of consensus. These eight areas are:

13. The structure of our socioeconomic system does not inherently produce a high-level stable equilibrium of population, material output, and resource use. It

can produce either growth or decline, and the historical pattern has been cycles, first of growth, then decline, then low-level stagnation, then new growth. To produce a sustainable system with high quality of life requires both an explicit social goal of sustainability and a conscious structural redesign.

14. Food aid, and indeed, almost any direct commodity transfer from the rich to the poor, is counterproductive, except in times of emergency. It sets up a pattern of dependence rather than of self-reliance; it discourages the forces of self-help, innovation, and leadership already present in the cultures of the poor.

"Cooperative approaches in achieving individual or national goals often turn out to be more beneficial in the long run to all parties than competitive approaches."

---

15. Removing all government intervention in world trade is neither the panacea its advocates claim nor the disaster foretold by others. Freeing trade has very complex results, favoring some nations and industries and hurting others. Those helped and hurt cannot easily be classified into groups. The major change free trade induces is increased specialization — and hence increased efficiency, with increased vulnerability of each special part to a failure in other parts.

16. The Lima and Third Development Decade targets for economic growth in the Third World are so imprecisely defined they are difficult to measure or model; insofar as they are defined, they are not achievable, and they are so aggregate that, even if met, they may not imply any improvement in the state of the poor.

17. Exotic new technologies such as synthetic food and fusion power are not necessary to solve world problems and are probably too expensive to implement.

18. Macroeconomic growth rates, as measured by GNP or GNP per capita will probably be lower in all regions than simple extrapolations would suggest — and that news is not particularly upsetting, since GNP is not a useful measure of human welfare or progress.

19. Just about any good-hearted change in the system intended to help the poor manages to get twisted to help the rich instead. The system is rife with negative feedback loops readjusting any change back into the same patterns of distribution.

20. The vital arena to understand in order to work on almost any global problem is that of values, goals, individual, social, and political will — why people are what they are, make the decisions they make, and especially how such things can be changed. (3)

Global models tell us we live in an interdependent world; that change in the status quo is certain; that improvement in the state of the world is by no means impossible and by no means guaranteed. We are a long way from knowing all we need to know, but we know enough about where we want to go and how to get there to begin the journey. In fact, we have already begun the journey, whether we like it or not.

In one sense these broad, qualitative messages about the world are not surprising; all of us know about them at some level. Yet in another sense, they are revolutionary; if everyone internalized them and acted upon them, the world would be in a different place.

The Impact of Global Modeling

Sweeping statements about the impact of global modeling would be presumptuous. But it is possible to point to specific examples of heightened global awareness. Future-oriented "twenty-first century studies" and the growth of grass-roots movements, emphasizing a global perspective, can be traced to the process of consciousness raising, regarding global interdependence, in which global modeling has played a part.

Twenty-First Century Studies. Government and privately sponsored twenty-first century studies are a major and highly visible activity that has been motivated by global modeling. The United States government's Global 2000 report was first. Since Global 2000, more than twenty national, regional, and world level studies have been initiated.

The Global 2000 report to President Jimmy Carter (1979) echoed concerns that had been expressed by the Club of Rome and some of the early global models. These concerns were now given the additional visibility and weight attached to an "official" government study:

> If present trends continue, the world in 2000 will be more crowded, more polluted, less stable ecologically, and more vulnerable to disruption than the world we live in now. Serious stresses involving population, resources, and environment are clearly visible ahead. Despite greater material output, the world's people will be poorer in many ways than they are today . . . unless the nations of the world act decisively to alter current trends. (4)

The massive China 2000 has been one of the more successful studies. The project had the enthusiastic support of Premier Zhao Ziyang and the ambitious second phase is being conducted at his request. (A draft of the second phase is reported to be thirteen volumes in length.) A recent visitor to China was repeatedly told that the China 2000 study had a considerable impact on China's top leaders and on the final draft of the seventh five-year plan (1986 through 1990). (5)

Many twenty-first century studies, including Global 2000, have had a relatively narrow environmental focus. However, there is a trend toward examining interrelationships among environment, development, and war and peace issues. This return to the breadth of concern expressed in early statements of the Club of Rome's problematique is exemplified by

"Common Future, The Report of the World Commission on Environment and Development." Work on the report was initiated in 1983; it will be presented to the UN General Assembly in 1987.

Major themes of the report were recently discussed by Commission Chair and Norwegian Prime Minister Gro Harlem Brundtland. Her statement echoed concerns expressed in more than a decade of global modeling:

> We share a world economy; a world environment, which is the basis for the present and future world economy; and a stake in world development and a decent and dignified human condition of life.

> We must learn to think globally and in a long-term perspective. The world is shrinking rapidly. No single region or nation can isolate itself from the rest of the world. They share the responsibility for a common future. We need to dig deep into our political consciousness and make the environment and sustainable development a prefit, not a retrofit. We must change our perceptions so that sustainable development and the conservation of our planetary heritage come to the forefront.

> We must come to see that many of our current approaches add up to a sort of piracy against our children that a truly civilized world can no longer tolerate. (6)

"We must come to see that many of our current approaches add up to a sort of piracy against our children that a truly civilized world can no longer tolerate."

Grass-Roots Organizations

A great number of nongovernmental organizations concern themselves with international development issues. Not long ago I compiled a list of these as part of a sourcebook on just one global issue — world hunger. The list was longer than the book itself. Therefore, instead I chose to only list directories of organizations. Seventeen directories were identified, printed in ten countries (including India, Nigeria, and Mexico), listing thousands of organizations. (7)

Lists focusing on other dimensions of the problematique would be similarly large. And there is considerable overlap. Organizations that focus on development are increasingly concerned with environmental and war and peace issues. Many organizations have been raising consciousness about the environmental issue of "nuclear winter."

I believe it can be said that in less than two decades, the initial goals of the Club of Rome and the Global Modelers have been achieved. Issues of long-term global development are becoming a matter of public discussion. But new ways of thinking required for national policies to be shaped by a global perspective have not yet become part of public consciousness.

Ways of Thinking That Are Inconsistent with Global Interdependence

While I have not done a comprehensive survey of the more recent twenty-first century studies, none that I have examined contradict the twenty basic messages we need to respond to. Most of the messages sound like common sense. But a list of the broad assumptions on which public policy is based in many nations (including my own) would read quite differently. This list would include statements such as the following:

1. Growth in physical capital and material output can and should continue indefinitely.

2. All problems of scarcity will be handled in a timely manner by national-level market mechanisms without significant social or economic costs.

3. It is better to postpone changes in social and technological systems until the necessity for change is demonstrated by a major crisis.

4. Most major global problems have technological solutions. The more costly, complex, and centralized the technology, the more likely it is to be used successfully.

5. The actions, successes, and failures of one nation or transnational economic institution are basically independent from those of others.

6. The future is predetermined by forces that are beyond the control of individuals.

7. Most human beings are basically selfish and narrowly focused; they are unconcerned about the future, about the environment, or about other human beings on the planet.

8. There isn't enough of anything to go around; each nation and group should protect what it has rather than sharing.

9. The most important priority for any nation is to protect itself from potential adversaries by building up its military power.

10. Competition between nations is the only viable form of international behavior. (8)

During the past twelve years I have spoken about the messages of global modeling to citizens and public officials throughout the world. Across cultures, walks of life, and classes, the majority of reactions I hear are the same. There is broad agreement with the basic messages, but there is also the belief that only a small minority shares that agreement. There is a feeling of powerlessness, whether the individual speaking is peasant, corporate executive, or cabinet minister. There is a belief that constraints imposed by social, political, and economic institutions prevent people from acting in accordance with the messages of the global models. The assumptions which shape present policies are unexamined, but taken for granted as true.

Perhaps the most pernicious unexamined assumptions are exemplified by items 7 through 10 above. Such philosophies have become manifest in resource allocation priorities by nations around the world, and are both decried as immoral and accepted as essential. While the Brundtland Commission report may detail our global aspirations, the following sam-

> *"The most important message is that changes in human values, modes of thinking, and visions of the future are needed for us to live more sustainably and harmoniously — indeed to survive — in an interdependent world."*

pling of information more accurately reflects what our values and priorities have manifested on the planet:

> The megatonnage in the world's stockpile of nuclear weapons is enough to kill 58 billion people, or to kill every person now living twelve times.

> In the Third World, military spending has increased fivefold since 1960 and the number of countries ruled by military governments has grown from twenty-two to fifty-seven.

> The US and USSR, first in military power, rank fourteen and fifty-one among all nations in their infant-mortality rates.

> The budget of the US Air Force is larger than the total educational budget for 1.2 billion children in Africa, Latin America, and Asia, excluding Japan.

> The Soviet Union in one year spends more on military defense than the governments of all the developing countries spend for education and health care for 3.6 billion people.

> There is one soldier per 43 people in the world, one physician per 1,030 people.

> It costs $590,000 a day to operate one aircraft carrier while every day in Africa alone 14,000 children die of hunger or hunger-related causes.

> In a world spending $800 billion a year for military programs, one adult in three cannot read and write; one person in four is hungry. (9)

How can we transform the world we have into the one most of us say we want? Global models do not provide an answer to this question, but they point the direction where the answer may be found. The most important message of global models is not about specific future projections or even about global interdependence. The most important message is that changes in human values, modes of thinking, and visions of the future are needed for us to live more sustainably and harmoniously — indeed to survive — in an interdependent world.

Towards a New Mode of Thinking

In 1982 Donella Meadows, Gerhart Bruckmann, and I completed a book about the first decade of global modeling. The title of the book, *Groping in the Dark*, referred to the Sufi fable of the man searching for his front-door key under the lamppost, not because he lost it there, but because the lighting is best there. Our point was that global modelers would prefer more light, but feel they must work where the critical problems lie.

Our book shared not only the technology, but the personal experience of building global models and working with other global modelers. The most important consequence has been a fundamental transformation in our personal worldview. Living in an interdependent world will require greater levels of trust and cooperation. We know this is true, but must be willing to risk acting on this knowledge.

In the conclusion of the book, we tried to share our own experience of transformation and our views on the mode of thinking toward which global modeling points. That statement is an appropriate conclusion for this survey as well. (1)

The most basic message of the global models is not new
    and should not be surprising.

We do not need a computer model to tell us that:

    we must not destroy the system upon which our sustenance
        depends
    poverty is wrong and preventable.
    the exploitation of one person or nation by another degrades
        both the exploited and the exploiter.
    it is better for individuals and nations to cooperate than to fight.
    the love we have for all humankind and for future generations
        should be the same as our love for those close to us.
    if we do not embrace these principles and live by them, our
        system cannot survive
    our future is in our hands and will be no better or worse than
        we make it.

These messages have been around for centuries.
They reemerge periodically in different forms
    and now in the outputs of global models.
Anything that persists for so long and comes from such diverse
    sources as gurus and input-output matrices must be coming
    very close to truth.
The current condition of our globe is intolerable
    and we make it so.

It is changing
    because of what we decide

It could be beautiful
>   If we would only
>>   decide to get along together
>>   be open to each other and to new ways of thinking
>>   remember what is really important to us
>>>   and what is less so, and
>>   live our lives for that which is important.

As sophisticated, skeptical, scientific Westerners
>   We always react to statements like that by saying:

It sounds too simple
>   And is in fact impossible.
How could we ever decide to get along together?
>   You don't just decide things like that.
>   And how could we get everyone else to decide it?

(It couldn't be possible that everyone else is just like us
and is saying the same thing)

When everyone is so sophisticated
>   that they can't believe it could be simple to be honest and
>>   to care, and

Everyone is so smart
>   that they know they don't count
>>   so they never try

You get the kind of world we've got.

Maybe it's worth thinking another way
>   as if we cared and we made a difference
>>   even if it's just groping in the dark.

Security for All
in the Nuclear Age

Anatoly A. Gromyko

Director, Institute of Africa Studies; Professor and Member of Committee
of Soviet Scientists for Peace against the Nuclear Threat. Dr. Gromyko is a
Corresponding Member of the Soviet Academy of Sciences. He is the
author of over 200 papers and books, including *New Thinking in the
Nuclear Age*, coauthored with Vladimir Lomeiko, which reflects the spread
in the USSR of the philosophy of new thinking.

If I were to put the meaning of new political thinking in a nutshell, I'd
say it stands for a process in which we ought to recognize each other's
humanity, as we move to solve today's complex problems dealing with
political relations, economics, and social life.

Some will dismiss this move as utopian thinking and claim that even if
we see our opponent's humanity, he will not necessarily see the humanity
in us. After all, during past scholarly debates a favorite argument always
has been that opponents never previously in history have paid much attention to each other's humanity, that other motives always guide politicians
in their day-to-day activities.

But I ask: When in human history, other than now, have we had such
clear evidence, devoid of question, showing that we humans have arrived
at a limit? If we move beyond it, our continued survival on this planet is
imperiled. Does not this extraordinary situation we all face dictate equally
uncommon solutions that transcend our usual points of view?

New Thinking and New Politics

We all live on the same planet Earth, our common home. No matter
how widely we differ in our understanding of what is good and what is
just, and which path leads to freedom, equality, and happiness, we should
not try to change another's views by means of nuclear weapons. Now this

nuclear threat, like a two-edged sword of Damocles, hangs over the heads of all mankind, not a select few. Should it fall, it will spare no one.

The necessary philosophy for survival in this modern era contains several significant implications. For instance, we must learn to express opinions, no matter how unpleasant, without threatening or injuring the national and human dignity of those who do not share our opinions. Equally important, we must learn to express opinions without exciting in ourselves and others fear and hatred for those who think differently.

". . . we must learn to express [our] opinions without exciting in ourselves and others fear and hatred for those who think differently."

Here again special responsibility rests upon those with the potential to destroy everything through the use of nuclear weapons, primarily the US and the USSR. Some Americans do not like many things about the USSR; the same is true of some Soviet attitudes towards the US. And everyone is entitled to express opinions within, of course, the limits expected of any civilized society. Thus, conflicts will always exist, but in the present nuclear age, they can no longer be resolved by war and violence. This will require both new thinking and new action by the USSR and US.

New political thinking must be based on a reasonable practice of international relations. I would say we need a rational humanistic approach, based on our new information of nuclear danger and global interrelatedness, rather than a thoughtless continuation of faith in the permanency of many stereotypes that developed over recent centuries. And here let me quote Leo Tolstoy, who, reflecting on the correlation of reason and faith in man's world outlook, wrote:

> Misinterpreters of the truth usually say that reason can't be trusted because it speaks differently in different men . . . But such a claim is quite the opposite of the truth. Reason never speaks differently. It always speaks alike in all men . . . Whether God is said to have appeared in a pillar of fire, or Buddha to have ascended on sunrays, or Mohammed to have flown to the heavens, or Christ to have walked on water . . . rational men, always and everywhere answer in a similar manner: This isn't true. But, to the questions, "Is it right to do unto others as you would they do unto you? Is it good to love and forgive them, do good to them?" The reason of all men throughout time has said: "Yes, it's right and worthwhile." (1)

The strategy of survival in the nuclear age presupposes a new awareness of security for one's own country and for other nations, and consequently a new approach to international security. Assuming that all the members of the international community acknowledge and subsequently reject nuclear war as collective suicide, they should be interested in removal of those factors which make a nuclear conflict likely. The two most important and decisive factors being: the nuclear arms race and striving for military superiority.

The Logic of Nuclear Thinking

Many years of experience have shown that even with a sincere desire to stop the arms race and reduce armaments, it is still very difficult to reach an agreement — especially in an atmosphere of international tension and mutual mistrust. In the absence of agreement, a continuing arms race leads only to still greater tension and mistrust. The system, therefore, has built into it a spiraling or escalating effect.

What is the way out of this vicious cycle?

In my opinion, this will occur only when the new logic of international relations will be recognized and accepted: In a world of nuclear overkill and growing interdependence, it is impossible to secure a unilateral advantage for oneself to the detriment of the other side without ultimately impairing one's own interests. Recognition of this basic fact provides the basis for establishing one of the main principles of the new way of thinking.

"In a world of nuclear overkill and growing interdependence, it is impossible to secure a unilateral advantage for oneself to the detriment of the other side without ultimately impairing one's own interests."

The stark realities of the nuclear age demand a revision of such basic notions as strength, superiority, victory, and security. Nuclear war now, it is clear, cannot be the continuation of state policy by other means. Victory in a nuclear war is as much an illusion as is the idea that there can be security for one side to the detriment of the other.

Genuine security in the present nuclear age must always mean universal international security. This international security is based on the premise that both sides consider each other's interests and, while ensuring security for one side, see to it that the security of the other side is not compromised. Common security can only be possible when based on the principle of equality and equal security.

Naturally achieving this goal is difficult and will take time, for it means abandoning many old and habitual modes of thought. For years, a gain for one side implied a loss for the other. Moreover, it was considered beneficial when damage occurred to one's opponent. In fact, these principles are given expression by some military and political strategists who continue to hold to the concept of deterrence or the doctrines of a limited and protracted war, the ultimate goal being the infliction of grave or mortal damage to the other side.

Instead, the philosophy of survival in this age of nuclear overkill presupposes a shift away from present military and political thinking, based as it is on now-antiquated notions of strength, superiority, and winnable war. Thus, real differences between new and traditional political thinking involve more than the issue of a possible nuclear war, since there can be no winners and no survival under these conditions. It is hard today to imagine any sane person seriously believing it possible to achieve one's political aims by using nuclear weapons.

There is still another matter to consider. New and traditional thinking have clearly distinguishable and diametrically opposed viewpoints in their approach to a state of security. New thinking urges renouncing force in international relations and guaranteeing security only by political means. Old thinking seeks to preserve conventional power politics through the use of sophisticated military technology. The former viewpoint calls for a constructive and creative interaction of nations and peoples on a global scale. The latter envisions perpetual armed camps of "them" and "us" and hopes to create a Noah's ark on this planet in which "the chosen" can possibly sit out the "deluge" of mankind's global problems.

The main danger of war, even of a war fought with conventional weapons, lies in its unpredictability. Experience shows that during wars, the entire intellectual and physical potentials of the belligerent nations are concentrated on achieving one goal — defeat of the enemy. Even regional wars have resulted in the invention and employment of new conventional armaments which have then become most dangerous weapons. And how many times has the temptation to use nuclear weapons arisen during these conflicts?

Every regional conflict which flares in various areas of the world has its own specific danger. Such conflicts have a tendency to spread and involve a considerable number of other states. These conflicts tend to poison the international atmosphere. The time has come not only to understand their basic causes, but to root them from the soil of world politics. The Middle East, Afghanistan, and Nicaragua can become zones of peace and tranquility. This will occur only through joint parallel efforts of those governments affected by the conflicts. A policy which vigorously pursues the resolution of conflict must become a reality. In any case, the use of force in regional conflicts is no longer justified. The full voice of politicians and diplomats and not the roar of guns and rockets should be heard.

The question arises: Is it possible to halt the arms race and to reduce spending on arms? Reykjavik gave us an answer. At that meeting top Soviet and American leaders reached a basic, if not formal, understanding on the need to eliminate nuclear weapons in ten years, a relatively short time. At Reykjavik what had only been a "dream" in all our minds could have become reality. This itself is historic — a first important step on the road to disarmament was taken.

Our Common Home

That the Earth is our home is now common knowledge. But do we always remember that our planet is the home of all mankind, rather than for just two or several of its nations? Or do we at times behave in our common home as if it were our exclusive estate, regarding other nations as invited guests at best? Yet, large or small, the other nations, like ourselves, are the caretakers of our planet and have no less right to be safe and well-off while living on it.

> *". . . the use of force in regional conflicts is no longer justified."*

For all their importance, Soviet-American relations cannot overshadow the modern world's diversity, contradictions, and problems. This requires considering the concept of all-embracing international security. If we really want to conduct world affairs humanely, we should not be indifferent to Third World troubles. Reason, not just a natural compassion, bids us so. Africa, Asia, and Latin America's plight soon may turn into a tragedy which will affect industrialized lands too.

Apart from straining East-West relations, the arms race widens the gap between the North and the South, and is fraught with the danger of global upheaval in our interdependent world. New thinking in the nuclear age also demands awareness of the importance of these new problems and ways of solving them. This is all the more important since East-West confrontation represents the number one political issue in the minds of the majority of people in the Northern Hemisphere. On the other hand, people in the south regard this view as a manifestation of isolationism and a legacy of colonial rule.

Within the next few decades North-South conflict may grow into an awesome confrontation dwarfing many of today's problems, though many people in the North today are still unaware of such a dramatic end result. It is not a certainty, but a definite possibility, if conditions continue as they are. They cannot be overlooked since no problem of this sort has gone away of its own accord: a cure rather than a palliative is needed. Moreover, in this case conditions are worsened by the huge gap in development between the North and the South, and its associated hunger, poverty, illiteracy, and backwardness for a considerable part of the Third World population.

Remove the Cause — The Disease Will Pass

The ancients used to say: "Sublata causa, toletur morbus." Remove the cause — the disease will pass. We could paraphrase the applicability of this dictum for today's international relationships: "Stop the arms race in order to have a sound world economy and healthy politics."

It will take much time and effort to close the gaps between the economic levels for developed countries of the North and the emergent nations of the South. At present these keep widening. There can be no simple and swift solution here. Progress to this goal undoubtedly calls for the establishment of a new international economic order, for the restructuring of unfair and unequal economic relations between many industrialized developed powers and developing countries, and for penetrating social and economic changes in the Third World itself.

But these problems can only be resolved if the arms race is halted and subsequently ended. Then, the developed nations, released from the crushing burden of military spending, will be able to allocate more resources to aid struggling poorer countries.

The above abysmal gap between the North and the South is well illustrated by the following figures. About $800 billion is being spent on the arms race each year. This is more than the incomes of the world's fifty poorest nations, with 1.5 billion inhabitants. Fuel poured into combat vehicles, tanks, planes, and ships equals half of Third World oil needs. The developing states use less copper, lead, tin, aluminum, nickel, zinc, and platinum-group metals than goes into the arms race. Is this a wise order of priorities, not only for Third World development, but for international security as a whole?

The Time Bomb

Twentieth-century man's impact on nature has begun to assume dangerous proportions; as a consequence, an ecological time bomb is ticking on Earth. This ticking becomes ever louder as the environment deteriorates, most often through the misuse of major natural resources — water, air, soil, animal and plant life — and as environmental pollution spreads to threaten life on Earth. Concerns for the environment and actions to limit pollution must become part of our global plan as soon as possible.

A true picture of the scope and extent of needed changes for the present and in the imminent future can only be made by using approaches which recognize the complexities of relationships and interdependencies of man and his environment. Factors have combined to diminish our Earth's apparent size and to restrict its possibilities. These include: the growing world population (which doubled every 30,000 years at the dawn of civilization and doubles every thirty-nine years today), and drastic depletion of natural resources such as fresh water, fertile soil, animal and plant life, raw materials, and energy sources. Added to this is the recent discovery of depletion of our protective ozone layer over Antarctica, exemplifying yet another and human effect on planetary ecological survival systems.

Not long ago many believed that environmental protection was a primary concern only for industrialized countries where human intervention with the environment was most pronounced. But now we hear alarming predictions from futurists about doomsday-like accumulative effects from negative demographic, socioeconomic, and ecological trends resulting from many Third World country actions. Environmental degradation is proceeding in a most intensive fashion in these places. It is enough to provide just a single example like the desertification in Africa which has reached a tragic scale.

"Fuel poured into combat vehicles, tanks, planes, and ships equals half of Third World oil needs. . . . Is this a wise order of priorities, not only for Third World development, but for international security as a whole?"

Worsened environmental conditions in some parts of the Third World are already affecting global ecology. Consider the increased carbon dioxide content in the air, which may lead to global climatic changes within the next few generations. This development results from a mix of at least two tendencies: the continuing growth of worldwide hydrocarbon fuel use and the chopping down of tropical forests by developing countries.

Pondering ways to resolve present-day complex problems, more farsighted scholars draw two important and correct conclusions. First, unlike earlier societies, the world today is witnessing a growing interdependence of global problems, none of which can be resolved independently of the others. Second, a new thinking is needed in our age, prompted by worsening global conditions which confront mankind with the need to devise a new and lasting approach to their solution. These conclusions have been drawn, in particular, by Günter Kunz and Friederich Wester of the Federal Republic of Germany (West Germany). The latter, the leader of a Munich team of biological and environmental scholars, observed that our world is a very complex mesh of interdependencies, but that we often view every phenomenon and concept individually, out of the context of their interdependencies or, as he puts it, "out of their cybernetic interaction." (2)

Friederich Wester concludes: "We need new thinking with new dimensions." (3) Günter Kunz shares his view: "Only a serious and well-thought-out approach to complex systems based on new thinking can ensure that we will continue to live in peace with nature." (4)

These experts, like many others, rightly believe that our ecological problems are closely related to the problem of peace and can only be resolved under conditions of peace. Moreover, they recognize the special danger of the escalating arms race. Günter Kunz believes:

> As a consequence of technological progress, the arms race keeps increasing the risk of war which could escalate into a worldwide atomic catastrophe, not only because "accidents" at different levels cannot be ruled out, but also due to the temptation that still exists to use armed force to resolve disputes.

He draws a very important conclusion:

> Psychologically, [the arms race] promotes intolerable and outdated thinking and views in nationalistic or imperial categories, which facilitate brutal and violent actions (national arrogance, thinking in terms of prestige, hunger for world dominance, prejudice against foreigners, or violence in domestic politics). It perpetuates a form of relationship typical of the Stone Age (Law of the Fist) in state-to-state and often in domestic relationships. Such actions may be characterized polemically and not unjustifiably as "pollution of the spiritual environment." (5)

Even if we succeed in avoiding the worst of possible consequences — death in the fires of thermonuclear catastrophe or the snow of "nuclear winter" — continuing the arms race will doom the world to a chronic feverish state of military conflicts and crises and to ecological disaster. A "Noah's ark" strategy will be useless in this situation; there can be no safe place to hide, no "safe harbor." Instead, should those days come to pass, they will bring with them the horrors of the ancient prophesied apocalypse when "Men shall seek death and shall not find it; and shall desire to die, and death shall flee from them."

Nuclear War — Super Taboo

Where is the way out of the dead end into which the arrogance of power drives mankind? Shall we have enough determination and wisdom to curb the forces that we ourselves have created and use them for our own benefit instead of harm? Hardly anybody has a universal recipe to cure all mankind's wounds and ills. But one thing is clear: Cure them we must. We simply have no other choice.

In a nuclear world, it is impossible to cut the Gordian knot of tangled global problems at one stroke of a crusader's sword. The nuclear sword would certainly cut the knot, but it would also put an end to the human race in the process. Only by carefully untangling the knot of problems and by cooperative joint efforts will it be possible to find a way out of the maze of nuclear despair into a world of reason, trust, and cooperation.

Survival of the two different social systems must be accepted as a given. That is basic. First, change in thinking must be firmly established. Without acceptance of the long-term continuation of both capitalism and socialism — with all their multiple variations — no new thinking will prevail. That is the starting point. At the same time, we can explore all mutual means of survival.

It is fortunate that both countries have chosen this path. Present efforts by Mikhail Gorbachev and Ronald Reagan and their coworkers may lead to important agreements concerning eliminating rockets with nuclear warheads in Europe. The USSR and US are striving to reach agreement on nuclear disarmament. This process, however, may prove to be extremely difficult.

"Without acceptance of the long-term continuation of both capitalism and socialism — with all their multiple variations — no new thinking will prevail."

In this joint effort common sense is gradually prevailing. This prompts the realization that people should observe a possibility boundary — a "taboo line" for their activities. Nuclear war now means death for humanity — it's a "super taboo." Unfortunately humans have the capacity to cross over this limit. At the same time scientific studies have shown that there will be no survivors after a nuclear holocaust. This is why nuclear weapons are such a dread adversary of all state governments and their peoples. Either we eliminate nuclear weapons, or they will eliminate us. This leads to a very distinct conclusion for politics and diplomacy in the nuclear age: We must eliminate all nuclear weapons and any other means of annihilating people as soon as possible. By developing a political will to do so, the US and the USSR, along with other countries, can achieve this complex task.

The arms race must come to an end. Instead, efforts should be directed to create stable security for all. Nuclear deterrence will become completely unnecessary in the face of a comprehensive security system, deep reduction of arms, and total elimination of nuclear weapons. The immorality of nuclear deterrence will become abundantly clear.

The USSR and the US, as well as other governments, can explore space for peaceful purposes. To this end they could work to further mutually beneficial large-scale projects, including a joint manned mission to Mars.

Security for the international community can be based on "deterrence through verification." Strict adherence to national and international verification can prove highly beneficial in building required confidence for maintaining agreements on disarmament.

Moscow and Washington, along with other industrialized states, could use financial resources, realized from disarmament, to support a number of vitally important projects in the Third World, in such places as Africa, Asia, and Latin America. Specific projects in Africa could involve altering present practices of desertification, providing clean drinking water, abolishing tropical diseases, and constructing children's hospitals.

These projects as well as others leading to peaceful cooperation can become a reality. This will occur only if we truly have the desire to make them so. This realization will require new political thinking on our part. In the long run this process must be adopted by all politicians. The sooner the better for all of us. As long as we behave rationally in the future, all is not lost.

Problems with the
New Way of Thinking

Ales Adamovich

Professor and Corresponding Member, Byelorussian Academy of Sciences. Dr.
Adamovich is the author of twenty books and is a member of the Union of Soviet
Writers. His sometimes controversial writing has been at the cutting edge of new
thinking in the Soviet Union.

New View of War

First people perceived there was a problem and then they found words
to express it. Witnesses say that after detonation of the first nuclear device
American Professor Kenneth T. Bainbridge exclaimed: "Now we are all
scoundrels!" Thus physicists were the first to recognize the consequences
of bringing these weapons of cosmic power into a world already divided
and disturbed. Subsequently the rest of us have come to the same point,
albeit later and more gradually.

Several years ago one of our famous mathematicians phoned me and
accusingly read a quotation from my story *The Chastisers* which had just
been published. In it I state: "It's not yet known whose formulae — physicists' or poets' — will be used to blow up the earth." The mathematician
seemed pleased to read this self-criticism of us lyricists. And indeed there
will be no guiltless ones, if this most terrible event occurs. It appears as if
the public does not take this problem seriously, or has drifted into the
state described by Byelorussian novelist Eduard Skobelev in *Catastrophe*:
"Having lost faith, people repressed the thought of victims and being a
victim. No one climbed a pyre convinced that they would die and that is
why they all perished there."

121

Yes, a feeling of personal identification with the problem and a historical perspective is mandatory in today's world, not only for physicists who
have brought these doomsday weapons into existence, but also for politicians, military people, and we the public — the rest of the lyricists.

Today, everything depends on our thinking. Its content and character
will determine whether mankind itself has a future and whether there will
be a future for the world, as well. It all depends on our mode of thinking,
the ability, or the inability, of the majority of people to think in a manner
appropriate for the reality of our nuclear times.

Poets in the 1940s and 1950s complained — "It seems physicists are
respected and lyricists are shoved into the background."

Now times have changed and today poets are respected. It is to their
credit that they did not invent nuclear weapons. However, this happened
only because they did not directly participate. On the other hand they
have made recent positive contributions. They have worked effectively to
save the environment — to rescue the rivers, forests, soil, as well as cultural and spiritual values in our country. Still, their contribution to the
present critical issue, that of changing dangerous mind-sets concerning
war, is not even noticeable.

Writers certainly understand the meaning of growing up under military-
patriotic influences. But even today, if anyone says to them that it would
be better to have antimilitary-patriotic influences, notice their expressions.
Many will stare back in bewilderment, some even with fright.

If a military victory in the present nuclear age is impossible and is, instead, a crime against mankind, then it is logical to reason that the highest
level of patriotism, a wish for the best for your people, and others (insepa-
rable today), must coexist with a profound disgust for war. Outrage is not
for an enemy, but for everything that provokes war or hostility and for
anyone who is ready to unleash it.

There is some urgency to reconsider the way our literature is being
used, rather than in the way it is formatted. For example, in all the world
there is no collection of antimilitary literature which is better. No one
speaks, or can speak more eloquently about war's dangers, because of our
past experiences. Yet at the same time it is senseless to talk of maximized
security and greater military strength. We can no longer have it both ways.

What M. S. Gorbachev said at the 27th Party Congress is an example of
new thinking. He said it again at Reykjavik. He said it so clearly and
concisely that it will undoubtedly be recorded for posterity: "We cannot
accept 'no' as an answer to the question of whether mankind is to be or
not to be."

This is true regardless of how many times the other side says "no," true
even if they say it in a deliberately offensive and provocative manner; true
no matter how one would like to reply by slamming the door or answering

bellicosely and implacably in kind. We have no right to do so. In the final analysis, it is no longer a question of systems of socialism and capitalism, but of life on Earth itself — for "man to be or not to be."

New thinking has become our state policy. This fact is significant in itself, but this doesn't relieve any of us as individuals from the need to work for the goal of developing a new mode of thinking. It is not an easy process and cannot be done at once.

"In the final analysis, it is no longer a question of systems of socialism and capitalism, but of life on Earth itself — for 'man to be or not to be.'"

In 1984 the magazine *Friendship of People* published an unexpected article. The author, a major-general and doctor of philosophy, obviously belonged to the military-scientific establishment and had won over the editorial staff. He wrote:

At present one thing has been clearly demonstrated: with local wars imperialism has not attained a single major historical objective against revolutionary forces. Viewed from political goals, there is an ever more obvious trend for diminishing the effectiveness of predatory and unjust imperialist wars against revolutionary forces. Unjust wars cannot resolve the historical contraindications of imperialism.

This would all seem convincing. But let us read further:

On the other hand, if the effectiveness of the use of military force by aggressive circles decreases, just wars by revolutionary forces remain important and sometimes an essential means for struggle against imperialism. (1)

For the person guided by class contradictions, this latter situation makes everything simple. It provides the perfect excuse. There is still hope of inventing military solutions — possibilities already cancelled by the nuclear age. During the war there was a saying that can be paraphrased: A Russian is special. He can bear and endure conditions which would cause the death of even his most vicious enemy.

But one should carry the thought through to its end: Where does this lead us in the present world situation? What if the most just war of all ends with a nuclear holocaust?

During World War II, grave mistakes and miscalculations occurred in the resistance movement. Good demolition men were blown up because of seeming trifles: A Bickford slow-burning fuse was very similar to a fast-burning one. The time was calculated correctly, but the fuse happened to be the wrong one. An explosion occurred in one's hands, or underfoot. We are moving to make these same kind of miscalculations today, but this time we risk losing our entire world.

Reality of Nuclear Age — War Is Obsolete

It didn't happen at once, but even the most far-sighted politicians have grasped the reality of our present nuclear age, stated so simply and precisely in the now famous Russell-Einstein Manifesto: "There can be no victory in a nuclear war!"

The manifesto also says: "In order to eliminate the threat of a nuclear holocaust, one should refrain from any wars." The logic is simple: If a conventional war starts anywhere, nothing can prevent it from escalating into a nuclear one. Even if nuclear weapons are eliminated, war is still a problem. Both sides will continue to live with fear and suspicion that the other side may once again restore its nuclear capabilities. Today this is a danger more than ever before, as the world sits on top of ever-growing nuclear stockpiles.

Is war obsolete? What about just wars? It is true there are many in the world who are robbed and deprived, even entire countries. There are also many who are ready to plunder others and profit at another's expense. But one thing is important today — the end of all war. No one knows what type of a fuse one has in his hands, where it leads, and how much time there is. One can ask a childish question: If there are permitted wars, what weapons are permitted? Clearly not nuclear. Then, chemical? This is not possible. Conventional? These forces are getting very close to nuclear in killing power. This means that the improvement in conventional weapons is abolishing any warfare. Therefore, those who live with the old thinking of yesterday's policies drive themselves and all of mankind into an ever more discernable trap. The superpowers must take this into account as they presently engage in small wars such as those in the Persian Gulf, Afghanistan, Nicaragua, Iran-Iraq, and Africa.

Diversity

Soviet experts who study the United States know very well how hard it is to converse with our Western opponents — our partners in survival. Whatever is discussed, the question always comes up: "Do you still want to bury us?" If not by military, then by other means. Do you want to standardize social systems, reducing them to one?

It is these facts that Western harangue uses as a basis for continuing the confrontation, whether military, economic, or psychological. This has produced large obstacles to overcome, fostering projections of what is going on over there, promoting fear, stirring patriotism, or anything else that might incite bad feelings. And sooner or later the precept is posed: "Better dead than red"; or in our dogma, "Better dead than nonred."

Once I saw a small poster carried by a schoolgirl in the Federal Republic of Germany (West Germany) that read: "Better Star Wars than to come under colonial rule of Moscow."

But let us think about the crux of the matter and put aside propaganda and its passions. If one does not submit to the hypnotism of stereotypes, there is a way out. This comes from the realization that our world is full of diversity. It is the strength of our survival, not an obstacle to it. This is most obvious when we view nature with its wealth of diverse biological forms and complexity of genetic makeup. These conditions are responsible for stability of the life process and guarantee the continued presence and a future for our flora and fauna. This same process applies to all mankind. V. I. Lenin said that diversity is a sure way to guarantee vitality. This statement certainly applies today.

"What if the most just war of all ends with a nuclear holocaust?"

The same applies to nations, cultures, and languages. Thank God we have already abandoned the simplistic notions that variety of nations, cultures, and languages hinders progress and the unity of mankind. It became obvious that from such wealth and variety, from the flourishing of cultures and languages, the groundwork had been laid for a genuinely open-ended future and the possibility for an increasingly united mankind. Clearly nature and society must have a choice of options; we cannot leave them only one single choice, or "thread." The thread could break, and also, nobody knows what the choices should be, or their impact in a hundred or a hundred thousand years.

How far ahead can people see if they are surrounded by the walls of their own time? Can they see far enough to decide for thousands of subsequent generations? Don't such considerations also apply to the issue of the variety of social forms as well? The old axiom applies to this situation: "Better to be different in life, than the same in death."

The time for such intolerance has passed, both for their side as well as ours. Although some social philosophers would hardly agree with such a course, we must leave tomorrow alone. The future will take care of itself. Our first concern is just to have this future be, to have it come. No one has a right to risk the life of billions of people out of an egoistic concern that they receive their future life in a specially packaged form. Future generations will sort everything out themselves when they come into this life! To let, to permit them to come — that is the most important thing.

At a meeting with writers participating in the Issyk-Kul Forum, M. S. Gorbachev said: "Look at the whole world — we are all different. Is this a disadvantage? It is reality. We must learn how to live with this variety and to respect the choice of each nation."*(2) Let's follow our leader's advice and that of the old proverb: "The sun will continue to rise and set, people will continue to be born and die."

How is the process of new thinking and new perception proceeding in a specific field such as literature? This can best be handled by breaking our discussion into three concerns: humanitarian issues, morality in the nuclear age, and specific artistic issues.

Humanitarian Issues. Tolstoy once wrote this thought: ". . . throughout history people worked, traded, waged wars . . . but what they were really doing all this time was finding out what is good and what is evil."

Yet, contemporary life has introduced an amendment to Tolstoy's observation. This is best expressed by contemporary author Sergei Pavlovich Zalygin: ". . . before we used to solve two equations — what is good and what is evil? The whole of world literature and æsthetics were occupied with this issue. Now we have a third equation: 'What is nothing?' That is the reality we are facing at the moment." (3)

This must inevitably exert a powerful influence on the whole of literature. But, what is really happening? It's not quite like that. In fact, we live as we did before, we write basically as we always have. This means that we write much worse from a moral perspective, than we did in the prenuclear age. From the perspective of that previous age, literature that was considered to be adequate, just right, sufficient, must today be judged totally inadequate. Even right now, we overindulge ourselves in our writing and philosophizing, mainly about trifles, neglecting the major concerns of the nuclear age. And many say: "Who really cares about that!" But fortunately things are beginning to happen in literature, if not consciously, then subconsciously.

This is occurring because the concept of humanism is changing, along with moral and artistic values. And slowly along with these have come changes in literary form and content. Humanism is ridding itself of various definitions that served as past limitations. Today its concern is for nothing less than all of mankind. Now formerly competing aspects and ideas have become partners in a system to promote survival and preservation of life. Why? Because no one individual can or will survive in the present nuclear age without and at the expense of others.

Finally, we fully understand the issue of so-called arithmetic humanism, debated so intensely just several years ago. Life in that process was disposable in order to obtain the goal. It was quite impersonal. In this scheme one can calculate how many lives might be sacrificed for the happiness of others: If more of those others are lost, then the goal is attained, since there would be many more survivors. This is so-called active humanism!

---

*Lake Issyk-Kul, near Alma Ata, capital Kazakhstan Republic, USSR.

What would "the tear of a child," or the sacrifice of a single child matter in such a case — survival of the group is all that counts, survival at any price!

It is now a different time. The atom bomb has erased arithmetic thinking. Behind every coldly calculated figure now looms the nothing of Zalygin. The gap between killing a single man and killing all of mankind has narrowed to a gnat's eyelash in the age of nuclear weapons.

This very notion of nothing jeopardizes our immediate future and inevitably permeates all moral values and categories and changes them — sometimes quite drastically.

Morality in the Nuclear Age. On an intellectual level, our species is back at the same stage at which primæval man started. Then, as now, the moral issue of the time was survival — "Is homo erectus to live, or not live?" was the question.

"The gap between killing a single man and killing all of mankind has narrowed to a gnat's eyelash in the age of nuclear weapons."

Having come full circle, humanity has returned to the situation it faced at that far distant beginning — that of survival. But now all life on the planet depends on whether or not we will continue to kill our own kind.

All previous commandments developed in the prenuclear age such as, "Do not kill," and "Don't do to another what you would not wish done to yourself and your own tribe or clan," still do not carry the import of today's mortal danger and threat and now we need to add: "Otherwise you will all perish." This time death will be absolute, all will die.

One can say: We are killing each other now and nothing has happened! We have made so many bombs and we are still alive! We live in debt to chance. As our minister of Foreign Affairs reminded the whole human community at the General Assembly of the United Nations — this debt to chance is more terrible than that demanded by Shakespeare's Shylock: If payment is demanded, we shall not get away with cutting off a piece of flesh: We shall have to pay with the life of every human being living on the planet.

That is why new humanism and new morality are not words hastily tacked onto the concept of new thinking. They are an integral part of the practical process needed for an adequate response to the unprecedented situation into which people have driven themselves: We must change in every way.

Specific Artistic Issues. Modern Soviet literature, with its best novels *Fire* by Valentin Rasputin*, *Sad Detective* by Viktor Astafyev†, and *The Executioner's Block* by Chingiz Aitmatov††, has become directly involved with today's controversies about how we must lead our lives. It has aroused considerable and diverse comment particularly from certain writers and critics who have judged their material from criteria of style — whether these novels were written according to previously accepted artistic rules; or content — whether their message had gone too far or was too extreme.

The Executioner's Block by Aitmatov provides a particularly interesting and instructive example of this process. It received mixed reviews from "Round Table" in *Literaturnaya Gazeta* and raised similar commentary from television critics. On one hand, readers said that Aitmatov's novel had failings in taste and language; very often his sense of proportion fell short of the mark. On the other hand it contained a power, unprecedented even for this writer. Where did this power come from? What fed it? How can one explain the nature and source of this power if this novel had significant shortcomings and some things weren't quite right and others simply bad? Nobody has provided a convincing argument one way or the other. I am sure that I would arrive at the same position using past criteria.

Two years ago when I had a friendly argument with Vasiliy Bykov, whom I tried to seduce into making antinuclear statements in the literature, we came up with the new word superliterature. After all, life faced a super threat to its existence from super weapons! So shouldn't we think about matching this with an adequate expression in literature — "superliterature"? Let the damned bomb blow up inside ourselves, in the consciousness of literature. Why not? We had failed to make any other adequate response to all that was happening and threatening existence in our outer world. It seemed quite clear. If our consciousness is moved to a new level, we would automatically start writing in a new way.

This approach has subsequently caused much debate among writers and critics, as would be expected. There is a lot of disagreement. First, this approach is considered both presumptuous and offensive to those steeped in classic literature. We postulate that the classic writers have missed something. And how can we, such geniuses, produce it? In reality it is most

---

*Considers moral values and changes in our modern age. Attacks the "comfortable position between good and evil." Individuals walk back and forth across the line constantly.

†Revival of family values. "Dynasties, societies, and empires turned into dust" as the result of family disintegration.

††Emphasizes individualism, criticizes party hacks. "Man must work for himself." Attacks mindless sloganeering against capitalism. Raises religious questions and the struggle against drug use.

confronting to us. We have been writing a lot up to now. But wasn't this merely going through the motions and therefore wasted effort?

Yet all the same — even more confronting and threatening is the truth that today our life depends on chance. Life exists due to the fact that nobody, as yet, has pushed the nuclear button. We live in a world where such a disastrous global calamity like Chernobyl is just a warning of the holocaust that menaces all of us, every moment of our lives. One cannot simply stand still and let it happen.

With such knowledge, it is no longer possible to work and write with an Olympian calm, hoping that your work will be recognized, perhaps if not now, then in a decade or a century. One might manage to squeak by, but what kind of writers are we then, and who needs that kind of literature?

It was just this kind of discussion that was aroused by *Fire* and the *Sad Detective*. The more recent publication of *The Executioner's Block* by Aitmatov started the process anew, again with critics attempting to measure it with the same old yardsticks. But let us think for a moment: What if the criteria and standards for measuring this literature are out of date? What if the critical yardsticks are wrong? Hence our ability to grasp things and to appreciate their literary worth is inadequate. The real merits, since they are not well understood, seem to be demerits. There seems to be shortcomings and lack of public appeal. This is understandable, since we have a greater tendency to praise things that are familiar, that fit old standards of reference. Take *The Executioner's Block*. It is a pyramid built of huge blocks, so why should we scan it for roughness that may need some polishing? Shouldn't we stop, instead, and admire the way the author cut out these blocks, put them together, and built the pyramid? But we lack the time and the urge to do so.

Actually such points as desire and skill in interpreting this kind of literature are not that important. The main point is whether literary criticism evidences an awareness of the truth concerning our modern world which is the central message of *The Executioner's Block*.

It is interesting sometimes to register the stream of one's own thoughts. To this end I feel like calling today's literature a superliterature because of the powerful flash of new consciousness it is capable of providing. I also realize that the image of this new literature emerged some time ago, at the 1983 Minsk conference on "war" literature. A discussion was held then on whether literature should deal with the truth about the nuclear threat. We came up with this expression: "Let the damned bomb blow up in the heads of writers, in the consciousness of literature."

A young girl who had no standing in literary circles a few years ago, has become today one of the best writers in the past forty years. It is Svetlana Aleksiyevich who wrote *The Face of War Is Not Feminine* and *The Last Witnesses*. She is skillful not figuratively, but literally. She likes to use a tape recorder, not a microphone. Following the leads of writers of the older generation, she went out to listen to life, to record it, and an old truth was reconfirmed: There is wisdom in life! You have to just listen and grasp this wisdom. Document the facts as they occur on tape and on play-back catch the nuance of voices, truth, and psychological state of the times, now passed.

At first I remember being astonished (later I accepted it as normal), by the overwhelming truth revealed about man and his soul through this process. They were contained in stories told by ordinary, often illiterate women, others in letters or diaries. It was as if this material had been written by Dostoyevsky. In many cases as if the person were quoting or retelling some unknown work of Dostoyevsky, or of Tolstoy! I would like to retell at least a couple of the best ones.

During the siege of Leningrad a woman was dying from starvation. She was surrounded by her children who crowded around her fear-stricken, waiting for the inevitable. As soon as she closed her eyes, they burst out crying. Their tears called her back to life. The suffering seemed to go on forever. Finally the eldest girl said: "Turn away! Let Mommy die!" Where can one go to find a measure of this compassion, or find a similar measure of this truth — only among the best material that has ever been written. It was previously only contained in the classics.

In the Byelorussian village of Borki where the fascists burned to death more than 2,000 people, in a new house built after the war on the very site where an older house had been burned down, we were recording a woman who remembered it all. She looked out of the window, as if the Nazis were still there, as if they were still coming to her doorstep (as happened in June 1942). She was recalling about a neighbor woman from next door who ran into her house with her eight-year-old boy, saying: ". . . my son, why did you put on these rubber boots? Your feet will burn for a long time in the rubber!"

I have been thinking for a long time: Isn't this same kind of oral history necessary for describing events in villages in the 1920s and 1930s. It could shed new light on and explain today's events as well. We could hear tales about the villages themselves, but a great deal more about life in those times would be revealed. This art form exists. It really works.

Thinking back upon events that occurred at the Minsk Conference in 1983, there seemed to be much argument (the ideas were still in a developmental stage) about whether one should frighten oneself and others and whether it is possible to create a literature while standing with one foot at the very edge of an abyss. Wouldn't it be better to step back a little bit and then create?

Today no one argues about this any longer, although in practice only a few are able to walk along the edge of the abyss. But it is they who have become the spokespersons for new perceptive literature and new thinking. (Or, as philosopher Yuri Karyakin says, with a new chronotype, a new breed in time.) This literature is slowly becoming the accepted norm, it has not retreated, but dared to meet the danger and more so because the bomb has exploded in it. This is Aitmatov's *The Executioner's Block*. As critics and the literary community fixate all the harder on the unevenness and flaws of the work, they are becoming increasingly irritated at their own inability to accept and interpret this new literary realism.

Of note is the fact that Chingiz Aitmatov was one of the first to be deeply touched, so deeply as to actually become obsessed, by the persistent and agonizing realization that there is a lack of clear expression as to what awaits people and the planet. How can this best be said, shouted, so as to be heard? How does one express the unspeakable? How does one write so that resultant literature will somehow influence the course of events? His articles, speeches, and communications were not just timely, but serious pieces of work that came from the bottom of his heart and from his deep concern, and his novel *The Executioner's Block* is proof of that.

> *"There are new and emergent forms in contemporary literature, mainly due to meditative and intuitive connections with something bigger than oneself."*

One must get used to such books as *The Executioner's Block*, *Sad Detective*, and *Fire*. The global problems that they introduce become the most important parts of their novels. Probably it was once also difficult to become accustomed to seeing new volcanic mountains. At first there surely were feelings of discomfort and disbelief. One would wonder: Where did this all come from? What is it? Later it would be just as impossible to imagine that those very mountains and landscape had not always been there.

Soul on Fire

At the time of such Roman tyrants as Tiberius and Nero, there existed, paradoxically, a moment of great personal freedom for their subjects, who were normally totally dependent on their brutal whims, wishes, and wild paranoia. This moment, however, was side-by-side with death. Preparing to commit suicide by order of the tyrant, a Roman citizen could sit down at a table and write what he would not have dared to even think about the day before. The whole truth. This last moment of life raised up to the human level anyone who had been bowing and scraping at the tyrant's feet.

It is exactly the same for a writer. To live every instant as if it were the last has always been important in literature: to write as if it were your last word, and to live life openly, so as to fear that nothing could not be re-vealed for everyone in the world to see.

This was the attitude of Dostoyevsky. Besides his painful conscience and rare gift of compassion, there was another point of his life to consider. In various recent academic publications of his works, there are hosts of dates listed when the author suffered attacks of illness.* We know how exhausting these attacks were and that each of them could have cost him his life.

These attacks combined with his talent created that burst of psychologi-cal energy that allowed Dostoyevsky constantly to look beyond the threshold of death. This closeness to death intensified in Dostoyevsky a feeling of catastrophe for the world as a whole. He sensed that this catas-trophe would occur unless people started to turn from self-involvement to look for truth outside of themselves and to kindness for their fellow man. A century before we contemplated the militarization of space, Dos-toyevsky foresaw this possibility in his writing, as embodied by an axe launched into outer space. He saw the similarity between this axe in space and the axe under Raskolnikov's cloak and the very bottom of the human soul.† He was reproached for being a pessimist and a misanthrope. Today we are astonished by his foresight.

Today we could compile a different list of attacks of illness afflicting entire countries, with the whole human race sweating in cold fear: a list of insane plans for nuclear bombing of cities — new crises like the one in the Caribbean. The literature we are talking about must not take its eyes off this list for even a moment.

There have always been liars in literature. Some even more than that. But what would you call the Roman citizen who, before his ordered death, with a blade in his hand, ready to commit suicide, would praise and flatter his murderer in his last message?

While in the United States, at the Kennan Institute to help in their Russian studies program, I raised the subject of spacebridges. I argued that they would eventually generate a new art form. There was a special conference devoted to the issue at the Moscow Art Institute.

I might have been naïve, but I started to dream how the very scale of this new art form might raise the level of truthfulness among nations and enhance social self-criticism: just imagine an audience of 2 billion to 4 billion people! Would anyone dare to keep mumbling the same old thing: You are all wrong, I alone am right? . . . One would have to be Khlestakov (Gogol's hero in *Inspector General*) on a planetary scale to be able to look into the eyes of all mankind and keep lying like that.

---

* Dostoyevsky suffered from repeated attacks of epileptic seizures.

† Main character and assassin in Dostoyevsky's novel *Crime and Punishment*.

Someone objected and stated that I was wrong: The larger the audience, the easier it is fooled. It is more difficult to deceive one man; while so many ways have been found to fool a crowd. History bears witness to this!

I was confused by this reasoning, but not for long. There are new and emergent forms in contemporary literature, mainly due to meditative and intuitive connections with something bigger than oneself. This is present in Aitmatov's novel and others like his. They provide a new yardstick for everything to be measured against. Yes, and for a sense of one's own responsibility to one's fellow man as well.

I recall Valentin Rasputin's words at Irkutsk University where we were making a public presentation a few years ago related to efforts to stop the damming of local rivers to provide water to Central Siberian deserts. He was asked a question: What if all these efforts of his and his friends' become stymied due to ministerial and bureaucratic barriers? Good intentions like these have been thwarted in the past. The writer answered very quietly, even growing pale. "Yes," he said, "these were not words spoken lightly." He was totally serious. He knew there was opposition: "An executioner's block will remain, there still is a 'scaffold'!" Rasputin and his colleagues took the risk. They won their battle.

"New thinking . . . means basic alterations in everything we think and do. It involves assuming a feeling of personal and historical responsibility for everything on the planet."

"Art . . . requires one to be like an ancient Roman. Instead of idle talk and going through the motion, it requires from its creators a total and complete dedication, including laying down of the artist's life," said Boris Pasternak, describing the poetic nature of a real artist. But never before has an artist's profession so seriously challenged him: He may burn to death, to try to get someone to put out the fire!

For me, as for most of us, the appearance of *The Fate of the Earth* by Jonathan Schell was of great significance. I also had the opportunity to see how very different people, from simple workmen to those high in the government, after having read that book, somehow became alike in the way they saw the realities of our world. One may think that these books and films should help people to understand each other in a new and better way.

New thinking requires a radical change. It does not refer to cosmetic changes such as buying a new calendar or setting the clock a few hours ahead.

It means basic alterations in everything we think and do. It involves assuming a feeling of personal and historical responsibility for everything on the planet. I repeat this for emphasis.

In the past, as individuals we used our creativity to invent, then produced anything we chose. Later, we came to understand that it was wrong. This certainly was the case with the atomic bomb. "I am death, the destroyer of worlds," said J. Robert Oppenheimer, the father of nuclear weapons.

New thinking compels us to calculate our steps in advance. We can no longer do anything we choose. We must now reject those ideas and creations that are not for continuing the life process before they lead us to the verge of disaster. And logic alone is not sufficient to achieve this goal. What is needed is the intuition generated by a great love of man for others. This is more essential today than anything else.

This has always been the subject matter and concern of literature. What is new is the urgency of the task: We must not be too late!

Realism and Morality in Politics

Andrei V. Kortunov

Institute of USA and Canada Studies, Academy of Sciences of the USSR. Dr. Kortunov is author of chapters in eight books and more than thirty papers and coauthor of the book *American Model on the Scales of History*.

Be good in thinking — this is the main principle of morality.

—Blaise Pascal

Realism has always been considered an important virtue for a state leader. Understandably, a reputation of a dreamer, or even worse of an unrestrained adventurer, would not win anyone's support. It is particularly unsuitable for any man responsible for the destiny of a country.

Today realism in politics takes on special significance. The time of prophets and magicians has passed. The continued existence of life on this planet depends on the direct and consistent application of realistic principles to international relationships.

Concepts and practices of original realists in foreign policy, Niccolo Machiavelli and Hugo Grotius, or the "Realpolitik" of Austrian Prince Metternich are again achieving popularity in the modern world. This is understandable, since no one wants to run the risk of embarking on a totally unknown path in politics, particularly when the stakes are high. Under these conditions, the future is predicted by a straight-line extrapolation from the past. Present actions are then not determined by what might be, but by what has already happened or is happening at the moment.

Yet this kind of attachment to the past correlates very poorly with the real world. If this type of realism had been followed in science, in the arts, or in society in general, then civilization would have stagnated. Copernicus's concepts of orbital mechanics in astronomy cannot be logically deduced from Ptolemy's. Descartes's reasoning concerning the physical laws of nature cannot be extrapolated from Aristotle's thoughts. Nor can Einstein's observations of the laws of the universe be regarded as a direct consequence of Newton's. In a similar way Gauguin's paintings are not a modern day adaptation of Raphael's techniques, and Christ's teachings are not a direct result of the system developed by the ancient Greeks.

Realism in politics and dogma were never meant to be identical. Political realism, when practiced properly, first stood for an objective analysis of the existing political problem; then for the choice of the central or principle means for its solution; and finally, for a realistic estimate of the possibilities for achieving this aim and its subsequent implementation.

This means that the practice of realism can never be set in concrete. It has to be flexible and change with the character of political life and facts of history. What was good yesterday may be totally useless today. Today, what is accepted without question may appear senseless tomorrow. Today's success may lead to disaster, if used in the near future.

But a change of habitual patterns is often difficult, whether it involves the hard sciences or patterns of social life. In politics it is probably even more difficult. The applicability of a theory or practice in science can be demonstrated by performing an objective experiment. Findings can be compared after a series of observations and errors are evaluated. The opposite is true for the politician — history gives him only a single chance. The failure of a social experiment usually is not only a personal catastrophe for the individual politician, but of the basic concept he was fighting for, as well.

On the other hand, certain things are easier for politicians. Politicians don't need to spend nights in a laboratory or watch blips on a screen of an oscilloscope, pore over notes of previous experiments or depend on new insights from repeated statistical analysis of their data. The only thing usually needed is an alertness to the constantly asked question: Are we trying to introduce "Newtonian" politics into an "Einsteinian" world that has completely changed its manner of operation?

The world is constantly changing. Today the rate of that change has become so rapid as to require development of new approaches and decisions which are consistent with the times. Though it will not be possible to cover all events fully, it is possible to detail some of the phenomena which have become driving forces for new approaches in realism in foreign policy.

The World Is Striving for Diversity. It was never true that one could imagine various countries as identical billiard balls that were colliding with one another on the world political scene. Yet it is true that those countries which determined the nineteenth century's classical "balance of power" had much in common. They were united by a similar socioeconomic base, a common past (European), a common culture (Age of Enlightenment), and a common religion (Christianity). The ruling elites, whether in Petersburg or Madrid, also had a common language (French).

The situation is quite different today. The past few decades have failed to confirm predictions that the world is moving in a direction of greater standardization and unification and that modern-day economics and attendant political relations would wipe out historical modes of interactions, nationalism, cultural differences, and ideologies. Instead, it has become clear that with a certain level of social development, humanity can afford to choose different life-styles and approaches on the world scene. This in turn means the days of messianic universal dogmas and ideologic crusades are completely a thing of the past.

" The past few decades have failed to confirm predictions that the world is moving in a direction of greater standardization and unification . . . the days of messianic universal dogmas and ideologic crusades are completely a thing of the past."

Diversity denotes not only differences in function, but of interest, as well. Sometimes it is this diversity that is the source of greater stability of the overall system. For example, in a forest each tree, bush, or blade of grass has its own unique spot and competition takes place among its own kind rather than with others. This principle also applies in the international arena where differences among countries may not sharpen competition. Instead it may enhance possibilities for cooperation. Take, for example, the present state of economic cooperation between the East and the West. Its development has enormous possibilities. For the most part this is due to structural differences in the systems and related growth potential between socialism and capitalism. As a result, economies of East and West do not actually contradict one another, but rather mutually supplement each other; for example, present progress in space sciences. The USSR has placed emphasis on the development of a space station, while the US has emphasized development of the space shuttle.

Over the Years International Relations Are Becoming More Complex. Reduction of world politics to "bipolar" or "multipolar" concepts is not only an oversimplification, it is a delusion. Contrary to the recent past where at most a dozen states dealt with the rest of the world in a classic balance of power posture, there are now two hundred that can and do act in this manner. Thus balance of power in the modern world must be based on a newer and more useful long-term model. World politics under these conditions must be an open rather than the closed system of the past. Not only must nation-states be included in this process, but international organizations, transnational business groups, means for international dialogue, political and public movements, as well. The former hierarchy of foreign-policy priorities is also losing its clear lines of distinction. New problems are appearing on the world community's agenda. To analyze the events and trends of today through the prism of old-style "political realism" is like trying to pour water from a pail into a bottle with a narrow neck. Of course some water will get into the bottle, but the loss will be tremendous.

Growing Interdependence of Nations. The chain of interdependence does not consist of just one or two links: Therefore, economic decisions taken in one part of the world can have significant unforeseen consequences at other sites, near or remote. In the past when interactions were chiefly political and military, a high degree of economic independence was present. Foreign trade was totally dependent on politics and was only a minor aspect of any country's overall economic structure. Today the reverse is true. The internationalization of world economic ties has reached such a high degree of interdependence that any steps to undermine trade brings enormous hardships to all participants, even those not directly associated with the changes. This is particularly the case for most middle- and small-sized nations who regularly have over half of their gross national product tied to exporting goods. The notion of national "power" takes on new meaning under these conditions and is relative to a great number of variables, including the extent of foreign-policy agreements, the amount of capital invested outside the country, and the amount of business conducted with or in a specific country. In some cases these may be assets for foreign policy, in others they may become a source of significant vulnerability. For example, while a creditor can exert tremendous pressure on a debtor, it can also become a hostage of the debtor country.

Differences between Foreign and Domestic Policies Are Fading. Although foreign policy was always meant to be an expression of domestic policy, previously there were often significant differences. Since international problems did not seem to touch the personal lives of a country's peoples (except during war), those in power were able to exercise considerably more freedom in foreign-policy decisions than in any other sphere of activity. Over the centuries, this allowed state figures and diplomats to plot their designs for foreign relations on a private chessboard, playing the game by unwritten rules of their own design, motivated solely by their own national self-interests.

Today, diplomats and generals no longer have a monopoly on determining foreign policy. Businessmen, bankers, scientists, and figures from the arts are all participating in this process. Today the mix of a state's foreign and domestic policies represent a complex interaction of internal and external factors played out on the world scene, heavily affected by bureaucratic influences from government, private enterprise, and public organizations. The concept of "national interests" in these circumstances becomes moot since the interests of the parties participating have become so contradictory. There is no single "national interest."

War Is Not Working as an Effective Means for Conducting Foreign Policy. During the past period of "balance of power," war played an important role. It determined equivalence for those with similar military forces and legally determined the international, economic, and political hierarchy as well. War then was acceptable — legally, economically, and morally. It was romanticized, with the soldier presented as a brave handsome figure as in the Renaissance paintings of Velasquez. Today war is seen differently. As imaged by Salvador Dali, it has become a monstrously absurd "Autumnal Cannibalism." In the nuclear age, it is a dead-end passage with no safe path of return for either the aggressor or the victim. If used, nuclear weapons will destroy all humanity and perhaps all life on the planet.

As a consequence, there is no longer any rationale for participation in even small conventional wars. Each one is capable of escalating into a full-blown nuclear exchange. In the past, national security was gauged by establishing a better border and creating buffer states to protect one from an aggressor. In the nuclear age such geographic factors have no meaning. Geography provides no protection against intercontinental ballistic missiles. Besides, each regional conflict now bears with it the seed of a nuclear catastrophe.

These are the realities of our times whether we like them or not. One can be deeply attached to the historical past, with its sacred alliance and "balance of forces," but the world has changed. This has happened irrespective of our individual wishes or desires. Now we must move to respond positively and creatively to these forces. We have no other choice. To resist by closing one's eyes and withdrawing into the past can serve no purpose but guarantee doom. Science has amply shown that man can conquer his environment when he obeys, rather than flaunts, the rules of nature. The man who tries to fly by jumping off a cliff will like all others fall to the earth and pay with his life.

Force of Law or Law of Force?

When you read the works of historians or students of politics, or listen to the speeches of political figures, you get the impression that basic problems of international relations stem directly from developments in international law. This law appears to them as the only reliable regulator of world politics, and for a movement in the direction of order in the world. On this basis it seems natural to consider establishing new legal norms for regulating modern-day spheres of interactions between nation-states. It is felt that eventually a place must be reached where each state clearly knows what is good and what is bad, what is favorable and what is unfavorable, devoid of ambiguities and uncertainties. Under these conditions everything becomes simple and easy to understand, like a multiplication table, because everybody knows that it is useless to argue with the absolute facts given in a multiplication table.

Is such a perspective realistic? I don't think so. At any rate, present international practices do not favor it.

First, it's not so very easy to reach legal agreement regarding some of the most important international problems. A sadly recurrent theme can be seen to occur: The more important the problem is, the more difficult it is to find an acceptable legal solution. For example, the Soviet-American SALT II Treaty was under consideration for seven years, yet, it was never ratified by the US Senate. Dialogue concerning the international Law of the Sea went on for many years, but the final convention, agreed upon after all the years of effort, is still not signed by a number of leading countries of the world.

Second, international legal norms do not have a single interpretation as with a multiplication table. Sometimes they are prone to quite opposite interpretations, as has been the case with the basic provisions of the charter of the United Nations, which is interpreted so differently in the East compared to the West.

It is doubtful whether it will ever be possible to draw up a specific treaty which excludes all opportunities for starting rumors, arbitrary interpretations, and juggling. And, of course, any country can find lawyers and experts who, by intricate manipulations of words, can readily give all the responsibility of breaking a treaty to the other side.

Third, conduct of international relations is so complex in today's world that it is simply impossible to work out simple rules and procedures, and agree upon legal norms under all conditions. Attempts to constrict the richness of international dealings into conformity with the prescribed codes, treaties, and rules of international organizations — is the same process as attempting to turn a live cell into a dead crystal. If prescribed law is not responsive to the markedly dynamic situations present in today's world, it would be quite naïve to think that it will be responsive to the politics of tomorrow.

Is international law worth striving for? Do we want relations in our family, with our friends and acquaintances, colleagues, and people in general regulated only by courts and bulky volumes of civil and criminal laws? Do we want our every step to be checked with corresponding instructions, directives, and approved rules? One has to agree that there is a tacit and humiliating assumption in such a perspective, that people are inherently evil and unable and unwilling to get along with one another.

Historical experience confirms a humorous remark of Voltaire's that multiplicity of laws in a state is the same as having a large number of doctors treating a person — they are a sign of declining health. Very often the force of codified law has been substituted in directives for the force of moral law. Societal development has been tied to the judicial system and written history to criminal codes.

Very often international rules of conduct have been futile attempts to stop the process of international system disintegration, creating an illusion of reliability and stability where they had never existed. Hegel used the analogy of the Minerva owl which flies in the twilight. In other words, wisdom comes late. The international legal system, created in the Roman empire, reached its peak at the time of Justinian when "Pax Romana" was in evident decline. The international legal system in feudal Europe took shape only after the Peace of Westphalia (1648), long after feudalism's golden age. The Versailles-Washington structure after World War I, modeled after the most recent legal information, with all necessary treaties, protocols, and procedures turned out to be a total failure and lasted less than two decades.

The large amount of legal activity during the period between World War I and World War II allows one to draw the conclusion that many countries felt very uncertain about the future and instinctively moved to preserve the existing order in the international arena. At the time of crisis and catastrophe, state leaders regarded the paragraphs of treaties and items of agreements as a private repository for gradual accumulation of today's hopes and conquests and which could be safely counted on for their nation's security. The 1930s was a period when so many international conferences were conducted, and with so many pacts, treaties, agreements, and conventions — bilateral and many-sided, open, and secret. And the result? A universal disease of "pactomania" which did not prevent a world war and became only a belated symptom of the growing military threat.

Over the centuries the force of law has always been supplemented by the law of force. In fact, rules of international conduct were most often determined by the state of military affairs existing at the moment.

Today, the law of force is rapidly losing its dominant role. The invention of nuclear weapons has turned a worldwide war into collective suicide. International interdependence and globalization of social change have turned notions of "local conflict" and "regional war" into sheer non-sense, and with it a still greater devaluation of the meaning of military force in foreign policy. The same may be said of any process for exerting economic pressure under conditions where production is under international control. In a word, it is not possible for the law of force to assume the role of universal law in international politics.

On one hand, international relations cannot remain as a jungle of "power struggles" by states, nor on the other can states develop under a totalitarian yoke of all sorts of codes, rules, directives, and systems of regulations. Therefore, today the problem of developing a moral-ethical structure for relations between states is of more vital importance than ever before.

Law and Morality: General and Special

Obviously we cannot believe that moral-ethical considerations have never played a role in international life. On the contrary, such notions as "moral duty," "justice," and "national honesty" have always exerted a certain influence on states' politics. Nevertheless, these moral slogans were often a form of cover-up for political aspirations rather than a source of inspiration. Such things occurred so frequently that morality became a weapon and a force for the weak, while moral revenge was sometimes the only answer to political defeat.

Easy manipulation of foreign policy by moral-ethical categories is clearly shown by the following two circumstances. First, maintenance of a low educational and cultural level in a given population makes it possible to impose any kind of mind-set on them. Second, moral isolation of peoples provided their rulers with a certain monopoly for moral education of their subjects. For example, the decree of the Peace of Augsburg (1555) stated that the religion of the ruler determined the religion of his subjects.

Today, we have in principle a new situation. Mankind's cultural development has led the individual to an ever increasing moral independence. Culture is not only knowledge but also a consolidation of contributions by all of its human members. A tragedy by Sophocles and a theory by Einstein, a novel by Dostoyevsky and a computer program — all of them equally liberate our thoughts and strengthen us spiritually, and facilitate our moral development as individuals.

On the other hand, development of the mass media and the widening person-to-person contacts between countries is gradually eradicating spiritual isolation between peoples. Barriers give way as we begin to understand the common character of our aspirations, our common ideals, and our values. It is difficult to overestimate the importance of this point. We see the mind-set of "ours-not ours" being transformed into old and useless concepts. And realize how this concept of "opposites" in its different forms ("Greeks–barbarians," "Christians–pagans," "civilized nations–

savages") has had a decisive influence on forming the patterns for political and moral interaction of individual societies over our entire past history. National borders were viewed as fortress walls behind which could be found either an enemy's values or absence of values. Today the enemy may exist in one's own midst and anywhere else in the world, with those holding fast to old stereotypes and the use of force to resolve conflict.

As knowledge has grown and the individual has been freed to become more independent, it has become more difficult to manipulate moral values and they are changing gradually to become an independent factor influencing the development of world politics. Politics cannot evade moral judgment while morals, in their turn, cannot remain apolitical. Morality as a form of social consciousness and social relations has much in common with law. Both morality and law form an international point of view representing a combination of relatively stable rules and directives. Legal structures have come to reflect levels of general progress in international relations, as well as human civilization; morality as evidence of an individual's idea about what is absolutely required and just in dealing with other human beings.

"Politics cannot evade moral judgment while morals, in their turn, cannot remain apolitical . . . moral restraints are more comprehensive and applicable than legal restraints."

At the same time, there are serious differences between morality and law. Law, first of all, is the written rule of conduct fixed in corresponding treaties, agreements, and regulations of international organizations. Morality is an unwritten code existing in the form of world public opinion. If necessary, rules of international law are executed by enforced measures (economic and political sanctions, use of UN Armed Forces, etc.); but moral requirements are supported by the power of common customs, public opinion, or personal conviction of the people. Thus, moral sanctions are executed by a measure of spiritual influence, which becomes supported by others around the world, not by special legislative edict of individual states but by the whole of mankind.

In many aspects, international relations are regulated both by the rules of law and moral codes. For example, military aggression is the breach of a universally recognized legal code, as well as a moral crime. However, moral restraints are more comprehensive and applicable than legal restraints.

All of us, undoubtedly, have met people who do not violate laws, who honor the criminal code and fulfill all resolutions, decrees, and instructions but at the same time they provoke unpleasant feelings — even disgust. An execution of legal norms can surprisingly be associated with egoism, inattention to concern or care for others, or use of people for personal gain. These individuals cannot be arrested or tried in civil proceedings, and moral censure is the only means of influencing them.

Similar situations very often appear in the international arena. Since international legal standards are unable to regulate all aspects of relations between countries, there are many ways of getting around laws. There are no laws (and probably it will be impossible to ever invent them) which prohibit an artificial increase of a nation's currency rates with the aim of bankrupting financial operations of competitors. There are no laws to prevent a "brain drain" from developing countries to developed ones. It would be very difficult, even if possible, to work out a system of legal standards which would clearly define the concept of "subversive," destabilizing propaganda. The significance of such "nonlegal" spheres in international relations will inevitably grow as the scientific and technological revolutions continue to develop, leading to ever-widening contacts at all levels between states. Moral-ethical considerations may become their primary regulators. Moral condemnation of a "national self-interest" policy may turn out to be more effective means of regulation than attempts to prove its illegality.

Morality has another important difference from law. A treaty can be signed under pressure. Formal equality in the agreement can conceal a factual dependence of one state on the other; yet morality, in principle, is impossible without the independence of states. The choice of freedom is impossible without independence and there is no ethics without freedom of choice. But morality also limits the independence of actions of states in the international arena because it presupposes that all states act responsibly and do so willingly.

And there is yet a final consideration which is important. Morality, unlike law, is always the result of individual action. Moral behavior by a state is based on the conduct of its citizens, not on the declarations of its leaders. This includes the sum total of collective as well as individual actions taken separately. And if the overwhelming majority of us consider ourselves as amateurs in international law, in the sphere of morality all of us are pros. This is a fact and there is no irony in this. When an international treaty is concluded, one can talk about his incompetence, lack of knowledge in the details of legal law, and absence of information. One can digress from the theme, wait in the next room, loaf in the corridors, smile at foolish things. In a word, entrust our leaders to speak on our behalf and make decisions for us. But when we move to estimate the moral consequences of an event in world politics, no one has the right to abrogate his responsibility. No one, be he or she a scientist, engineer, soldier, economist, peasant, or housewife, can be satisfied if he or she sloughs off the required decision-making process to a political entity. Everyone is responsible for everything.

Inevitability of a Moral Conflict

Dostoyevsky was asked: Is it enough to define morality as simply following one's own convictions? "No," he answered, "this is only honesty. We must also constantly ask ourselves: Are my convictions true?"

This differentiation between morality and honesty is, unfortunately, very often lost. They have significant differences in principle. We can, for example, assume with a great degree of certainty that there are many political leaders in the Republic of South Africa who actually think that black people are an inferior race, that blacks must be restrained, and that the policy of apartheid is the only possible course to secure domestic stability in their nation. And these people follow their convictions quite honestly. It's very hard to reproach them with dishonesty: They honestly speak about their views and honestly try to implement them in life. But firm adherence to their convictions does not make them moral. Supporters of racism, like supporters of nuclear war, deserve moral condemnation by all the world's inhabitants.

"Traditional morality teaches that it is impossible to be a patriot and, at the same time, sharply criticize one's country's policy. Nuclear-age morality teaches that a patriot must critically assess the policy of his state . . ."

A unique feature of establishing standards for moral conduct is the fact that they become such only when they pass through the conscience of each and every person. As a rule, this process does not proceed smoothly, but rather with inner resistance manifest in a form of moral conflict, splitting of conscience, and an understanding of the necessity of healing this split which requires the making of a firm decision.

There are, at least, three types of moral conflicts. First, moral requirements can come into conflict with legal standards. We can find at times that an international treaty or agreement seems amoral to us and one-sided, despite the fact that it was concluded in full conformity with all international legal formalities. This is certainly the case in developing countries. Do they have a moral, as well as legal, obligation to pay back formal loans that were made to them in good faith?

Second, moral requirements can clash with immediate needs and benefits. Can the world's great powers morally justify continuing the supply of arms to any country on the planet, knowing the full implications of military conflict in the present nuclear age?

Finally, a conflict is possible between different systems of moral values. This conflict is, perhaps, the most difficult and painful kind because it can be solved only by the individual himself. On the world scene, this conflict presently takes its form from the collision course occurring between "traditional" morality and nuclear-age morality. Traditional morality primarily demands support for the security of one's own country, and only subsequently for solving other international problems; while nuclear-age morality is building towards universal security which can be the sole guarantor of national security. Traditional morality teaches that diversity among nations and conflicts that may arise from such differences can and must be used for the benefit of the motherland, thus weakening them; nuclear-age morality teaches that partiality towards one's own state can and must be sacrificed for humanity's interests. Traditional morality teaches that it is impossible to be a patriot and, at the same time, sharply criticize one's country's policy. Nuclear-age morality teaches that a patriot must critically assess the policy of his state and that acknowledgement of mistakes and learning from them are most favorable actions for himself and for all others, and the only way to prevent their continued recurrence in the future.

The resolution of a moral conflict does not resemble the solution of a chess problem or a legal case. People feel a moral conflict keenly and quite deeply. We very often prolong our sufferings by putting off the necessity of taking the needed moral step and making the needed decision. We remain passive, hoping that the conflict will pass with time, or that someone (government, experts in international affairs, lawyers, history, or God) will solve all our problems for us.

Perhaps all of us have experienced such a state of being and indecision. It is very tempting to project an annoying inner conflict into our outer world, making it an outer conflict, thus preserving our inner state of harmony and calm. Unfortunately, or maybe fortunately, such attempts usually end in failure. Sooner or later we have to make a choice, and sooner or later we are forced to face the need for personal responsibility.

Naturally enough, moral conflicts have more than just a personal character. Very often, moral conflicts occur between large groups of people, political parties, classes of individuals, and even states. In these cases people have an easier choice: They can simply join one or another side. However, such choice also requires great personal courage and results in an inner moral conflict.

Up to now we have addressed answers to old questions. Realizing that the nuclear age has placed us in a totally new situation, with totally new questions we have never faced before, we must even change the manner of posing our questions. We must ask these questions realistically and without holding out false hopes.

Competition or Confrontation? Being realists, we must recognize that contradictions and differences between countries do and will continue to exist. Moreover, the development of international cooperation can increase contradictions and expose areas where cooperation was more supposed than real. There are no two states in the world whose interests are, or ever will be, absolutely identical and who have "full unity of opinions" on all problems. This latter cliché is nothing more than a substitute for continuing business in the previously old intolerable manner of relations.

But if states are doomed to rivalry, this doesn't mean that they cannot choose the forms for such rivalry. This means that the inevitable conflict can be expressed as competition, rather than confrontation. The principle differences in these approaches deal with attitude. Confrontation presupposes each side wants to conduct their interactions according to the laws of a "zero-sum game" (one wins, while the other automatically loses); while competition can be accomplished over the course of parallel, independent actions, even involving a third party, without need for direct or even hostile interaction, and according to the rules of a "positive-sum game" (all sides win).

". . . conflict can be expressed as competition, rather than confrontation. The principle differences in these approaches deal with attitude."

As a rule, subjective, principally political factors play a determining role in confrontation, whereas objective, mainly socioeconomic factors constitute the basis for competition. Confrontation excludes any possibility of cooperation, except in the narrow sense when efforts are directed to handle the confrontation itself or prevent its occurrence. Competition, on the other hand, requires full cooperation of both sides at all levels of mutually agreed upon tasks and strives to find ways of maximally utilizing the experience and capabilities of the other side.

Estimation of Capabilities or Estimation of Intentions? Traditionally, political figures have based their course of action on a "worst case" scenario, considering this approach to be the most probable situation that could occur. But is this really the way life is? If our relations with other people are to be based solely on assessing the magnitude of harm they "in principle" can inflict upon us, then life becomes totally unbearable. Every passerby then becomes a potential robber, rapist, or murderer. The strategy of "deterrence," which is presently so heavily favored by "political realists," becomes absurd when we try to apply it to everyday life. But why is this faulty logic still applied to the relations between the West and the East? Maybe it's high time to switch from relying on worst case scenarios and hypothetical estimates of "the potential enemy" to the most probable case and to uncovering the real intentions for each side.

Primary Aims or Primary Means? When firm agreements are not present, perspective is lost. Actions become more reflexive in character. Without a clear definition of a national interest, power politics quickly moves in to fill the vacuum. Left in the hands of the political realists, national interest quickly becomes redefined to mean "national power" and the maximization of that power. Foreign-policy goals become limitless and can be contained only by resistance from other states. If it is possible to design some kind of armament system, it must be designed, and corresponding doctrinal substantiations will be tended to later. If it is possible to intrude into some area of the world, it must be done, and later invent arguments to prove that it is a "zone of vital interests," "strategic bridgehead." It's high time for all state figures to clearly define their countries' real interests, and only then begin to reach out in search of their achievement.

Dialogue of Governments or Dialogue of Civilizations? There is a traditional point of view that governments can reach an agreement easier than between peoples. It is also felt that state figures are better informed, less emotional, and more realistic, therefore it is they who must lead the people to dialogue. There is some correctness in this, but to paraphrase Clemenceau – "international relations are too serious a matter to leave them solely to politicians." State figures may be driven by self-interests which differ markedly from the peoples they represent.

Therefore, the most productive dialogue is that between peoples or civilizations, though it is more difficult than the dialogue of governments. Only then can the "image of the enemy" and its dehumanization be overcome. Only through dialogue can an atmosphere of cooperation be created that can withstand all the fluctuations of day-to-day political life. Only through this process will the hold of present-day logic be broken, which makes us powerless and isolates us from one another.

One need not be an expert to adopt an ideology which stresses our common goals and desires, rather than one which pits us against each other.

We all want our life to have meaning, and history a purpose.

We all want to participate in the discovery and realization of this meaning.

We all desire that all peoples share in the shaping of our future human destiny and it not be determined by a handful of leaders.

At present, we fully realize that mankind has not yet restructured its system of international relations to function on a just and democratic basis. We have not yet achieved universal disarmament, we have not provided adequate help to economically backward countries, nor have we arrived at common solutions to many global problems. These await us in the future. But, as Goethe said: "What we desire today already includes the possibilities of our ability to accomplish them tomorrow."

Further, one must refrain from visualizing the modern world as being in a simplified black-and-white state, where all moral virtues are collected at one pole, while all moral vices at the other.

". . . there are no experts or specialists who can . . . free us from the responsibility of deciding the future of our countries and of all humankind."

A morality of survival is nothing but a moral necessity stemming from the task of preventing the destruction of our civilization. It is another matter entirely when moral standards are being followed, not due to outside pressure, but by inner agreements set by society itself and its members. In this case, international moral standards are transformed into national conviction. Application of this type of morality to international relations would result in a qualitatively different world order based on a good-neighbor policy and mutual assistance by all peoples of the world.

It is necessary to clearly understand that neither science, law, military strategy, economics, nor sociology can substitute for moral standards of political conduct by a state. Therefore, there are no experts or specialists who can relieve any one of us from the required moral choices we each face, or free us from the responsibility of deciding the future of our countries and of all humankind.

Jerome Frank, Richard Lagerstrom, William
McGlashan, Craig Barnes and Andrei Melville

Vladimir Ageev and William McGlashan

Yuri Zamoshkin   *Andrei Melville*   *Fyodor Burlatsky*

SECTION THREE

Process of Change
Individual Action and Collective Transformation

OVERVIEW

I. Survival as the Superordinate Goal

In the Long View of History Cooperation Is Spreading

For most of human history, we have thought of war as a given. For centuries, war within, say, Western Europe has been a constant. Today, it is unthinkable. In certain areas of the globe, there has been an evolution from stable war toward stable peace. Worldwide, most human activity is peaceful and cooperative: eating, working, loving, building, studying, planning, communicating. Internationally, when boundaries have stabilized stable peace has evolved. Habits can and should build into taboos, and taboos into unwritten agreements which reject war. This is one way stable peace will grow. ("Moving from Unstable to Stable Peace," Kenneth Boulding)

Moving from Unilateral to Multilateral Decision Making

Despite the fact that "peace" and "security" are usually discussed together, their real correlation is not so clear. They do not necessarily go

151

together. For many years we have concentrated on security, strategic parity, and preserving a high level of mutual danger. Today, the whole understanding of what is security must be revised. Universal security is not a ready-made package, but it has been studied and "common security" is becoming a viable concept. For this, nation-states would have to abandon deterrence through terror, or psychological stalemate, as the basis of security. There are also real limitations on national sovereignty in a nuclear and interdependent world. Any attempts to use military means for the solution of disputes of a political and ideological nature must be ruled out by both the American and Soviet sides. Security can be achieved only through cooperation and can only be global in scope. ("The Concept of Universal Security: A Revolution of Thinking and Policy in the Nuclear Age," Alexander I. Nikitin)

Reorientation!

In the nuclear age many traditional beliefs, perceptions, and views must change. The problem is global and involves the whole civilization, which is now at risk. The challenge here is to the linear development of society. Nuclear apocalypse would be the end of history, the end of everything. The crucial fact is that both sides are totally vulnerable. That changes the nature and character of war. It forces a reevaluation of the correlation between force and politics. Old notions of security are turned upside down. We are challenged to make a radical reorientation in our consciousness. It is an unprecedented, difficult task which entails a resolute break with historical, political, psychological, and ideological traditions. We have to move past the psychological defense mechanisms of denial, of overstating absolute ideals, or of underrating nuclear weapons as if they were only conventional weapons. ("Nuclear Revolution and the New Way of Thinking," Andrei Y. Melville)

If Survival Is the Goal Cooperation Is Inevitable

Antagonists don't have to like each other to cooperate. They don't even have to be rational. They don't have to have a backlog of trust. It is only necessary that they expect to share the future. Given that overwhelmingly important expectation, cooperation naturally evolves, with or without ideological agreement. That has been the experience from soldiers in the trenches of World War I to international commercial enterprises today. Those are also the results of a surprising computerized tournament that demonstrates how cooperation not only evolves, but spreads. Cooperators seek each other out. Groups of cooperators grow. They bolster each other, while noncooperators tend toward isolation or mutual retaliation which inhibits growth. Cooperators survive. They have in history, and computerized simulations show why. ("The Evolution of Cooperation," Robert Axelrod)

II. Resistance to Change

Brain Functioning and Reorientation

Change is a universal phenomenon. But it is not comfortable. It is resisted. Studies of electrical currents in the brain show that the brain seeks stability. It functions less well in times of high stress, thrives on stimulation but not overstimulation; it may overreact, and shut down in an unhealthy, passive stability. When it does, it resists change mightily. It slips into psychic numbing. What is then required is not just a soft push, but rather a massive jolt. Without this stimulus on the one hand, and active involvement by the individual on the other, the brain will resist and stay in the unhealthy state. It is the action, however, which literally transforms the mind. Involvement is healing. Anyone can cure psychic numbing by acting personally. Such healing action can begin with as little as verbalizing the problem, and is more pronounced when one actively seeks a solution. ("Dangers and Opportunities for Change from a Physiologist's Point of View," Natalia P. Bekhtereva)

Projection of Blame onto an Enemy

It is natural for humans to form into groups and to value their groups above all others. It is the historic way to survive. Groups provide protection. Other groups can be dangerous. The net effect can be to idolize one's own group and demonize the other. Sometimes, images of the enemy mirror each other. The images become excuses for staying in an old reality, resisting change, blaming all our problems on the other group, now characterized as an "enemy." Then, often, it is said that it is only the "leaders" of the opposing group who are the problem — the people are good. These exaggerated images gradually blur and distort the vision of both sides and reality is lost. The escalation of enemy images disrupts communication. The result is the idea that one can deal with the enemy only by force. Thus, the image of the enemy itself breeds the arms race and carries adversaries toward war. ("The Image of the Enemy and the Process of Change," Jerome D. Frank and Andrei Y. Melville)

Hiding Behind Idealism.

We sometimes use ideals, not as a guide for action, but as a shield against action. The greater the gap between words and deeds, the louder and more insistent the words become to protect the psyche from seeing one's own behavior. Any ideology, not excluding Christianity and Marxism, can be used for this purpose. On the other hand, when an individual or a society faces the fact that the current course can lead to death, there is a chance for transformation. That is the situation with the nuclear threat today. The ideal is that nuclear weapons be eliminated. The reality is that to survive, the ideal must be achieved. Thus leaders who seek this goal can be both practical and idealistic at the same time, and the real and the ideal can become one. ("Nuclear Disarmament: Ideal and Reality," Yuri A. Zamoshkin)

Fabricating Resistance to New Realities

National policy is often based upon perceptions of military power rather than upon realities. There is a perception, for example, that more nuclear weapons make one more secure, but military strategists know that the reality is that more weapons have no more impact on security. To deal with this difference between fact and perception the human has a high capacity to tolerate ambiguity. There have been two key responses of the defense planners. One, to suppress the awareness of the reality that numbers of weapons do not increase security; the other to suppress the idea that nuclear weapons are more dangerous than conventional weapons. Interviews with some Soviet and American experts and observers reveal that both indulge in these twin efforts to deny the nuclear reality. Both have, in the past, discussed the idea of "winning" a nuclear war. There is encouragement in the fact that in the late 1980s, both are trying to adapt to new realities created by the nuclear revolution. ("Nuclear Reality: Resistance and Adaptation," Steven Kull)

III. Bringing New Thinking to Life: Building Public Support

Important Governmental Changes Depend upon Public Support

The most important achievements in arms control are those which have been backed by a public constituency. When that is there, as in the case of the ABM Treaty, there has been progress in arms control and moderation of the commitment to the MX missile. When the public support has not been active, as in the case of SALT II, or is ambivalent, as in the case of nuclear weapons testing, then there has been little or no progress in international negotiations. An enduring, energetic, informed, and politically aware arms control constituency is not just a good idea, it is essential. The arms control record is the evidence. ("The Impact of a US Public Constituency on Arms Control," Sidney Drell)

Restructuring of Soviet Society

The democratization that is going on in the Soviet Union today is both economic and political. The two are tied together, and there cannot be one without the other. There are multiple candidate elections taking place in all the republics of the country, including elections for factory managers and new direct-election, secret ballot procedures for local level party leaders. The attempt is being made to increase the influence of citizens, employees, and ordinary party members, so that power comes from the bottom up, rather than from the top down. Newspapers, radio, and television are changing. They are beginning to publish accounts of misdeeds of public officials, Western articles or interviews, and statements of foreign leaders. In economics, there is decentralization of management, and, very recently, new forms of adaptation to supply and demand. Here again, the principle is to lessen the influence on enterprises from above, giving more independence, and more rewards to those at the factory, plant, or local level. These changes are revolutionary. ("Restructuring of Soviet Society," Alexander I. Belchuk)

New Thinking Spreads One Individual at a Time

We are more likely to buy a new car or a computer because of a friend or peer than because of any other influence. In some degree, the same is true in adopting the idea of a world in which war is obsolete. The actual process of adopting a new idea is built upon individuals who learn from one another. An idea spreads from innovators to opinion leaders to the population at large. When it has been adopted by at least 20 percent, it cannot be stopped. It will grow and expand throughout the society. The role of the media is important — but not as much as one would think. The media builds awareness. Adoption, that is, the actual personal identification with the idea, "That is what I believe," is a result of activity, discussion, and example among friends. The role of each individual is, therefore, more important than that of any other influence. ("Diffusion of the Idea of Beyond War," Everett M. Rogers)

The Value of Diversity.

Diversity and unity are two sides of a picture. Our world is infinitely diverse, geographically, culturally, and economically. There is extraordinary variety. Prejudice against those who are different, who are strange, is extremely widespread. The foreigner is the enemy. To overcome this powerful psychological barrier will require a revolution in consciousness. Is it possible? In the Soviet Union there have been major changes in attitude concerning, for example, ecology and alcohol. Can the same sort of change occur, not only here but everywhere, with regard to the distrust of whatever is foreign? One is accustomed, in answer to this question, to look for what is similar between two peoples. An alternative is to look, not for what is similar, but to acknowledge and respect the differences. Studies at the University of Moscow show that we can look into the culture of another, become more conscious and understanding of them, and, at the same time more conscious and understanding of our own culture and values. ("Similarity or Diversity?" Vladimir S. Ageev)

We Must Adapt to the Reality of Conflict

There have been two distinct tendencies in Soviet history since the 1920s. The struggle between these two tendencies, two ways of understanding socialism, has continued from that time forward until the present day. One model was developed in the conditions of a cruel civil war under which all market mechanisms and transactions were abolished. The other model, beginning with the New Economic Policy, was one in which various types of enterprises — state, cooperative, and private — competed, and the peasant freely sold his production on the market. It is the latter tendency which is again emerging in the dramatic changes which are now going on in the Soviet Union. Contradictions in socialism have often been thought of as something to be eliminated. In fact, contradictions, or internal conflicts, are the most important engine of development, the source of dynamics and competitiveness in a society. Values are created by the people through pluralism, competitiveness, and democratization. ("New Thinking about Socialism," Fyodor M. Burlatsky)

Moving from
Unstable to Stable Peace

Kenneth E. Boulding

Distinguished Professor Emeritus of Economics, University of Colorado, Boulder.
Dr. Boulding is a past President of the American Association for the Advancement
of Science and the American Economic Association. He is a member of the
American National Academy of Sciences.

Phase Boundaries

Our world has changed, and so must our perceptions and relations to it.
Virtually all the systems with which we are familiar have the capacity for
change, some so slowly as to be hardly perceptible, others more rapidly,
still others so rapidly as to exhibit "phases." Many chemical substances
have a solid, liquid, and gaseous phase — such as ice, water, and steam.
Even within these larger phases there may be subphases, such as the varie-
ties of ice crystals. The phase in which a substance exists depends on its
environment, for instance, pressure and temperature. We can also usually
identify phase boundaries in our physical environment. Crossing such
boundaries normally causes a phase to change, as when ice melts or water
boils.

Biological systems likewise exhibit phase boundaries, such as between
life and death or health and sickness. These environments are more complex, since they include not only pressures and temperatures, but also
available materials (like water and food of different kinds) and energy
sources (predators, prey, and so on). Ecosystems also have phase boundaries between them, rather like the boundary between the tundra and the
forest.

Social systems also exhibit phases and phase boundaries in great variety
and complexity. These are most easily seen in terms of the niche a particular institution occupies in a given social system. For example, the niche for

157

stock markets in the communist countries has shrunk practically to zero; the niche for communists in the United States, while it exists, is extremely small. On the other hand, both the communist and the capitalist worlds have niches for steel mills and the organization which surrounds them, for department stores, and for armed forces. If we listed all the social species, like families, churches, political parties, retail stores, taxis, and so on, in the so-called First, Second, and Third Worlds, we would find both important differences and very large similarities.

Of all social systems, organizations, patterns, and structures, war and peace probably have the sharpest phase boundaries. Most historians can tell you with some confidence whether country A and country B were at war or at peace on a given date. There are a few fuzzy boundaries. We might not be quite sure exactly when the United States got into war with Vietnam, but there is a certain fuzziness in all systems that exhibit complexity beyond a certain level. We may not be able to identify the exact date at which a marriage disintegrates, although we can usually put a pretty accurate date on the moment of divorce, another phase boundary. Wars are seldom declared any more, but we can identify pretty sharply the date at which the Iraq-Iran War started or the moment at which a war ends, though there may be a somewhat fuzzy boundary between a cease-fire, an armistice, and a peace treaty.

Inclusive Peace

Both war and not war (what I have sometimes termed "inclusive peace") have different qualities and subphases within them. War may be limited, in the sense that some means of available destruction are not used. Thus in the first few months of World War II there was no civilian bombing. There is a somewhat hazy boundary between war and terrorism, since one is tempted to define a terrorist as a soldier without a government. Civil wars involve a considerable variety of situations. Wars of "national liberation" or of revolution begin as internal wars and sometimes end in the formation of a new state, like the United States, or a new regime, like that brought to power by the Russian Revolution. Sometimes it is hard to distinguish internal from external war when external states support internal conflict in another state. Peace also has many different phases within it. It can encompass greater or lesser justice, oppression, competence, enrichment, impoverishment, and so on.

Possibility Boundary

The transition from war to peace is very much involved in what might be called the "taboo line." This is an important and surprisingly neglected aspect of human behavior. Economists are familiar with the concept of a "possibility boundary," which separates what we can do from what we cannot do. At the moment I am writing this in California. Tomorrow I could go to New York, but I could not go to the moon. The possibility boundary is defined partly by physical, partly by biological, and partly by social limitations.

Taboo Line

Within the possibility boundary, however, there is a taboo line which divides everything I can do into two parts: what I do not refrain from doing and what I refrain from doing. For example, there are no physical or biological obstacles to spitting in someone's face, but I have never done it. A great deal of social interaction and behavior is governed by taboos. These we learn, some in childhood, some in later life; some are imposed by fear of the law and of the consequences. For these reasons I rarely drive more than five miles above the speed limit and I have refrained all my life from robbing banks. Sometimes we refrain from going over the taboo line for fear of external consequences, such as disapproval or punishment; sometimes we refrain because of internal consequences, a sense of shame or guilt. However, unless taboos are internalized, they are apt to be rather ineffective, for we cannot hold external consequences in our minds all the time.

The essential difference between peace and war lies in the position of the taboo line of political and military decision makers. A country with what I call a "unilateral national defense organization," that is, a military organization, may have the power within its possibility boundary, certainly in the physical and biological sense, to invade its neighbor, bomb its neighbor's cities, sink its ships, and so on. Similarly, a person with a kitchen knife has within his or her possibility boundary the act of killing somebody. The world indeed has overkill in table knives. Peace, therefore, is a taboo on the use of armed forces. Of course, if armed forces did not exist, this taboo would become part of the possibility boundary. We cannot use weapons that do not exist. Over most of human history, however, it has been the taboo line rather than the possibility boundary that has prevented the utilization of the means of destruction. It is perhaps a linguistic matter as to whether we regard this taboo line as a social possibility boundary. Whatever we call it, it is very different from a physical or biological possibility boundary.

We can divide an economy, whether of a country, a region, or the whole world, fairly clearly into what might be called a "war industry" and a "peace industry." An economy consists of that part of human activity which involves the production, consumption, evaluation, transfer, and exchange of human artifacts: food, clothing, furniture, bicycles, houses, and weapons. It also involves the use of these things: wearing clothes, driving cars, living in houses, and using weapons. The war industry, which is fairly accurately measured by military budgets of states, rebels, and terrorists, is presently on the order of 6 to 8 percent of the world economy, with a larger percentage in some countries than in others. It is also a highly fluctuating proportion over time. For example, in the US, the war industry was less than 1 percent of the economy in the 1920s and the early 1930s, 42 percent by 1944, 14 percent in the Korean War, some 7 to 8 percent today. This situation is similar for the USSR.

Threat System

Threat, especially when it is legitimized, is the basis of all political systems. Without it, people would certainly not pay their taxes, and hence the political system would not be able to buy the foods and services that it needs without inflation. Within a nation-state, however, these threats are directed mainly at individuals: "You pay your income taxes or you will go to jail." In the international system, they are directed against other governments and the groups which they represent. Civil war, as we have seen, is a somewhat intermediate case.

The dynamics of the threat system depend on the responses to threat. There are at least six different classes of responses:

1. People can submit, as when we pay our taxes.

2. People may defy the threatener, which throws the action of the system back to the threatener, who has to decide whether or not to carry out the threat. This is often very costly to the threatener as well as to the threatened.

3. The threatened party can run away out of reach of the threat. This has been very important in the spread of the human race around the planet.

4. The threatened party can develop threat-reducing devices: armor, castles, city walls, bullet-proof vests, and bomb shelters. This also includes disarming behavior: "You wouldn't do that to me, would you? After all, we are good friends and I can do good things for you."

5. The threatened party can also develop devices and behavior which destroys the threat capability of the threatener by destroying his weapons. This is sometime called "defense," but it is very different from defensive structures and has a very different effect. It might more properly be called "counterforce."

6. Finally, there is counterthreat: "You do something nasty to me and I'll do something nasty to you." This may lead into deterrence, in which each side abstains from carrying out its threat for fear of the consequences.

All six of these phenomena have been important in human history. The responses that are most likely to lead to crossing the phase boundary from peace into war are defiance, counterforce, and counterthreat. Submission may lead to an uneasy and unstable peace unless it is legitimized by integrating the threatener and the threatened into a larger social unit. Flight is only successful if there is somewhere to go and if it takes the threatened party out of the range of the threatener. Threat-reducing devices, such as a mediæval castle, may stabilize a system of unstable peace somewhat. Historically, however, they have had very temporary effects, because they always seem to have been overtaken by threat-expansion devices, such as the cannon and the nuclear weapon.

"The responses that are most likely to lead to crossing the phase boundary from peace into war are defiance, counterforce, and counterthreat."

A fundamental principle which underlies all these systems is that threat has a cost of transport and hence diminishes in intensity and effectiveness as we move away from the threatener. The importance of flight in human history testifies to this, as do the limits that evolve in the area of conquest. As a conqueror moves into a hostile territory, the conqueror's threat becomes weaker and the countermeasures stronger. This is as true of the spread of ideologies as it is of empires.

Deterrence

Deterrence is a situation in which neither party destroys the other's means of threat, but each has the capability to damage the other if the peace is broken. An impressive example is the nuclear deterrence based on mutual assured destruction (MAD) that we have had between the US and the USSR now for forty years. There have been many previous examples of short periods of peace through deterrence, but these periods have seldom exceeded one or two decades. But there is a very good reason for the ultimate instability of deterrence: If deterrence was stable in the long run, it would cease to deter in the short run. We can see this certainly in the present situation, where if the probability of nuclear weapons going off were zero, they would not deter anybody. Deterrence, therefore, always has a positive probability of breaking down and anything which has a positive probability will happen if we wait long enough. Peace through deterrence in the prenuclear era was something like a twenty-year flood, that is, a flood with an annual probability of 5 percent, which is fairly probable even in twenty years and extremely probable in forty or sixty years. Nuclear deterrence may be more like a one-hundred-year flood, with a probability of 1 percent per annum (this is just a guess), but even this would have a 63 percent probability of occurring in a hundred years and a 98 percent probability in four hundred years. It is an illusion, therefore, to think that deterrence can be ultimately stable.

Of the various responses to threat, the two that seem most likely to bring peace are submission and disarming behavior. Of course, submission has a bad name and gives peace a bad name, although we do it all the time in private life. For example, when a police car approaches us from the rear with its lights flashing, we pull off the road and submit. We pay our taxes. We obey our employers and our teachers, and occasionally even our spouses. Indeed, without a certain amount of submission, social life would be impossible.

Turning 'Them' to 'We'

What is very important in history is the development of a combination of submission and disarming behavior which turns "them" into "we." We can see this phenomenon in the rise of the national state and in the development of courtesy and manners, both of which turned the threatener and the threatened into a "we" group. Historians have been singularly insensitive to these processes, and we need a very careful study of what might be called the evolution of "gentleness." It is quite significant, for instance, that the baron became a "gentleman," that the Vikings turned into the modern Norwegians, that we gave up wearing swords, that dueling disappeared, and so on.

A very significant innovation, mainly in the twentieth century, is the combination of defiance with disarming behavior, particularly associated with the name of Gandhi and with nonviolent struggle. This is perhaps less successful in developing larger integrative structures, as its principle objective was to gain national independence. This may or may not achieve stable peace. Thus, India and Pakistan do not have stable peace even today.

There are difficult problems here which are far from being resolved, such as the optimum structure of political organization and the optimum integrative structure. This goes back to the whole problem of the relation of the "I" to the "we" and the long seesaw conflict, perhaps more apparent than real, between individualism and collectivism. This in turn involves the skills of conflict management, the legitimation of the institutions of property, and a whole host of social problems which we cannot go into here.

A very important question in the interpretation of history is how we see war: as an interruption in the evolution of peaceful behavior, or as the essential dynamic of history, where peace is just an interval between wars. I would argue strongly for the former of these two positions. Over the history of the human race, I would guess that peaceful pursuits — plowing, sowing, reaping, producing, falling in love, having children, dancing, singing, having fun, learning, studying — represent somewhere between 85 to 95 percent of human activity, and that over the years war has rarely been more than 5 to 15 percent. Adam Smith says in *The Wealth of Nations*: "Among the civilized nations of modern Europe . . . not more than one-hundredth part of the inhabitants of any country can be employed as soldiers, without ruin to the country that pays the expense of their service." (1) The basic truth is that war is a parasitical part of the economy, particularly when it becomes professionalized. Professional armies cannot feed or clothe themselves or even provide themselves with weapons. This has to be done by the civilian population. Even looting is a very poor way of getting rich. There is abundant evidence from history that maintaining an empire impoverishes the imperial power, eventually to the point where the empire collapses.

> *"A very important question in the interpretation of history is how we see war: as an interruption in the evolution of peaceful behavior, or as the essential dynamic of history, where peace is just an interval between wars."*

Since the rise of science and its applications to production, the inefficiency of threat systems has become even more striking. In the nineteenth and twentieth centuries it was not the imperial powers that got rich rapidly. Instead it was countries like Sweden and Denmark, which abstained from building great armies and expanding and devoted their resources to minding their own business. Both Britain and France have increased their rate of economic development substantially since they gave up on their empires. If I had to express this in a one-sentence interpretation of history, it would be that wealth creates power and power destroys wealth. It may have taken us 5,000 years to catch on to this truth.

Just as the transition from peace to war or from war to peace involves the crossing of a phase boundary in the behavioral character of social systems, so one can detect phase boundaries in the total system of war and peace itself. I have distinguished four such phases. (2) At some times and places we have had stable war, in which war is virtually continuous over considerable periods. Southeast Asia, which has had almost continuous war for at least forty-five years, is perhaps the major example of this in the twentieth century. Stable war, however, is so debilitating and destructive that it tends to be interrupted by periods of peace. This might be called unstable war, a situation in which war is regarded as the norm but is interrupted by periods of peace. Examples of this are plentiful. In the twentieth century, the Middle East is perhaps the best example. Unstable war frequently passes almost imperceptibly through lengthening periods of peace and the rise of more integrative structures, into what might be called unstable peace, in which peace is regarded as the norm but is interrupted by periods of war. European society from 1648 is an example.

Since the Napoleonic Wars, however, we have developed a somewhat new phenomenon in the world, curiously unnoticed, which could be described as stable peace. An increasing number of independent states have no plans whatever to go to war with each other. Stable peace can almost be measured by the amount of dust on the plans for invasion in the various war offices.

"Stable peace can almost be measured by the amount of dust on the plans for invasion in the various war offices."

It seems to have begun in Scandinavia, sometime after the Napoleonic Wars, when the Swedes and the Danes stopped fighting each other, after they had done so for centuries. The Danes, of course, were involved in a war with Germany over Schleswig-Holstein, but the Swedes did not intervene. Stable peace spread to North America by about 1870, perhaps through a succession of lucky accidents. Certainly the United States did not have stable peace in the War of 1812. However, this war was followed by the Rush-Bagot Agreement of 1817 between Britain and the United States. This remarkable event, which disarmed the Great Lakes, has gone almost unnoticed, even in the United States. It was followed by the settlement of the boundary between Canada and the United States, in spite of a presidential election and the slogan "54–40 or Fight!" which reflected the fact that the United States wanted what is now British Columbia, and the Canadians and British wanted what is now Washington and Oregon. Eventually this dispute was settled and the forty-ninth parallel went peacefully to the Pacific. In my opinion, what finally established stable peace between Canada and the United States was the fact that Britain did not intervene militarily in the American Civil War, even though it came close to doing so. It seems that it is very hard to persuade historians that what did not happen, sometimes almost by a hair's-breadth, is often much more important than what happened.

One thing that limits the expansion of states and empires is their desire not to be too heterogeneous. This may explain why the United States got stable peace with Mexico after the Mexican War of 1846 and the Gadsden Purchase of 1853. Stable peace arrived in Western Europe after World War II, assisted no doubt by the development of the Common Market and the enormous expansion of trade and tourism. It is not often realized that the volume of international trade increased about sixfold between about 1950 and 1980. We now have what I have called a great triangle of stable peace, stretching from Australia to Japan, across North America, to Western Europe, Scandinavia, and Finland, with about eighteen countries that have no plans whatever to go to war with each other.

Conditions for a Stable Peace

If we ask ourselves, "What are the necessary conditions for stable peace?" the answer turns out to be surprisingly simple. The major condition is that change in national boundaries should be completely removed from the political agendas of the countries concerned, except by mutual

---

"If we ask ourselves, 'What are the necessary conditions for stable peace?' the answer turns out to be surprisingly simple. . . . change in national boundaries should be completely removed from the political agendas . . ."

---

consent. Again, this is an operation of taboo. This preserves a degree of national sovereignty with the development of what Karl Deutsch calls a "security community," in which each country finds its own security in the security of the others. (3) National sovereignty is a kind of political property, and property mutually agreed upon is a great source of peace. The English proverb that "good fences make good neighbors" perhaps only works if the neighbors can talk across the fence. But certainly secure boundaries make good neighbors. Oddly enough, national boundaries may be taken off the agenda for two quite opposite reasons: either because they are natural boundaries, like the water separating Sweden and Denmark; or because they are completely artificial, like the forty-ninth parallel between the United States and Canada. If we can get people to regard national boundaries as rather insignificant accidents of history and national states as arbitrary conveniences, a great deal of the sting will go out of the whole system. A second condition for stable peace is that there should be a minimum amount of intervention by one country in the internal affairs of another. Just where this minimum lies is hard to say. It is probably not zero, but it should not be threatening to the sovereignty or the integrity of either country.

Perhaps the greatest question facing the human race at the moment is: Can we expand the present triangle of stable peace to include the Soviet Union? The area of stable peace would then include the whole temperate zone. Understandably, the Soviet Union, after its long history of invasion, feels very insecure about its boundaries. If the Kellogg Pact of 1928 had outlawed boundary change, this would have been much more effective than outlawing war itself. The next question is: How do we expand stable peace into the tropics? There are difficulties here, especially in Africa, where the national boundaries resulted from the geographical ignorance of the European powers when Africa was divided among them in 1878. These boundaries often divide tribal, cultural, linguistic, and religious groups. Even so, there has been surprisingly little international war in Africa since independence, with the exception of Ethiopia and Somali, some rather minor incursions elsewhere, and a good deal of internal war, for example, in Nigeria, Angola, and Uganda.

"One of the tragedies of the world is that many of the people in powerful positions are still dominated by the experience of World War II, which is now almost totally irrelevant."

The nuclear weapon has changed the international system so profoundly that the immediate past is a very poor guide to the future. One of the tragedies of the world is that many of the people in powerful positions are still dominated by the experience of World War II, which is now almost totally irrelevant. To find a parallel to the present situation, we would really have to go back to the Thirty Years War in Central Europe. In this war we might say, the nuclear equivalent was the development of the enormously destructive cannon. It is a fundamental principle that what can be defended with weapons depends on the nature, particularly on the range and the deadliness, of the deadly missiles. The development of the effective cannon around the year 1500 brought the feudal system to an end, almost within a generation. The baron who stayed in his castle got blown up with it. Germany, of course, did not become a national state at that time, which is one reason why it was the battleground of the Thirty Years War. This was an ideological war with no serious economic conflicts behind it. Similarly, the conflict between the USSR and the US is an ideological conflict: There is virtually no economic conflict between them. Then in 1648 the conflicting powers said "Let the Protestants stay Protestant and the Catholics stay Catholic, and let's not fuss about it." As a result, change in existing boundaries was taken off the agenda. The settlement still holds. Prussia and Scandinavia are still Lutheran; Austria, Bavaria, and the Rhineland are still Catholic; and nobody seems to be much worse off for that. So what we have to look for between the capitalist and the communist world is what I have called a "Westphalian solution," which says in effect: "Let's each do our own thing and see how it works out. But let's declare the boundaries to be fixed."

The alternative, as we all know, is total, perhaps irretrievable catastrophe. The combination of the nuclear warhead, the guided missile, and the worldwide accurate information system, has turned the whole world into a battlefield. How bad the "nuclear winter" will be we do not really know, but it is quite possible that a nuclear war would mean irretrievable catastrophe for the evolutionary process on earth. Nuclear war, however, will be an inevitable result of the existing system of national defense. National defense is now the greatest enemy of national security. I confess I want

---

"National defense is now the greatest enemy of national security."

---

national security because I do not really want a world state. I want diversity, I want experiment, I want people to be able to pursue their own identities, I want people to have a homeland and homes. Above all, I want variety, for this is the essence of evolutionary change, a fundamental condition of it. Stable peace is now the only security that is available. Star Wars, the Strategic Defense Initiative, is nonsense, as are Soviet plans to counter it. Both would increase the probability of war. In the nuclear age, there are no castle walls nor suits of armor. An increased threat against the threatener can only increase the probability of war. There are no technical solutions to this problem. There are only political and moral solutions. Fortunately, these are available. Anything that exists must be possible. Stable peace exists, so it must be possible. It is not only possible, it is necessary, and it must be expanded.

The Concept of Universal Security: A Revolution of Thinking and Policy in the Nuclear Age

Alexander I. Nikitin

Senior Research Fellow, Institute of USA and Canada Studies, Academy of Sciences of the USSR. Dr. Nikitin is a member of the Executive Committee of the Soviet Political Science Association. He is coauthor of *American Model on the Scales of History* and author of *Evolution of American Globalism* and more than twenty papers on international relations, world order, and international security issues.

National Security

"Peace is the greatest good that people can wish for in this life." When the great humanist Cervantes wrote this he was stating the principle position of pacifism, where attainment of peace is regarded as the highest possible value to which all other aspirations should be subordinated. Yet history is full of examples where peace has been consciously sacrificed for attaining other goals, for preserving faith and principles, and for materialism and ideology.

Ever since relations between people assumed a political form, peace has been constantly balanced against other values such as independence, territorial integrity, sovereignty, and security. And just as Cervantes's famous hero Don Quixote who wanted peace and the triumph of good constantly engaged in armed conflict against injustice, so have people of the world in practice repeatedly sacrificed their peaceful lives for the sake of forcibly asserting other values and interests which were considered more important at the time.

Although concepts such as peace, security, and disarmament may be constantly placed side-by-side in political appeals and treaties and are therefore considered to be inseparably connected, their correlation in real life has become quite complex and ambiguous. Peaceful relations often fail to guarantee security. Very often the path to security is visualized as through armaments, rather than disarmament.

Due to concrete historical developments following World War II, the problem of a possible nuclear confrontation between the US and USSR assumed a key position in the area of international security. Despite recognition of the importance of economic, political, diplomatic, and ideological means for strengthening and preserving security and independence, each side has used military force and the concept of nuclear deterrence as a fundamental basis for development of security policies.

In practice, national or state security was the sole determinant of security policy. Due to the continued stockpiling of weapons, the US and the USSR attained nuclear strategic parity by the late 1970s. Yet, as one of the great parodoxes of our times, both sides began to depend on the use of a high level of imposed threat as a way of preserving their national security. Until the 1980s the concept of mutual assured destruction (MAD) was looked upon largely as a model of Soviet-American relations. It did not involve other countries, as they saw it.

This situation has changed considerably over the present decade. Information provided by the International Physicians for the Prevention of Nuclear War (IPPNW) and data from computer modeling in the US and USSR regarding climatic, physical, and other global consequences of a possible massive nuclear strike, has made it quite clear that Mutual Assured Destruction has in fact become Assured Universal Destruction. (1,2) This means that a reciprocal nuclear exchange between the superpowers will not only destroy both countries, but will make the very existence of life on this planet problematic. Today world opinion is paying more attention to the security doctrines of the two sides, since the security of all other states has become hostage to the security plans of the US and USSR. As a consequence, the redefining of national and state security has become an imperative for all countries and prompted replacement of previous concepts by the new alternative approach of universal security.

Universal Security

It would be wrong to consider universal security as a totally new proposal, or a ready-made set of ideas or practical proposals. In fact the principles and ideas incorporated in universal security have been circulated and discussed over the past several decades by politicians, scholars, and concerned citizens. Other concepts such as "collective security," "mutual security," and "common security" have also been posed as alternative possibilities for national or state security. When the concept of universal security did take form in the 1980s, it did so as an amalgamation of the most important and viable of these previous proposals.

An important contribution to the emerging concept of universal security was made by the independent (nongovernmental) Commission on

Disarmament and Security created by Swedish Prime Minister Olaf Palme. He brought together public figures from seventeen countries of Europe, Asia, America, and Africa. As a result of the Commission's work the concept of common security for the 1980s was formulated. (3)

The Palme Commission analyzed the causes and failures of the system of collective security under the United Nations Charter. It emphasized that sociopolitical confrontation between the East and West after World War II actually blocked implementation of Articles 39 through 51 of the UN Charter. That portion of the Charter called for creation of an effective UN armed force contingent and other measures for achieving collective influence (primarily by the UN Security Council) on individual sovereign states. "Instead of actions aimed at maintaining collective security as discussed in 1945, priority was given to other functions of a more limited nature." (4) Lacking an effective reliable international means for maintaining security, states in the post-World War II era regressed to former procedures based on time-honored military methods, instead of political or legal means.

The main idea of common security on the world scene involves abandoning the principle of deterrence as a political and psychological state of relations between major nuclear powers. As pointed out in the Palme report: "States can no longer strive towards strengthening their security at another's expense. It is only possible to achieve it through joint effort." (5)

The reality of today's international politics demonstrates how security and even our chances for survival in the nuclear age are sacrificed daily for self-motivated sovereign political, ideological, and military decisions. Examples include conditions operant in Nicaragua, Afghanistan, Iran-Iraq, and Africa. Yet, at the same time there has developed now a broadening strata of public and perceptive leaders who are coming to accept the imperative of a new standard of behavior. This standard demands that governments recognize that they exist in a nuclear and interdependent world. Despite ideological differences and political rivalry they must completely acknowledge the priority of universal security and survival over their political and ideological goals.

Principles of universal security obviously impose limits on an individual state's sovereignty to take unilateral political, military, or ideologic steps which might bring the world to the brink of a nuclear conflict. This is true even if such actions are consistent with the country's narrower internal political and ideological interests. In the last decade, a number of political leaders in the East and West have proposed and accepted certain principles codified in the concept of universal security. Among them are: recognition of the impossibility of survival in an all-out nuclear war and that there can be no victor after a nuclear exchange. President Jimmy Carter, after signing the SALT II treaty in June 1979, stated that each side would, from that moment on, have to consider the subsequent presence of military parity. No longer could there ever be nuclear superiority or a victory in a nuclear war. (6)

Acceptance of Universal Security

Starting in the late 1970s, Soviet leadership repeatedly proclaimed its recognition of the impossibility of ever achieving a victory in a nuclear conflict, or of gaining nuclear superiority. The Reagan administration, after a number of confronting statements in 1981 through 1983, has since also officially confirmed this position. This was established in a joint statement at the 1985 Geneva Summit and demonstrated major progress towards revising our understanding of security.

In today's world of nuclear "overkill" it is reckless for the USSR or the US to resort to military means for resolving any conflict, whether of a political or ideological nature. This is true whether it be a local conflict or an all-out confrontation, and whether it involves use of conventional forces, since "little" wars now have the potential of escalating to a full-blown nuclear exchange. This is certainly the case in our present nuclear age where the bulk of nuclear capability is concentrated in the hands of two sides that have competing social systems and ideologies. This calls for unparalleled restraint and caution by both countries.

"In today's world of nuclear 'overkill' it is reckless for the USSR or the US to resort to military means for resolving any conflict."

The acceptance of universal security will also lead to a change in the concept of parity as a guarantee of security in a nuclear world. We have reached a limit where parity ceases to be a factor for military-political deterrence. In a nuclear interdependent world parity and the principle of equality and equal security have become obvious liabilities, when armaments are at present "overkill" levels. This leads to the conclusion that the only way to ensure one's security in today's world is an immediate and drastic reduction of military arsenals. The concept of "reasonable sufficiency" has been put forward as an answer to this problem of parity. For the Soviet Union this has meant that nuclear weapons be limited to the minimum necessary for security.

The Path toward Universal Security

No one country has a monopoly on providing effective concepts for creating a complete and all-embracing security. Present discussions in the Soviet Union are but one step in changing existing concepts of security under pressure posed by the present nuclear danger. There is still much work to be done. Furthermore, reform of Soviet foreign political practices and military doctrines, so as to bring them in line with contemporary concepts of security, will not be a simple or an easy matter. It is also obvious that universal security cannot be carried out unilaterally, or just by several countries — parallel joint actions by many countries will be needed.

". . . the concept of a zero-sum game . . . is not only invalid in today's world . . . it will inevitably lead to a nuclear exchange."

The actual scale of the nuclear danger (and consequently nuclear security) is not national, but global in scope. It would be particularly helpful if this new idea of universal security received broad discussion which could be facilitated by including it on the agenda of the UN General Assembly. This would provide for open discussion on this new proposal by all nations possessing nuclear weapons and all concerned states. By its very nature, the new concept of security is not amenable for use at the national or state level, but is applicable only internationally. It has been formulated in response to the new conditions we face in an interdependent world and is provided as an alternative to prevailing versions of national security concepts.

To obtain an advantage by inflicting damage on one's enemy through a massive nuclear strike turns out to be as impossible in today's world as ensuring security of any one single country — whether it participates in the conflict, or is neutral, since the consequences involve all countries on the globe, including the one that initiated the attack. Delivering a first strike (which could have been regarded as ensuring national security in previous stages of stockpiling of nuclear weapons) is proving to be a suicidal act, even if the other side does not retaliate. A "nuclear winter" with global climatic changes could ensue when as little as 5 to 10 percent of the nuclear weapons now present on the planet are exploded, even if only launched by one side.

In this decade the fear of nuclear winter has become more effective than fear of a retaliatory strike as the chief factor for deterrence. But faced with the possible destruction of all life on the planet, there is need for the complete rethinking of the meaning of deterrence. We are all being held hostage to the continued stockpiling of nuclear weapons, their possible accidental use, terrorist activities, and the escalation of any conventional conflict to a full-blown nuclear exchange. These threats provide the most serious obstacle for developing political trust on the international scene. In turn, this leads to a vicious cycle which then results in a new spiral, or escalation, of the arms race. Control, or prediction, of any military or political outcome rapidly diminishes under these conditions. As a result, political leaders and scholars have long realized the existence of a threshold in the arms race where further development of armaments and their delivery systems would not lead to greater security, but make deterrence much more ineffective. We now have come to that threshold.

Taking the required steps towards arriving at a solution will not be simple. Deterrence has occupied a central position in policies promoting peace and security, primarily through the concept of a zero-sum game stratagem — benefit for one side automatically assures loss for the other. This concept is not only invalid in today's world, it is dangerous and must be surrendered, since it will inevitably lead to a nuclear exchange.

"The most important point is the recognition that reduction of an adversary's security . . . under today's conditions results in reducing one's own security."

It would also be an oversimplification to assume that adopting the principles of equality and equal security will automatically lead to cessation of efforts to gain military superiority. If one uses as a model the concept that greater security on one side immediately leads to a greater sense of insecurity on the other side, then any discrepancy in the levels of security is considered dangerous. Here equality is the main concern, no matter on what level. The model incorporates, as a legal right, that both sides may take corrective action to engage in a retaliatory buildup of weapons. This logic is inapplicable in the concept of not only equal, but, mutual, or universal security.

The new model of universal security gives priority to overall system security before considering the illusionary possibility of separately assigning security to its elements. The most important point is the recognition that reduction of an adversary's security (increasing a threat to him) under today's conditions results in reducing one's own security. Under these conditions the reduction of a threat to an adversary, over wide limits, does not necessarily make oneself more vulnerable, or provide tangible advantage to the other side. In other words, mutual security in the nuclear age is tied to a concept of "reasonable sufficiency" and rejects both the "equality" and zero-sum game models.

Required Change

New thinking calls for new action and policy particularly in dealing with military doctrines and the structure of existing armed forces. This implies that the principles of universal security be incorporated into international relations; that nations accept that there can be no victory, or defense, in a nuclear war; that instead of seeking equality of nuclear capability, they move to a reasonable sufficiency of arsenals.

Transition to a mode of universal security demands new attitudes towards political and ideological differences between powers. Demands of security not only concern matters of territorial integrity of sovereign states, but also require protection of existing social systems from outside interference. Changes in such systems must not be subject to forceful action from the outside, but are internal affairs of the respective states and amenable to change through their own internal conflicts and domestic movements. In practice, the foreign policies of the US and USSR should be redefined to accept these principles.

"This model is very far from the old Trotskyite call for world revolution."

One should not continue to assume that real security is unobtainable until all political and ideological contradictions between socialism and capitalism are resolved. This is old thinking. The principal task before us in our present nuclear, interdependent world is the development of universal security, irrespective of present and future incidents, or even profound contradictions between social systems. For this reason, one needs to distinguish between levels of social-system-to-system and state-to-state interactions. This needs to be viewed anew. Differences in social systems and ideologies should not become a source of friction between states. One should not attempt "to make another state better than it is." In the present nuclear age, individual states — particularly the US and the USSR — should not feel they have the right, or use force , to define the outcome of competition between socialism and capitalism in the world community.

In the process of changing old security stereotypes, one needs to overcome the simplified and often inadequate understanding of goals and motivation of the social systems of the other side. Competition in the form of different cultural and social system models should not be perceived as a threat to each other's national security. Promotion of security for socialist or capitalist countries should not require the alteration of the other social system. The principle goal for interaction and competition between these systems should be peaceful coexistence and provide for a maximal development of each system's potential in the areas of social development, economics, and politics. The sides should not engage in forcibly changing, curtailing, or even eradicating the other system. This model is very far from the old Trotskyite call for world revolution. Unfortunately this newer model of Soviet goals is not well recognized in the

West. The Soviet Union is striving to make it clear that it sees competition between capitalism and socialism proceeding along lines that exclude the use of military force, as a way of challenging the other side.

The process leading to a change in thinking, perceptions, and attitudes has just started. Both East and West are facing the necessity of rejecting many traditional dogmas in national strategy and security perceptions.

The security of each state and each social model can be achieved, but not at the expense of the other. This can only follow from a policy of cautious, civilized, coexistence which includes the cooperation of different states and social models in the framework of a self-aware world.

Nuclear Revolution and the New Way of Thinking

Andrei Y. Melville

Section Head, Institute of USA and Canada Studies, Academy of Sciences of the USSR. Dr. Melville was awarded the 1981 Gold Medal of the Academy of Sciences of the USSR for the best work of a young scholar. He is the author or coauthor of five books and a large number of papers on political consciousness and problems of war and peace.

Today we are often reminded of Albert Einstein's words: "The unleashed power of the atom has changed everything except our ways of thinking." Also we are reminded that the birth and development of nuclear weapons has drastically changed the conditions of human existence. These weapons have necessitated not only new norms of behavior in international relations but new principles of thinking relevant to the realities of the nuclear age. (1)

Unprecedented Task

But do we also realize that this is an unprecedented and difficult task which involves a resolute break with many historical, political, psychological, and ideological traditions that come from prenuclear times? Not only people, but whole societies carry with them the burden of the past, and eliminating it is usually a difficult and painful job. A great deal in our political traditions — in all their diversity — constitute a serious obstacle to adopting new political thinking.

Becoming conscious of the radical changes in the world demands not only political courage, but a certain degree of emotional readiness. This requires mental effort along with substantial psychological reorientation. This, then, is a task for all of us who were raised in the traditions of the past, and are often inclined to consider such traditions as being the only norm. (2)

The difficulty of this task is also due to the fact that on the journey to new political thinking there are not only "visible" political and ideological obstacles but "invisible" barriers as well.

These are the psychological and emotional barriers which are a result of the natural reluctance of the human mind to accept change. Such psychological defense is often intellectually attractive, saving one the trouble of thinking through the difficult problems of the nuclear age, and instead permitting one to use well-known ideas and concepts.

The New Era

The starting point here should be coming to grips with the fact that new types of weapons of mass destruction have divided human history in two periods — prenuclear and nuclear. Many ideas that were normal in the prenuclear age turn out to be absolutely unacceptable in the nuclear age. Many traditional categories of politics now do not make sense or have substantially changed their meaning. War and peace, victory and defeat, superiority and vulnerability, menace and security, strategy and force, balance and stability — these and many other concepts are acquiring new meaning today.

Moreover, the nuclear era is seriously changing the very notion of logic and rationality inherited from the past. The use of political ideas and concepts of the prenuclear era today become almost pseudorational. Formerly everything seemed logical, but today it is in essence absolutely senseless. The gap between technical and scientific development and the level of human thinking has created drastic changes in the world. These often force us to use ideas that are hopelessly outdated, even though we are already living under conditions where traditional political thinking becomes unavoidably contradictory. It becomes contradictory and irrational because it fails to come to grips with the new reality. Being rational only in form creates an illusory picture of the world and dictates solutions and actions which are dysfunctional. (3)

Nuclear Realities

So we are faced with the necessity of bringing our concepts and ideas in accord with the new realities of the nuclear age and the revolutionary change it has produced in the world. By mentioning revolutionary change we are not just making sensational exaggerations. We have all the reasons which qualify the nuclear revolution as a break with past traditions. The revolution demands a serious reestimation of many, if not all, our political concepts, first of all those related to the problems of war and peace.

The importance of problems of war and peace can be explained by the fact that the threat of war has acquired a qualitatively new dimension. Although the prevention of nuclear war is the primary aim of Soviet and American national policy, it, of course, does not exclude other national goals. However, the problem of preventing nuclear doomsday has today a great significance of its own and is of the utmost importance in the list of national priorities. This issue has become the specific context for all other major problems of today. (In this sense one can say that problems of war and peace and other global issues have become indivisible.)

". . . for the first time in history, the decision for total nuclear suicide can not only be made, but can be implemented by a relatively small group of people."

The nuclear revolution has ended the limits of the destructive capacity of weapons of mass destruction and has ended the possibilities of traditional defense against them. For the first time in human history, war with the use of nuclear weapons threatens to become not genocide but omnicide — total extermination of humanity. For the first time, the potential of mutually assured destruction has been acquired. This eliminates any possibility for the aggressor to win, even in a hypothetical situation. The military arsenals are ready for immediate use, and no mobilization or restructuring of industry is needed to begin a war. And for the first time in history, the decision for total nuclear suicide can not only be made, but can be implemented by a relatively small group of people.

Previously the problems of war and peace generally concerned relations between particular states, nations, classes, or social groups. Today for the first time they have become a global problem for all of civilization.

History becomes world history little by little. In a positive sense, this global character consists of economic, political, and spiritual interdependence. But in the case of the nuclear threat, the global character of human history acquires a negative connotation in the sense that the possibility exists for the destruction of human history itself. In this same negative sense, the nuclear revolution and the threats it entails has united human civilization to a greater extent than even the internationalization of the economic process, the growth of interdependence, or the development of mass communications — all of which could perish in nuclear war.

In prenuclear times nations and peoples perished in wars, but this did not stop the natural thrust of historical development in general. Nuclear war, however, poses a threat of a dramatically different kind — it brings into question the future of the linear development of human society, the vectoral direction of history. In apocalyptic stories of the past, "the end of the world" usually occurred simultaneously with the "beginning" of a transition into some higher quality. But nuclear apocalypse is not a beginning of anything else, it is just the "end" of history, the end of everything. (4)

Military Force and Politics

It has already been noted that nuclear revolution has totally changed the nature and character of war. Nuclear war or the threat of nuclear war can no longer serve as a means of resolving international, social, political, or ideological conflicts or contradictions. The traditional correlation between the objectives and the means of war becomes senseless. War with the use of nuclear weapons can no longer be considered a rational continuation of "politics by other means."

"Under these new conditions, an increase in military power does not enhance security, but, on the contrary, undermines it."

The task of reevaluating many concepts and ideas which have become outdated due to the nuclear revolution concerns a whole spectrum of key military and political categories. First of all is the question of the correlation between military force and politics. The change in character of war engendered by the nuclear revolution must be analyzed in its global context — the changing role of force and the threat of force in achieving political ends. The nuclear revolution brings into being a paradox of security by turning upside down the traditional correlation between a nation's military force and its security. Under these new conditions, an increase in military power does not enhance security, but, on the contrary, undermines it. Moreover, the political influence of a country on the international scene is no longer directly related to its military potential. The military force of a nation cannot be equated with the quantity and quality of its nuclear potential because that potential cannot be implemented in practice — neither in a direct military sense nor for achieving political aims.

The determining factor of the above-mentioned shift in the relationship between military force and politics is the total vulnerability created by the nuclear revolution — the inability to defend oneself against the threat of nuclear destruction by the use of any technical or military device. This is why the concept of national security has so dramatically changed. In the first place, security is relative since under the circumstances no nation, not even the strongest militarily or otherwise, can assure itself absolute security considering the total vulnerability brought about by the nuclear revolution. In the second place, one-way security is impossible. It is unachievable without substantial political cooperation and mutual understanding with the adversary.

The Security Dilemma

Before the nuclear revolution, nations were encouraged to deal with the so-called "security dilemma." In essense, the efforts of any state to increase its security, no matter what its subjective intentions, often objectively result in diminishing the security of others. In other words, the stronger a state became militarily — the more it strengthened its own security by one-way military measures — the more vulnerable and less secure were its potential adversaries. But the nuclear revolution has given this security dilemma a qualitatively new dimension.

The situation of total vulnerability, once created, is irreversible. It cannot be changed by any military efforts, defensive efforts included. The scientific and technical development of defensive weapons cannot eliminate the fundamental fact of the nuclear revolution — the vulnerability of the nation's territory and its civilian and industrial centers to the possible nuclear attack. Under the circumstances, the assurance of even relative security becomes militarily impossible.

Mutual vulnerability deters actions which could definitely lead to a military conflict. Moreover, vulnerability and constant potential menace to one's security deter not only direct nuclear attack but also actions which under other circumstances could lead to escalation of conflict. It is significant that in the past the uncertainty factor related to war often stimulated aggression. But under the nuclear revolution, that uncertainty, the unpredictability of possible escalation, becomes a deterring factor.

In this sense, the weapons created by the nuclear revolution are not strictly speaking military weapons, since under no hypothetical situation can they be used to achieve those aims which used to be achievable with the help of weapons. The concept of force acquires special ambiguity in relation to nuclear weapons: weapons are capable of destroying but are incapable of assuring traditional political influence. In any event, with the "nuclear revolution" the interrelation between military force and political influence ceased to be simple and linear. After a certain point, any increase in the capability to destroy becomes excessive and cannot be used for political goals.

Offense versus Defense

The nuclear revolution has destroyed the traditional competition between offensive and defensive means. It has established forever the superiority of offensive weapons. Thus all efforts to create a defense against nuclear weapons in the usual sense are meaningless. This leads to a phenomenon unknown in human history. Now the mutual possession of nuclear offensive weaponry makes both sides equally defenseless. This phenomenon becomes one of the crucial factors in creating, again for the first time in history, a real strategic dead end — one that eliminates any sense of the traditional concepts of military strategy and the use of military means for achieving specific aims.

". . . the acquisition of military superiority has no military significance . . . no relationship to real security."

Total vulnerability eliminates the traditional rationale for the idea of "defense" by devaluating it. Defense in the sense of assuring national security ceases to be military in nature and becomes instead a political and a psychological problem. Total vulnerability means that the acquisition of military superiority has no military significance, it has no relationship to real security. Hence the notion of superiority or vulnerability now lacks meaning in the traditional sense.

Nuclear weapons create another paradox — the contradiction between their enormous destructive force on the one hand and the incapacity to totally destroy the adversary's nuclear potential on the other. That gives the enemy a' guaranteed possibility of launching a second strike to exterminate the "winner" even after he himself was hypothetically "defeated." This brings into existence a new strategic situation without a traditional military meaning. In prenuclear times one army could defeat another and impose on the loser its political will. However, nuclear weapons with all their destructive power cannot assure "victory."

Another fact deserves attention: To search for practical technological solutions to existing problems now contradicts reality since those solutions no longer work. The understanding of this dilemma often entails psychological tension and a search for some way out of the dead end, even if illusory. One of the common reactions to this new situation is the effort to get rid of the sense of nuclear vulnerability by spending resources on various technological projects by reviving "defense" in its traditional meaning. But in practice, all attempts to create a universal defense against nuclear weapons (either in space or by civil defense) are in essence the same efforts to get rid of the painful feeling of total vulnerability. New norms of political rationality in the nuclear age make the principle of zero-sum game in international relations meaningless especially in relations with a potential adversary. The traditional political principle that says "what is bad for the enemy is good for us" has become hopelessly outdated.

Deep modifications of the "image of the enemy" are urgently needed. We need a new attitude about our adversary — not only political but psychological and emotional as well. Psychologically this may be one of the hardest tasks. This will be particularly difficult due to deeply rooted ethnic, sociopsychological, political, or ideological prejudices but also due to the arms race which is in itself a source of misperceptions. "Absolute" weapons need an "absolute" enemy who would be so "evil" that the use of these weapons would be morally and psychologically justifiable. (5)

Dehumanization of the enemy and its perception as an "absolute evil" is extremely dangerous in our present situation. It is very important and necessary today to avoid situations where the adversary could feel insecure, unsure, or vulnerable. The feeling of security of the other side is as important today as the preservation of one's own security. A new concept of common human faith should be based on this principle of internationalization of national interest, which is an outgrowth of giving top priority to global human needs and interests.

The paradoxes and dilemmas of the nuclear age undermine traditional political thinking and lead to unresolvable contradictions which cannot be overcome in the framework of old political logic.

But are such radical changes in our way of thinking possible at all, and what are the obstacles in the way?

Yes, the changes are possible and the obstacles are numerous. First, there are political and ideological obstacles, such as the resistance of those who quite consciously, due to specific interests, are against the new thinking. But there are also psychological obstacles which are not always fully realized. (6)

In great measure, these obstacles are produced by the fact that our thinking processes work in accordance with traditional perceptions and tend to elaborate their own psychological defense against the new reality too painful for it to face. These mechanisms of defense create an illusory psychological calmness and block consciousness. This results in a sort of "psychological deafness."

In human perception, one of the most common forms of resistance to nuclear realities is conventionalization of nuclear weapons, a tendency to perceive them as "usual" but more powerful, as weapons which can be dealt with by traditional military and political means. Such conventionalization can be attractive psychologically and intellectually because it forces out of the mind information which is too painful. It permits us to use well-known concepts and categories which were applied successfully in the past. (7)

Another form of resistance is the appeal to ideological absolutism and purism. This is when one declares abstract, absolute ideological goals that allow us to not face the realities of the nuclear age. Here, in particular, we see modern variations of a "crusade" or "holy war," ideology extremely dangerous in the nuclear age.

The military-technological fetish is another variation of resistance when people avoid accepting radical changes now called for by the nuclear revolution. This resistance takes the form of using refinements of technological development — an increase in accuracy, invention of smaller warheads, and other improvements so that nuclear weapons can once again acquire "military" feasibility. An example of such a "fetish" is the idea of creating an exotic technology of "space defense" against nuclear weapons.

". . . there exists another serious obstacle on the way to creating this new thinking . . . between rhetoric and action . . . there is danger that 'new thinking' will become only a cliché."

Tendencies to think in old political categories are evident in cases where the absolute parameters of nuclear weapons are ignored. A glaring example is in negotiations where we are still discussing the number of warheads, their accuracy, time of reaching the target, the number of targets, and their defense. What should openly be declared now is the absence of limits on the destructive power of nuclear weapons, the fact that both sides are totally vulnerable, and that projects to assure absolute security are unrealistic. (3)

Among unconscious psychic mechanisms of resistance one should mention semantic traps, that is, linguistic formulas of artificial "nuclear esperanto" that in practice have no relation to nuclear reality but nevertheless are proposed for dealing with it. For example, when we hear such phrases as nuclear exchange, escalation, counterforce, window of vulnerability, or nuclear umbrella, we must realize that these are euphemisms that create an illusion of rationality for a situation which, in essence, lacks all rationality.

Comprehension of the nature of the nuclear revolution is a most important precondition for a transition toward the new paradigms of thought we now need in order to survive. But there exists another serious obstacle on the way to creating this new thinking. That is the gap between rhetoric and action when grand declarations about the necessity of new thinking are made simultaneously with totally unchanging behavior. It is when old politics are justified by new rhetorical assurances. If this persists, there is danger that "new thinking" will become only a cliché.

At the same time one should note a certain "schizophrenia" of the old thinking. On the one hand it seems to accept the fact that nuclear weapons are not weapons in a traditional sense, and in respect to these weapons traditional ways of thinking and behaving have lost their meaning. But on the other hand it continues to regard nuclear weapons as if they were conventional ones. This is done in order to create an impression about one's firmness and decisiveness in the enemy's eyes, in order to press the other side politically and psychologically. (8)

In other words, obstacles to new political thinking are numerous and diverse. But by not overcoming these obstacles, we are left with the dead end created by old political thinking and behavior. This could also lead to a continuation of the escalation of tension in Soviet-American relations which, in turn, could result in disaster.

It is important to understand that we cannot elude this dead end with the help of technology. The very problem of the nuclear revolution is not primarily a military one. That is why there is no hope for some "miracle" in the field of new weapons or in the field of arms control.

Another approach is more realistic: Only by a radical change in the political and psychological climate in Soviet-American relations can we promote arms control and diminish our common nuclear danger.

That is why relaxing tension in the world, eliminating hostility, and developing confidence between countries and peoples are tasks that are comparable in significance with the task of disarmament. These are the most important elements in developing new political thinking in Soviet-American relations.

This is certainly a distant goal on a long road. But this is also the most noble and most practical course for the human species.

The Evolution of Cooperation*

Robert Axelrod

Professor of Political Science and Public Policy, University of Michigan, Ann Arbor. Dr. Axelrod is a member of the American National Academy of Sciences and the American Academy of Arts and Sciences. His honors included a MacArthur Foundation Fellowship for the period 1987 through 1992.

Under what conditions will cooperation emerge in a world of egoists without central authority? This question has intrigued people for a long time. We all know that people are not angels, and that they tend to look after themselves and their own first. Yet we also know that cooperation does occur and that our civilization is based upon it.

A good example of the fundamental problem of cooperation is the case where two industrial nations have erected trade barriers to each other's exports. Because of the mutual advantages of free trade, both countries would be better off if these barriers were eliminated. But if either country were to eliminate its barriers unilaterally, it would find itself facing terms of trade that hurt its own economy. In fact, whatever one country does, the other country is better off retaining its own trade barriers. Therefore, the problem is that each country has an incentive to retain trade barriers, leading to a worse outcome than would have been possible had both countries cooperated with each other.

---

* Adapted from Robert Axelrod, *The Evolution of Cooperation*. New York: Basic Books, 1984. Reprinted by permission.

The Computer Tournament

This basic problem occurs when the pursuit of self-interest by each leads to a poor outcome for all. To understand the vast array of specific situations like this, we need a way to represent what is common to them without becoming bogged down in the details unique to each. Fortunately, there is such representation available: the famous Prisoner's Dilemma game, invented about 1950 by two Rand Corporation scientists. In this game there are two players. Each has two choices, namely "cooperate" or "defect." The game is called the Prisoner's Dilemma because in its original form two prisoners face the choice of informing on each other (defecting) or remaining silent (cooperating). Each must make the choice without knowing what the other will do. One form of the game pays off as follows:

Player's Choice	*Payoff*
If both players defect:	Both players get $1.
If both players cooperate:	Both players get $3.
If one player defects while the other player cooperates:	The defector gets $5 and the cooperator gets zero.

One can see that no matter what the other player does, defection yields a higher payoff than cooperation. If you think the other player will cooperate, it pays for you to defect (getting $5 rather than $3). On the other hand, if you think the other player will defect, it still pays for you to defect (getting $1 rather than zero). Therefore the temptation is to defect. But, the dilemma is that if both defect, both do worse than if both had cooperated.

To find a good strategy to use in such situations, I invited experts in game theory to submit programs for a computer Prisoner's Dilemma tournament — much like a computer chess tournament. Each of these strategies was paired off with each of the others to see which would do best overall in repeated interactions.

Amazingly enough, the winner was the simplest of all candidates submitted. This was a strategy of simple reciprocity which cooperates on the first move and then does whatever the other player did on the previous move. Using an American colloquial phrase, this strategy was named Tit for Tat. A second round of the tournament was conducted in which many more entries were submitted by amateurs and professionals alike, all of whom were aware of the results of the first round. The result was another victory for simple reciprocity.

The analysis of the data from these tournaments reveals four properties which tend to make a strategy successful: avoidance of unnecessary conflict by cooperating as long as the other player does, provocability in the face of an uncalled-for defection by the other, forgiveness after responding to a provocation, and clarity of behavior so that the other player can recognize and adapt to your pattern of action.

"The soldiers of these opposing small units actually violated orders from their own high commands in order to achieve tacit cooperation with each other . . . cooperation based upon reciprocity can develop even between antagonists."

Live and Let Live in World War I

One concrete demonstration of this theory in the real world is the fascinating case of the "live and let live" system that emerged during the trench warfare of the western front in World War I. In the midst of this bitter conflict, the frontline soldiers often refrained from shooting to kill — provided their restraint was reciprocated by the soldiers on the other side.

For example, in the summer of 1915, a soldier saw that the enemy would be likely to reciprocate cooperation based on the desire for fresh rations.

> It would be child's play to shell the road behind the enemy's trenches, crowded as it must be with ration wagons and water carts, into a bloodstained wilderness . . . but on the whole there is silence. After all, if you prevent your enemy from drawing his rations, his remedy is simple: He will prevent you from drawing yours. (1)

> In one section the hour of 8 to 9 A.M. was regarded as consecrated to "private business," and certain places indicated by a flag were regarded as out of bounds by the snipers on both sides. (2)

What made this mutual restraint possible was the static nature of trench warfare, where the same small units faced each other for extended periods of time. The soldiers of these opposing small units actually violated orders from their own high commands in order to achieve tacit cooperation with each other.

This case illustrates the point that cooperation can get started, evolve, and prove stable in situations which otherwise appear extraordinarily unpromising. In particular, the "live and let live" system demonstrates that friendship is hardly necessary for the development of cooperation. Under suitable conditions, cooperation based upon reciprocity can develop even between antagonists.

Conditions for Stable Cooperation

Much more can be said about the conditions necessary for cooperation to emerge, based on thousands of games in the two tournaments, theoretical proofs, and corroboration from many real-world examples. For instance, the individuals involved do not have to be rational: The evolu-

---

"For cooperation to prove stable, the future must have a sufficiently large shadow . . . the importance of the next encounter between the same two individuals must be great enough to make [noncooperation] an unprofitable strategy."

---

tionary process allows successful strategies to thrive, even if the players do not know why or how. Nor do they have to exchange messages or commitments: They do not need words, because their deeds speak for them. Likewise, there is no need to assume trust between the players: The use of reciprocity can be enough to make defection unproductive. Altruism is not needed: Successful strategies can elicit cooperation even from an egoist. Finally, no central authority is needed: Cooperation based on reciprocity can be self-policing.

For cooperation to emerge, the interaction must extend over an indefinite (or at least an unknown) number of moves, based on the following logic: Two egoists playing the game once will both be tempted to choose defection since that action does better no matter what action the other player takes. If the game is played a known, finite number of times, the players likewise have no incentive to cooperate on the last move, nor on the next-to-last move since both can anticipate a defection by the other player. Similar reasoning implies that the game will unravel all the way back to mutual defection on the first move. It need not unravel, however, if the players interact an indefinite number of times. And in most settings, the players cannot be sure when the last interaction between them will take place. An indefinite number of interactions, therefore, is a condition under which cooperation can emerge.

For cooperation to prove stable, the future must have a sufficiently large shadow. This means that the importance of the next encounter between the same two individuals must be great enough to make defection an unprofitable strategy. It requires that the players have a large enough chance of meeting again and that they do not discount the significance of their next meeting too greatly. For example, what made cooperation possible in the trench warfare of World War I was the fact that the same small units from opposite sides of no-man's-land would be in contact for long periods of time, so if one side broke the tacit understandings, then the other side could retaliate against the same unit.

In order for cooperation to get started in the first place, one more condition is required. The problem is that in a world of unconditional defection, a single individual who offers cooperation cannot prosper unless some others are around who will reciprocate. On the other hand, cooperation can emerge from small clusters of discriminating individuals as long as these individuals have even a small proportion of their interactions with each other. So there must be some clustering of individuals who use strategies with two properties: The strategy cooperates on the first move, and discriminates between those who respond to the cooperation and those who do not.

If a so-called "nice" strategy (that is, one which is never the first to defect) does eventually come to be adopted by virtually everyone, then individuals using this nice strategy can afford to be generous in their open-

"Once the US and the USSR know that they will be dealing with each other indefinitely, the necessary preconditions for cooperation will exist. . . . The foundation of cooperation is not really trust, but the durability of the relationship."

ing moves with any others. In fact, a population of nice strategies can also protect itself from clusters of individuals using any other strategy just as well as it can protect itself against single individuals.

Evolution of Cooperation

The tournament results give a chronological picture of the evolution of cooperation. Cooperation can begin with small clusters. It can thrive with strategies that are "nice" (that is, never the first to defect), provocable, and somewhat forgiving. Once established in a population, individuals using such discriminating strategies can protect themselves from invasion. The overall level of cooperation tends to go up and not down. In other words, the machinery for the evolution of cooperation contains a "ratchet," that is, it increases. Many institutions have developed stable patterns of cooperation based upon similar norms. Diamond markets, for example, are famous for the way their members exchange millions of dollars worth of goods with only a verbal pledge and a handshake. The key factor is that the participants know they will be dealing with each other again and again. Therefore any attempt to exploit the situation will simply not pay.

In other contexts, mutually rewarding relations become so common-place that the separate identities of the participants can become blurred. For example, Lloyd's of London began as a small group of independent insurance brokers. Since the insurance of a ship and its cargo would be a large undertaking for one dealer, several brokers frequently made trades with each other to pool their risks. The frequency of the interactions was so great that the underwriters gradually developed into a federated or-ganization with a formal structure of its own. The potential for attaining cooperation without formal agreements has its bright side in other con-texts. For example, it means that cooperation on the control of the arms race does not have to be sought entirely through the formal mechanism of negotiated treaties. Arms control could also evolve tacitly. Once the US and the USSR know that they will be dealing with each other indefinitely, the necessary preconditions for cooperation will exist. The leaders may not like each other, but neither did the soldiers in World War I who learned to live and let live.

The foundation of cooperation is not really trust, but the durability of the relationship. When the conditions are right, the players can come to cooperate with each other through trial-and-error learning about possi-bilities for mutual rewards, through imitation of other successful players, or even through a blind process of selection of the more successful strate-gies with a weeding out of the less successful ones. Whether the players trust each other or not is less important in the long run than whether the conditions are ripe for them to build a stable pattern of cooperation with each other.

The Value of Provocability

Cooperation theory has implications for individual choice as well as for the design of institutions. Speaking personally, one of my biggest surprises in working on this project has been the value of provocability and that it is important to respond sooner, rather than later. I came to this project be-lieving one should be slow to anger. The results of the computer tourna-ment for the Prisoner's Dilemma demonstrate that it is actually better to respond quickly to a provocation. It turns out that if one waits to respond to uncalled-for defections, there is a risk of sending the wrong signal. The longer defections are allowed to go unchallenged, the more likely it is that the other player will draw the conclusion that defection can pay. And the more strongly this pattern is established, the harder it will be to break it. The success of simple reciprocity certainly illustrates this point. By re-sponding right away, it gives the quickest possible feedback that a defec-tion will not pay.

The response to potential violations of arms control agreements illus-trates this point. Each superpower has occasionally taken steps which appear to be designed to probe the limits of its agreements with the other. The sooner the other detects and responds (in moderation) to these probes, the better. Waiting for probes to accumulate only risks the need for a response so large as to evoke yet more trouble.

The speed of response depends upon the time required to detect a given choice by the other player. The shorter this time is, the more stable cooperation can be. A rapid detection means that the next move in the interaction comes quickly, thereby increasing the shadow of the future. For this reason, the only arms control agreements which can be stable are those whose violations can be detected soon enough. The critical requirement is that violations can be detected before they can accumulate to such an extent that the victim's provocability is no longer enough to prevent the challenger from having an incentive to defect.

A Self-Reinforcing Ratchet Effect

Once the word gets out that reciprocity works — among nations or among individuals — it becomes the thing to do. If you expect others to reciprocate your defections as well as your cooperations, you will be wise to avoid starting any trouble. Moreover, you will be wise to respond appropriately after someone else defects, showing that you will not be exploited. Thus you too would be wise to use a strategy based upon reciprocity. So would everyone else. In this manner the appreciation of the value of reciprocity becomes self-reinforcing. Once it gets going, it gets stronger and stronger.

". . . simple reciprocity succeeds without doing better than anyone with whom it interacts. It succeeds by eliciting cooperation from others, not by defeating them."

This is the essence of the ratchet effect: Once cooperation based upon reciprocity gets established in a population, it cannot be overcome even by a cluster of individuals who try to exploit the others. The establishment of stable cooperation can take a long time if it is based upon blind forces of evolution, or it can happen rather quickly if its operation can be appreciated by intelligent players. The empirical and theoretical results might help people see more clearly the opportunities for reciprocity latent in their world. Knowing the concepts that accounted for the results of the two rounds of the computer Prisoner's Dilemma tournament, and knowing the reasons and conditions for the success of reciprocity, might provide some additional foresight.

From National Competitiveness to Global Cooperation

Robert Gilpin points out that from the ancient Greeks to contemporary scholarship all political theory addressed one fundamental question: "How can the human race, whether for selfish or more cosmopolitan ends, understand and control the seemingly blind forces of history?" (3) In the contemporary world this question has become especially acute because of the development of nuclear weapons.

Today, the most important problems facing humanity are in the arena of international relations, where independent, egoistic nations face each other in a state of near anarchy. Many of these problems take the form of an iterated Prisoner's Dilemma. Examples can include arms races, nuclear proliferation, crisis bargaining, and military escalation.

Therefore, the advice to players of the Prisoner's Dilemma might serve as good advice to national leaders as well: Don't be envious, don't be the first to defect, reciprocate both cooperation and defection, and don't be too clever.

There is a lesson in the fact that simple reciprocity succeeds without doing better than anyone with whom it interacts. It succeeds by eliciting cooperation from others, not by defeating them. We are used to thinking about competitions in which there is only one winner, competitions such as football or chess. But the world is rarely like that. In a vast range of situations, mutual cooperation can be better for both sides than mutual defection. The key to doing well lies not in overcoming others, but in eliciting their cooperation.

Dangers and Opportunities for Change from a Physiologist's Point of View

Natalia P. Bekhtereva

Director, Institute of Experimental Medicine, Leningrad; Member of Committee of Soviet Scientists for Peace Against the Nuclear Threat. Dr. Bekhtereva is a member of the Soviet Academy of Sciences, the Soviet Academy of Medical Sciences, and a corresponding member of the Austrian Academy of Sciences. She is holder of the 1985 State Prize of the USSR, the McCullough Award of the American Society of Cyberneticists and author of 250 scientific papers, including eight books, in the field of neuro-physiology.

An American businessman, who has contributed very much to people's health and whom I consider a friend, sent me a story written by Mark Twain titled: "My first lie and how I got out of it." It was about the human tendency to avoid seeing what we do not want to see. Twain addressed an instance of widespread "lying" of that time — the failure to see that slavery was a problem.

It has been only recently that physiologists studying the human brain have begun to understand the reasons behind Twain's observations. These discoveries have profound implications for human survival. They reveal that our brains, when functioning properly, have the creative capacity to produce solutions to today's most urgent problem — the arms race and the potential for nuclear catastrophe. They also reveal why so many millions today are prone to "lie" about that threat — to convince themselves and others that no special action is needed; that the threat of war is not really a problem.

Careful studies of electrical potentials in discrete zones of the human brain have demonstrated the power of sustained negative emotions, such as fear of approaching disaster, to "unbalance" the brain's normal state. (1, 2) An imbalance causes the electrical levels to rise too high or fall too low. When that happens, a person can become either excessively excited on the one hand (close to "mental breakdown") or emotionally shut

193

down on the other (emotional dullness, numbness). This robs the individual of the ability to fully respond to life situations and also robs society of that person's creative potential at a time when great creativity is needed to avoid devastation. The best therapy for the individual human brain turns out to be precisely what is needed by society as a whole: active engagement with others in the solution to our predicament.

Recent advances allowing measurement of the brain's electrical activity have led to a clearer understanding of the inner workings of the brain — how it perceives external events and how it processes direct information. These direct measurements have shown that most small areas of the brain (discrete "zones") are multifunctional — they participate in more than one activity — and that the brain works as a whole, integrating information from its various zones to provide the individual with the ability to function under the most favorable conditions possible. (3) The same zone that may participate in maintenance of mental processes, emotions, and body movements also may assist in the function of internal organs like the heart or intestines.

For any particular function, certain zones (sometimes called "rigid" or "skeletal" zones) are especially important because they must participate consistently for our brains to perform that function (e.g., to complete a certain action or to feel a given emotion). Other zones are optional, flexible (i.e. they do not participate consistently or regularly). If one of these supplementary areas "takes a rest," so to speak, its function is handled by another which is activated at the moment of need.

The essential point is that our minds have a potential flexibility and richness for maintenance of thought and emotion. To realize maximal capability, each human's brain must have most of its zones and their interactive capability in an optimal functional state.

Infraslow Physiological Process and Its Most Stable Part — The Steady Potential

How does a zone maintain its function in an optimal way? There is always a certain level of slowly changing activity in each zone, a small voltage called the "steady potential." Infraslow Physiological Process (ISPP) is a complex consisting of the steady potential as well as slow physiological modulations of different duration. Work has shown that this steady potential has a definite optimal range which is different for different brain zones. These steady potentials play a decisive role in the functioning of the normal brain. It has been shown repeatedly that defined areas of the brain exert their own particular kind of influence, or abstain from doing so, depending on the level of the steady potential.

Our clinical work demonstrates that when the steady potential for any brain zone becomes too high or too low, thus leaving its optimal range, the brain area either fails to act or its capacities for action drastically diminish. The rich endowment of the brain is lost. It may have to concentrate all of its energy to be able to maintain just one activity.

This discussion of the brain's functioning is based upon quantitative measurement of parameters directly obtained from the brain itself. (4,5) These were obtained clinically through a long series of investigations with patients over a twenty-five-year period where direct contact with the brain was accomplished using forty to seventy implanted gold electrodes, applied for diagnostic and/or therapeutic purposes. Measurements were taken during various states of the patients' emotional reactions under conditions linked with their main illnesses. These data were supplemented by additional investigations under presentation of emotion-inducing tests. These investigations as a whole proved very helpful in both diagnosing the patients' illnesses and their subsequent treatments.

> *"The best therapy for the individual human brain turns out to be precisely what is needed by society as a whole: active engagement with others in the solution to our predicament."*

In normal conditions, emotions play a predominant role among the factors which affect the ISPP, the level of steady potential in particular, and thus the brain's information handling capacity. Emotions can decrease the capacity of the brain to such an extent as to induce a state of disorder. The first and foremost function of the brain to be lost is creative thinking. Emotions "capture" the individual by taking possession of more and more cerebral areas.

The Effect of Long-Term Stress

Everybody knows how difficult it is to think when one is emotionally upset, or when our blood pressure has fallen or risen. We may read words in a text, reread them, trying to understand: "What is this all about?" "What is the matter with me?" But we are not usually aware of the decline in our brain's capacities if the condition has resulted from gradual changes in steady potentials which have occurred under the constant influence of negative emotion-inducing factors. Such factors may be personal troubles, the continuing arms race, or failure of superpower disarmament meetings. Under these conditions, the steady potential changes in most of the brain zones, which inevitably leads to decreased brain function, first of the less "enduring," supplementary zones and later of the whole brain.

The unhealthy response of the human brain to long-term emotional stress may be in either of two directions. The brain may evolve over time toward an overexcited state, the extreme being a nervous breakdown. Or it may evolve in the opposite direction — toward psychic numbing due to overactivity of the brain's own defenses. Psychologically, either of these unhealthy states results from the steady potential of the brain moving out of the optimal range. If it goes too high, the condition is overexcitement; too low produces emotional numbing (dullness).

The Overexcited Brain

First, let us consider the case of the brain already suffering from abnormally high steady potential in multiple brain zones. This first shows up as an excessive response to emotional stress. Under these conditions, an additional very weak emotional stress can induce shifts of the steady potential, not only in the zones mainly associated with emotions, but in most other areas as well. The "emotionalized brain" becomes larger, which literally blocks the brain's ability to perform the regular integrative mental tasks which allow an individual to function normally. Usually minor events, such as a delay in the arrival of an airplane, late preparation of a meal at home, or an argument with a co-worker, become major "attacks." The integrative-balancing state of the brain is lost and with it the possibility for creative thinking. There is a gradual hampering of all the complex processes associated with the thought process. The creativity of the human brain decreases dramatically.

Emotional Dullness (Numbing)

Now let us consider the second possible unhealthy reaction of the brain to emotional stress — psychic numbing — in which the steady potential in most of the brain areas decreases below the optimal range. This is the result of overactivity of "protective" reactions of the brain trying to guard against emotional stress. Our data have shown that this reaction is directly correlated as a counterbalance to repeated negative emotion and its associated elevation of brain steady potential. Sometimes a person may seem to be on the verge of an emotional breakdown, but the storm passes by. The protective mechanisms, the "power brakes" of the brain, have worked to rein in this horse galloping at full speed. However, if this "brake" mechanism malfunctions or the emotion-stimulating factor is too powerful, or too continuous, the reaction may itself develop into an unfavorable state. Precisely this excessive "protection" (excessive "braking") may lead to emotional stupor, or emotional dullness.

The laboratory data are quite clear. As a patient having a strong fear episode brings his or her fear under control, one can watch on a recorder reciprocal shifts of the steady potential of the brain and later its return to previous levels.

Everything is fine until the protective reaction becomes excessive. Then the steady potential dips below optimum in many brain zones. It becomes increasingly difficult to experience joy or sadness. The colors of the world fade. The creative potential of the brain in this second extreme situation decreases as well. For the individual, the world no longer holds previous fears (though the search for stronger emotions with all its negative consequences is quite likely to happen). If these conditions continue for a period of time, brain potential in most brain areas decreases and the person has become emotionally numbed.

A high threshold to emotional reaction, reaching emotional dullness, is a serious problem even though at first glance it may seem to be the way out of the emotional stress faced by the individual. He or she remains literally deaf to problems, both individual and those of other people. It is particularly dangerous for society when this condition develops in people having major social or political responsibilities. They may ignore the necessity for making decisions of extreme importance for humankind.

"If these conditions of the overexcited brain and emotional numbing are allowed to happen in a large number of human beings and our intelligentsia, humanity will see a significant decline in the planet's creative potential."

If these conditions of the overexcited brain and emotional numbing are allowed to happen in a large number of human beings and our intelligentsia, humanity will see a significant decline in the planet's creative potential. One can visualize this as a sort of "scissor" graph. The ascending line of the graph is the growth of the planet's creative potential in connection with the ever-growing increase in the pool of knowledge. The descending line, on the other hand, is humanity's creative potential degeneration from the impact of the knowledge of our impending doom. The degeneration can possibly outweigh the potential creativity, thus robbing the planet of its creative potential, a unique and most precious treasure. Creativity is needed now more than ever and must be reoriented to the task of preserving humanity as well as all other life on our planet.

The Brain Seeks Steady States

One final point about brain functioning needs to be made. The human brain seems to seek stable states, either normal or — after a period of destabilization due to disease — unhealthy. It is as though the brain adopts a "memory" and gravitates toward the stable state. Stability is a protective mechanism in a normal case and adaptive in a diseased one. Though the brain achieves a stable state in this latter case, it is constant negative emotions which have driven the brain into this pathological condition. These stable pathological states are hard to overcome since they are fixed in the long-term memory of the brain. The conclusion is sobering: Increasing numbers of human brains in stable pathological states can lead to global instability.

Vigorous Activity: Therapy and Survival

What does it take to break out of this state? It requires more than a minor perturbation. One possible way to prevent a stable pathological state is through activity. In addition to physical activity, oral speech helps. In our clinic we have observed how motion and speech sometimes bring the unfavorable state of the brain back to normal. The steady potential level can again become optimized and the spectrum of brain areas grows richer.

"Increasing numbers of human brains in stable patho—logical states can lead to global instability. . . . to break out of this state . . . requires more than a minor perturbation."

Activity directed toward the source of negative emotion can be especially effective. Large numbers of people engaged in discussions and actions to prevent the extension of the arms race and the extinction of humanity would help assure the creativity and the goodwill to achieve a world where humanity's survival is assured.

Since it takes more than a minor perturbation to break the stable pathological states, such as neurosis or psychic numbing, into which many people have fallen, the activity level will have to be high. A focused and dramatic movement to shift the course of history is what is needed. By struggling for the welfare of humankind, we would be counteracting the disastrous shifts in our own brain while helping to "awaken" the brains of others who have already become psychically numb. Such a process of change is physiologically sound, practical, and urgent. Everyone must get involved!

The Image of the Enemy and the Process of Change

Jerome D. Frank

Professor Emeritus of Psychiatry, Johns Hopkins University School of Medicine, Baltimore, Maryland. Dr. Frank has been President, Chairman, Director or Fellow of numerous psychological and psychiatric organizations. He is the author or co-author of over 200 papers and five books.

Andrei Y. Melville

Section Head, Institute of USA and Canada Studies, Academy of Sciences of the USSR. Dr. Melville was awarded the 1981 Gold Medal of the Academy of Sciences of the USSR for the best work of a young scholar. He is the author or co-author of five books and a large number of papers on political consciousness and problems of war and peace.

"Since wars begin in the minds of men, it is in the minds of men that we have to erect the ramparts of peace" is written in the UNESCO Charter. Indeed, the relations between states and peoples have been regularly accompanied by mutual misunderstanding, tension, suspicion, and hostility. The price that humankind has paid for that has always been high. But today, in the nuclear era, it has become unacceptable because of the unprecedented threat of a nuclear doomsday. In the face of this threat, it is extremely dangerous to exaggerate suspicion. Such an attitude makes international relations even more unstable; it works against rational and responsible behavior.

In this circumstance, it is a task of extraordinary importance to let go of ideological and psychological prejudices and stereotypes. We must work out realistic perceptions of each other. This is especially important for the relations of the two greatest nuclear powers — the USSR and the US.

Difficulties in Change

The task of bringing our consciousness to conformity with the radical changes in the world and achieving new ways of political thinking is highly complicated and often painful. It demands not only great political cour-

199

age but also certain emotional readiness. It is a task made difficult by many of our traditions and norms from the past. Difficulties arise not only from the fact that there are "visible" political and ideological obstacles, but also "invisible" psychological and emotional barriers. Traditional thinking naturally attempts to exclude painful and traumatizing new information. Psychological defenses permit one to operate with familiar and habitual concepts. They provide protection from rigorous intellectual engagement with the outstanding reality of the nuclear age: mutual vulnerability.

In the past, major causes of war were efforts of rival tribes or nations to gain control over tangible resources such as territory, national resources, or human labor. The two chief rivals on the world scene today — the USSR and the US — do not covet any tangible resources possessed by the other. Instead, their conflict, which poses a massive threat to the continuance of civilization, if not humanity itself, is over which of the two political and socioeconomic systems will prevail.

In such a conflict, ideological clashes, mutual perceptions, and misperceptions assume much greater importance than disputes over material assets. Many of these determinants are aspects of what has been termed the image of the enemy — a phenomenon displayed by almost all antagonistic groups. (1)

The Image of the Enemy

For humans as for all social creatures, the group, not the individual, is the unit of survival. Humans can survive only as members of organized groups. Groups provide protection against hostile environments and external enemies, and also provide a sense of psychological security. Since the majority of a group's members share the same customs and norms, they can readily understand each other's behavior, and the group carries the values that give meaning and significance to their lives. A threat to the group's integrity, especially when posed by a group with a different worldview, strikes at the very basis of its members' psychological as well as biological survival.

Many people experience the thought of submission to an alien ideology and social system as more intolerable than death itself, a major reason for the escalation of wars. Hence humans share with all social animals the predisposition to fear and distrust members of groups other than their own. When two groups compete for the same goal, this distrust often rapidly escalates into the mutual perception of each other as enemies.

Mirror Images

The perceptions of the enemy very often tend to mirror each other — that is, each side attributes the same virtues to itself and the same vices to the enemy. We could find people on both sides of the East-West conflict whose images are in many aspects identical, as illustrated by the American film *Rambo* and the Soviet film *Solitary Mission*. In each case, "we" are trustworthy, peace-loving, honorable, and humanitarian; "they" are treacherous, warlike, and cruel. In 1942, when Germany and Japan were enemies of the United States, the first five adjectives used by Americans in public opinion surveys to describe the enemies included warlike, treacherous, and cruel. None of these words appeared among the first five describing the Soviets, who at that time were allies of the United States. In 1966, when the Soviet Union was no longer an ally, among the first five adjectives describing the Soviets were warlike and treacherous. These adjectives also were applied to the Chinese, but had disappeared from the lists of adjectives applied to the Germans and Japanese, who by then were allies of the United States. (2)

". . . 'we' are trustworthy, peace-loving, honorable, and humanitarian; 'they' are treacherous, warlike, and cruel."

One should also note that enemy images are not monolithic — there are variations. For example, it is often said that "the people are good; it is only the leaders who are evil." It is much easier to hate a few evil leaders than all those people. This view may create a false hope that if somehow people could only get rid of a few evil leaders, then the problem would be solved. In fact, the problem is much more complex than that. In addition, whether it is the leaders or the people who are subject to the enemy images, the effects in either case on perception, feelings, and behavior are similar and the distinction is largely irrelevant.

Ways of Thinking

A key issue is the degree and type of thinking that has decisive influence on the formation of the policy of the state. A derogatory political cartoon is a symptom of an underlying attitude and a statement by a leader of the country officially endorsing the attitude is even more serious. While the ripple effects of the latter are greater, in fact, the two are mutually reinforcing, and one is probably not possible without the other. It is important for the public to be aware of each, and to be able to distinguish old thinking from new wherever it is found.

New ways of thinking, new morality, and new psychology lie in a dimension outside the traditional, accepted opposition between classes and social systems. The old ways of thinking emphasize divergent and even contrary social and political content, but new thinking strives for synthesis on the basis of common values. New thinking enables groups to unite rather than fight.

The enemy image impedes resolution of group conflicts in several ways. First, under the influence of mutual enmity, adversaries acquire the evil characteristics they attribute to each other; that is, the enemy image is a self-fulfilling prophecy. In combating what each perceives to be the other's cruelty and treachery, each may become more cruel and treacherous itself. This characteristic has its roots in societal evolution; nations that failed to recognize that their enemies were treacherous and warlike did not survive long. There was survival value in matching the tactics of the opponent, at least in the short run.

Disruption of Communication

While the image of the enemy once may have served an evolutionary purpose, it always has had serious negative effects. Escalation of enemy images profoundly disrupts communication. It isn't pleasant to communicate with persons one dislikes, and, since enemies can be treacherous, they may use communication for purposes of deception. In most societies, a common way of punishing children is to refuse to speak to them, and breaking off communication remains a way of expressing displeasure among adults. However, disruption of communication between adversaries reduces the chances of discovering areas of agreement or common interests.

These enemy images also act like distorting lenses that magnify confirming information and filter out incompatible information. This, in turn, increases the likelihood of serious misunderstandings of the enemy's intentions. Thus the mass media in both the USSR and the US often play up incidents which were regarded as manifestations of the other's treachery or cruelty and tended to ignore examples of humanitarian or honorable behavior. Similarly, the same behavior is often seen in the service of good motives if performed by one side and in the service of bad motives if performed by the other side. For example, although in wartime both sides always commit atrocities, the enemy's atrocities are evidence of his evil nature, whereas ours are portrayed as regrettable necessities.

Dehumanization

As the mutual formation of the image of the enemy develops, the adversary is progressively dehumanized. Members of hostile groups see each other as bestial and subhuman on the one hand, and diabolically clever on the other. In either case, this perception seriously weakens inhibitions humans may possess against attacking fellow humans. Destroying vermin or devils becomes a praiseworthy, even holy activity.

All this can progress to the point where the enemy is perceived as literally demonic, that is, as totally evil. If the enemy is viewed as the incarnation of evil, then whatever it perceives to be in its interest must by definition be disadvantageous to us. ("It" is an object; "we" are human.) In many cases, for example, the mere fact that either of the superpowers offered a proposal for arms control was sufficient to cause the other to reject the proposal out of hand. The "zero option" proposal for intermediate nuclear missiles in Europe is illustrative. Proposed by the US in 1981, it was at first rejected by the USSR. Later, repackaged, but offered in a substantially similar form by the USSR, it was at first rejected by the US.

"A universal feature of the enemy image is that the enemy can be influenced only by force."

The image of the enemy tends to impoverish each nation's own self-image in that each is tempted to define itself primarily as the opposite of its enemy. That is, the image encourages ideological rigidity and a self-image that is monolithic, lacking in depth and complexity, and not in keeping with reality. Therefore, transcending the image of the enemy inevitably requires rising to a new level of political thinking.

'Enemy' as Justification for the Arms Race

Furthermore, because of a human desire for consistency, whatever the enemy does is used to confirm the correctness of one's own behavior. A universal feature of the enemy image is that the enemy can be influenced only by force. If the enemy resists the effort to apply force, our side must double its efforts. If, on the other hand, the enemy seeks conciliation or compromise, this is a sign that force is having an effect. Alternatively, the enemy's conciliatory moves are seen as efforts to weaken one's own determination. In either case, conciliatory acts become justification to intensify the pressure. The enemy phenomenon is a powerful driver of the arms race and, ultimately, towards war.

There is a vicious circle. Arms races are the source of misconceptions and stereotypes. The atmosphere of militarism and preparation for war is an ideal medium for the emergence and confirmation of evil images. Further, in the nuclear age, absolute weapons need absolute enemies. As a result, the arms race and image of the enemy feed off each other in an upward spiral.

This interconnection means only one thing: Disarmament is impossible without fundamental changes in the psychology of international relations, and it is also impossible to get rid of the image of the enemy without stopping the arms race. That is why relaxation of tension, overcoming the image of the enemy and hostility, and establishing a basic trust between countries and nations are tasks as important as disarmament. They are among the main components for building up a new way of political thinking. The struggle against the threat of a nuclear holocaust demands a struggle against the ideology of hostility, demonology, and against the legitimation of the image of the enemy with the help of the rhetoric of "just wars." To win this struggle demands reorientation of the psychology of international relations itself.

Internal Implications

The image of the enemy is not only very dangerous for the stability and security of international relations but leads to highly negative consequences for the domestic life of countries. This happens because the hysteria about the outer threat is often used as justification for secrecy and suspicion, covert actions, policies creating "mobilized" societies, artificial national unity, "witch hunts," and policies suppressing dissent, all ignoring domestic problems and distracting attention from them. By projecting the blame for these on the enemy, each side protects its own self-esteem from the realization that it has been unable to solve its own problems.

". . . hysteria about the outer threat is often used as justification for secrecy and suspicion, covert actions . . . and policies suppressing dissent . . ."

Changing Images

Meanwhile, a hopeful consideration is that people can change with remarkable speed from enemies to friends, despite the apparent intractability of enemy images. This can occur when they decide that cooperation yields vastly greater benefits to both than antagonism. A most encouraging recent case in point is the rapid change in American perceptions of mainland China. According to public polls in the United States in 1976, three-quarters of the American public saw China as a hostile power. Only six years later, in 1982, the same percentage saw China as a friendly power and close ally, even though the Chinese leaders, like the Soviet ones, remained faithful to communism. (3)

Realistic understanding of the real doubts and problems of the other side may well be one of the ways to overcome the image of the enemy. Such understanding doesn't eliminate the differences or solve problems and contradictions, but enhances the possibility of finding compromise solutions. It demands an obligatory condition of maximum possible truth in depicting the other side and oneself, free access to information, without distortion or secrecy. For this effort, one needs political courage and psychological preparedness. This realistic approach is the starting point for transcending the image of the enemy.

Specific Requirements for Change

Two essential requirements for progressing to a world beyond war are to inhibit the formation of the reciprocal images of the enemy by antagonistic groups, and to inhibit antagonists from resorting to violence as a way of responding to the fear and frustrations created by images of the enemy.

To consider the second aim first, creating effective means for determining the outcome of disputes depends on the commitment to renounce violence in resolving international conflict. This commitment in turn must begin with the transformation of attitudes and values of individuals. Specifically, the precepts underlying nonviolent actions demand that its adherents acknowledge that their opponents share a common humanity and are activated by motives which in their own eyes are often regarded as just.

That such a massive inner transformation is somewhat rare, that its emergence cannot be predicted, and that its successes have usually been sporadic and temporary must be acknowledged. On the other hand, history supplies many examples of the enormous power of nonviolent actions, such as the examples in modern times of Leo Tolstoy, Mohandas Gandhi, Martin Luther King, and others.

New Technologies

The ability to progress beyond war around the world is greatly facilitated by new technologies equally as revolutionary as nuclear weapons. These technologies provide powerful means for heightening awareness of worldwide threats posed by nuclear weapons, for reducing national antagonisms, and above all, for fostering cooperation.

At least three new technologies are useful for achieving these ends: international telecommunication by satellite; international rapid mass travel; and exploration of outer space. With respect to the first, national leaders already use the hotline and surveillance satellites to communicate rapidly and directly without the distorting effects of intermediaries. This may reduce mutual fears by imposing restraints on secret preparation for hostilities.

Television and radio are by far the most effective means of communication ever invented. In contrast to the printed word, they jump the illiteracy barrier and have immediate and powerful emotional impact. Today, through television receivers in public places and transistor radios in the hands of individuals, communication satellites are already capable of reaching a significant fraction of the world's population. (4) The possibilities of international satellite communications are limitless for driving home on a worldwide scale the menace of nuclear weapons and promoting mutual — and more realistic — appreciation among the world's people. Television spacebridges such as those which have several times now occurred between Moscow and various American cities provide a glimpse of what the future holds.

Another technical innovation, rapid mass air transportation, can be used to bring a wide representation from different countries together in face-to-face interaction with each other. Some such programs are already operative, especially at the high school level, and they easily could be vastly expanded. That the official policies of both the US and the USSR now encourage exchanges of scientists and artists as well as students is heartening.

"The threat of nuclear annihilation should be useful to draw nations together."

To be realistic, increased communication, while a prerequisite for increased mutual understanding, does not automatically have this effect. It sometimes intensifies mutual hostile stereotypes. At the same time, there is abundant information confirming that interaction much more often results in mutual appreciation than hostility and mistrust. (5)

Superordinate Goals

A powerful way of breaking down enmity between groups and encouraging them to work together is to create goals that can only be reached by cooperation between them. The power of this approach has been illustrated by a classic sociological experiment at a boys' camp in which the mutual hostility of two rival groups was overcome when they had to cooperate to achieve goals that both wanted but neither could achieve alone. (6)

There are similar "superordinate goals" at the international level that could promote cooperative attitudes among nations and combat hostile ones. The most obvious one is survival — a goal surely shared by all nations and one increasingly jeopardized by the nuclear arms race. The threat of nuclear annihilation should be useful to draw nations together. Unfortunately, in contrast to the boys' camp, where joint measures for survival did not weaken either group, international measures for survival in the long run are perceived as jeopardizing survival in the short run. All nations want to survive and recognize that nuclear disarmament is necessary to achieve this goal, but none is willing to risk the radical unilateral measures necessary to get the disarmament process started.

Modern scientific and technological advances have created potential international enterprises that would not threaten the security of any nation, and nations working together on these projects would achieve much greater rewards than any one nation could attain alone.

At the international level, a spectacular confirmation of this may be the treaty about demilitarizing the Antarctic, and providing the cooperative exploration of the Earth's crust and oceans. (7) This treaty is self-enforcing. It is to each nation's interest not to violate it, because the gains from respecting the treaty's provisions outweigh the gains that might result from each nation attempting to militarize its own zone. Other recent examples of successful international cooperation to achieve superordinate goals are the cleaning up of the Mediterranean and the worldwide eradication of smallpox. Superordinate goals that urgently require immediate international cooperation are checking pollution of the atmosphere and oceans and halting the ominous destruction of the ozone layer.

Special mention should be made of outer space. While outer space tends to become a particularly dangerous arena of conflict, it also provides magnificent opportunities for international cooperation on projects that require resources that tax the facilities of even the wealthiest of nations, such as the Apollo-Soyuz space program. Outer space has the additional advantage of providing a positive outlet for the nobler martial virtues such as heroism and self-sacrifice.

Since such activities potentially yield enormous benefits to all parties involved, they can be expected to increase. Since prolonged participation in international cooperative ventures is incompatible with maintenance of mutual images of the enemy, these ventures provide the best immediate hope for freeing nations from the thrall of this image, thereby diminishing the threat of nuclear holocaust.

In the nuclear age, there must be a guard against old ways of thinking dominated by the image of the enemy, and a search for new ways of thinking based on the priorities of shared humanity, beyond class, political, and ideological differences.

Conclusion

The arms race is not driven by weapons alone. It is also driven by a very simple psychological phenomenon, the image of the enemy. Weapons of total destruction would be useless without such images. For such weapons to have any purpose, there must be people who may be totally destroyed. Adversaries must be transformed into demons. Once such images have been created, they, in turn, drive the arms race. People resist giving them up. There is a desire to see everything in a light which will reinforce the image. Images foster closed minds and reinforce resistance to change.

But change is possible. It has happened many times in history. Whole peoples have changed their views of one another. Even between the superpowers, areas of special accommodation have been achieved, agreements have been followed. New technologies offer new potentials for communication. New goals which transcend the narrow national interests of each will offer a framework for future common actions. In working out the way to achieve those goals the enemy images can be gradually lessened, perhaps even dissolved. If humankind is to survive in the nuclear age, there must be progress in this direction.

Nuclear Disarmament: Ideal and Reality

Yuri A. Zamoshkin

Chief Scientific Fellow, Institute of USA and Canada Studies, Academy of
Sciences of the USSR; Professor, Doctor of Philosophy. Dr. Zamoshkin is
author or coauthor of over 100 papers and five books.

This article is based on the author's profound conviction that it is necessary to eliminate nuclear weapons and all other means of mass destruction which threaten the existence of human civilization.

The Reality Gap

The unique nature of today's situation creates greater possibilities in the world than ever before for turning the ideal of nuclear disarmament into political practice. Yet the profound difference between this ideal and the political reality has in no way disappeared. Rather, while the popularity of the ideal grows, the infrastructures promoting the arms build up and the maintenance of the nuclear arms race are still powerful and actively at work throughout the world. The forms of traditional thinking and psychological principles stimulating the arms race still retain their inertia.

This obvious disparity between the ideal and the current reality creates the possibility for a personality type characterized by a seemingly sincere acceptance of the ideal of nuclear disarmament coupled with acceptance of all the prevailing forms of political practice which are in contradiction with the ideal.

The Ideal as Shield and Camouflage

This coexistence of contradictory trends within the same person may manifest itself in various neuroses, psychoses, or other unhealthy states of the psyche. Or it may take the form of psychological compensation in which attachment to the ideal neutralizes critical self-reflection of one's own practices which contradict the ideal. Such a person has a sudden temptation, and later a habit, of justifying himself, to silence within himself a feeling of guilt for such forms of practice. This psychological compensation manifests itself by the person constantly proclaiming the ideal, and by his reminding himself and others of his agreement with the ideal. And the greater the contrast between words and deeds, the louder, the more insistent, and even more sincere these words may sound.

We know from history that there have been both Christians and Marxists who have sincerely accepted noble ideals proclaimed by Christianity or Marxism, but who have been involved in practices inconsistent with those ideals. And, for many of them, their own subjective adherence to the ideal has not been a stimulus for critical self-reflection and a source of mobilization of their energy for putting their ideals into practice. On the contrary, the ideal becomes a shield for blocking critical self-reflection. This type of ideologue sees the contradictions in the world, but not in his own practice.

We also know that a person in this state of conflict between the ideal and his own practical behavior may experience severe fits of self-critique. But these fits will be in the style of repentance characteristic of religious revivalism: By loudly confessing his "sins" (the incompatibility of his conduct with the ideal) and praising the ideal, a person can feel purified and "forgiven," in order to return once more to the habitual and incompatible forms of behavior.

Another very dangerous psychological and behavioral feature is the purposeful and cynical proclamation of the ideal of nuclear disarmament, only to disguise military preparations and camouflage actions which are, in reality, aimed at preserving and expanding the nuclear arms race. Often this is done under the pretext of "rearmament for the sake of subsequent disarmament."

Long- and Short-Range Goals

Even among those who actively work to eliminate the threat of nuclear disaster, the obvious discrepancy between ideal and reality can generate contradictory types of behavior. One reaction, typical of some arms control advocates, consists of concentrating attention on concrete and very important steps such as reducing one or another type of weapon, or increasing confidence and mutual understanding between people, but with a complete lack of faith in the ability to achieve the long-range goal of total nuclear disarmament.

Another type of reaction is the mirror image of the first. Here, the necessity of achieving the ideal of nuclear disarmament is stressed, but without paying adequate attention to the immediate, concrete measures needed to restore confidence — confidence without which nuclear weapons will not be reduced significantly, much less eliminated.

Today, as never before, it is important to have a twofold combination in the peace movement — theoretical and practical, short range and long range. Working for the ideal of nuclear disarmament is not enough by itself. Neither is working to bring about concrete, immediate improvements. Only together do these beliefs and actions provide an effective means for step-by-step advancement along the difficult, contradictory, and lengthy road that leads to the ideal.

"Working for the ideal of nuclear disarmament is not enough by itself. Neither is working to bring about concrete, immediate improvements. Only together do these beliefs and actions provide an effective means for step-by-step advancement along the difficult, contradictory, and lengthy road that leads to the ideal".

Politicians as Idealists

The existence of the potential for nuclear annihilation creates, for the first time in history, a situation in which the traditional, practical concern of a professional politician for the security of his own nation may prompt him to a new, nontraditional way of thinking. The threat of the death of the entire human species, his own country included, may prompt the use of such heretofore idealistic concepts as "unity," "integrity of mankind," and "the preeminence of general human interests over any private interests" as working tools in the search for effective ways of resolving the very practical problems of national security of his own state. The problem of security for one's own state is vividly seen as the problem of creating conditions for universal and equal security for all nations. Political idealism and pragmatism have become one.

While there is much hope to be gained from this need for agreement between theory and practice, it makes the previously discussed psychological accommodations all the more dangerous. Vigilant self-reflection will be needed to realize the potential benefit that has been unlocked.

The Possibility of Revelation

In the philosophy of twentieth-century German and French existentialists (notably K. Jaspers), the term "grenzsituation" (border situation) has been used to designate an experience in which an individual comes face-to-face with the real possibility of death. Death is no longer merely an abstract thought, but a distinct possibility. Life and death hang in the balance.

Different human beings respond to the grenzsituation in different ways. Some become passive and put their heads on the chopping block, so to

"[When] life and death hang in the balance . . . some timid individuals have become heroes; some selfish individuals have become Schweitzers."

speak. Others experience something akin to a revelation and find themselves capable of feats they never before would have thought possible. In a grenzsituation, some timid individuals have become heroes; some selfish individuals have become Schweitzers. And sometimes, in so transcending their normal personalities, they cheat the grim reaper and survive where normally they would not.

Until now, this notion has been applied only to individuals. But I am convinced that today it can be purposefully applied to the world as a whole. The present day global grenzsituation resides in the possibility for global death and global life.

This situation, for the first time in history, directly, practically, and not purely speculatively, confronts human thought with the possibility of death for the entire human race. The continuity of history, which earlier had seemed to be a given, suddenly becomes highly questionable.

As with the individual, this global grenzsituation may contribute to a "revelation" in human thinking and to a positive change of character previously thought impossible for our species. The global grenzsituation could give rise to the critical self-reflection needed to resolve the contradictions between ideals and political reality. It could prompt rethinking the essence and importance of everything that constitutes the "human experiment." In this unique situation, and the hope that humanity will come to comprehend it, lies the real possibility for ideal to finally be translated into practice.

Of course there is also the possibility that, faced with a grenzsituation, mankind will go passive and put its collective head on the nuclear chopping block. But before we can learn our true mettle, we must bring the global grenzsituation into clear focus for all humanity. Society must see that it has but two possibilities, global life or global death. It is my sincere hope that this book will contribute to that goal.

Beyond Disarmament

Complete nuclear disarmament is an ideal. But it is not the ideal, the end state at which humanity can rest on its laurels, assured of a future. The

---

"Complete nuclear disarmament is an ideal. But it is not the ideal, the end state at which humanity can rest on its laurels, assured of a future."

---

destructive potential of conventional armaments is approaching that of nuclear weapons. Conventional bombs are even more destructive than many nuclear weapons if they are targeted on the hundreds of nuclear power plants in Western Europe, the USSR, and the US. Such attacks would release large amounts of radiation and poisonous materials into the environment. Radiation sickness would ensue. Crops would be damaged. Each of these hundreds of reactors could have worse effects than Chernobyl, where the fire fighters and clean-up crews had only to contend with nature, not hostile aircraft.

If we look further, we find that the fragility of humanity's existence extends beyond nuclear weapons, or even conventional war. When the complexity and fragility of the systems needed today to feed, clothe, and nurture humanity are considered, we have all reason to say that the global grenzsituation will hardly disappear after the elimination of nuclear weapons or war. Rather this condition is a new and essential feature of our existence. But nuclear disarmament will be a critical step in that it will show that mankind really is capable of learning to overcome the threats created by his own technological genius.

Nuclear Reality:
Resistance and Adaptation

Steven Kull

Fellow, Center for International Security and Arms Control, Stanford University.
Dr. Kull, a psychologist, holds a MacArthur Foundation Peace and Security
Fellowship. His research is based on in-depth interviews with over one hundred
Soviets and Americans in formulating and analyzing defense policy.

Whenever there is a significant change in environmental conditions, humans respond in an ambivalent manner. On one hand, they have an interest in comprehending this new condition so as to adapt to it more effectively. On the other, they feel an inertia and resistance that lead them to suppress awareness of the change and to resist facing the implications that flow from it. Both these tendencies can be seen in American and Soviet responses to the relatively new condition engendered by nuclear weapons. The condition of mutual vulnerability has prevailed in the Soviet-American relationship ever since both sides gained secure second-strike capabilities. This means that both sides have the capability to inflict an annihilating attack on the other even after absorbing a surprise all-out attack. The consequence of this new condition is that neither side can reasonably hope to achieve a meaningful advantage in a military conflict. Even in a limited conflict in which one side is doing relatively better, the other would still have the option of escalating to the next higher level of conflict, until both sides would be effectively destroyed.

At first glance, it may seem that the obvious adaptive response to this new condition is to simply eliminate military force as an option for state behavior. Such ideas were discussed in the years just after the first atomic weapons were built. However, as people began to think more about the

214

implications of such a policy, it became clear that eliminating military force would not be so simple. Military force is intrinsically bound up with the very concept of a state. The boundaries of a state and its ability to exert its will in the international arena have rested on its military power. In trying to eliminate the option of military force many questions arise, such as: "How do states protect their boundaries or resolve conflicts if they do not have military force as the ultimate arbiter?" While some have suggested the complete elimination of the state system, there is a growing consensus that this is not feasible.

Faced with these difficult questions, there have been two major responses. One has been a tendency to suppress the awareness of the fundamental change engendered by the condition of nuclear vulnerability and to continue to approach problems of security in ways that may have been appropriate in a prenuclear context, but are no longer applicable. On the other hand, there have also been attempts to adapt to this new reality in ways that recognize the implications of nuclear weapons and evolve naturally from present conditions. This paper will examine examples of each of these responses.

Resistance

Conventionalization. Several writers have described the tendency to resist nuclear reality by approaching nuclear weapons and nuclear war as if they are fundamentally no different than conventional weapons or conventional war. Hans Morgenthau, the realist political theorist, wrote in an article titled, "The Fallacy of Thinking Conventionally about Nuclear Weapons":

> . . . From the beginning of history to 1945, when mankind thought naturally in prenuclear terms, it developed certain conceptions about weapons and war, which have not yielded in the minds of certain theoreticians, or even in the minds of practitioners, when they have time to think in theoretical terms, to the impact of an entirely novel phenomenon, the availability of nuclear weapons and of what we call euphemistically a nuclear war.

> So we have a disjunction between the conventional ways we think and act about nuclear weapons and the objective conditions, under which the availability of nuclear weapons forces us to live . . . We have tried, then, instead of adapting our modes of thought and action to the objective conditions of the nuclear age, to conventionalize nuclear war . . . (1)

Robert Jervis also writes about this tendency to "conventionalize" nuclear weapons:

> The changes brought about by nuclear weapons are so painful and difficult that it is not surprising that people react not by making the best of new realities, but by seeking alluring, if ultimately misleading, paths which they think will lead back to traditional security. (2)

Maintaining a Balance. One of the most common manifestations of this tendency to conventionalize nuclear weapons is the intense concern about maintaining a balance of forces in the superpowers' strategic arsenals. In a prenuclear context the relative distribution of military forces on each side was of significant concern and could reflect the potential outcome of a battle. However, in a nuclear context in which both sides have a secure and flexible capability to inflict an annihilating attack, relative capabilities are largely irrelevant. Nevertheless, there is an intense concern about "who's ahead" in the superpower competition, a desire to "catch-up" or to acquire a "margin of safety."

". . . concern for equality, parity, or balance pervades the entire defense discourse. It has become a major stumbling block in arms control . . ."

Sometimes it seems that the notion of maintaining a balance has become fused with the notion of maintaining deterrence. President Reagan has said: "As long as we maintain the strategic balance . . . then we can count on the basic prudence of the Soviet leaders to avoid nuclear war." (3) Secretary of Defense Weinberger has written: "The critical point in deterring and preventing war is maintaining a balance of forces." (4) Defending the deployment of the Pershing II and cruise missiles in Europe, Margaret Thatcher told the House of Commons: "The principle is a balance in order to deter . . . we must achieve balanced numbers." (5) Soviet leaders have also stressed the importance of maintaining "parity," warning against grave military consequences from the failure to do so. More recently General Secretary Gorbachev has placed more stress on the notion of "reasonable adequacy" than that of "parity." However, in arms control negotiations both sides continue to stress the need for equality.

This concern for equality, parity, or balance pervades the entire defense discourse. It has become a major stumbling block in arms control negotiations because each side has taken a different position on how to measure the relative equality of the arsenals. As each side ignores the areas in which it is ahead, and focuses on those areas in which it is behind, the concern for equality has become a driving force in the arms race.

From a psychological perspective, it is not difficult to understand why this concern for the balance is attractive. Faced with the unnerving condition of absolute vulnerability, the defense establishments in both countries are charged with the task to "do something" to enhance the security of their countries. Being behind in the competition becomes associated with danger. (President Reagan has said: " . . . it is dangerous, if not fatal, to be second best." (6)) Restoring the balance, or gaining a "margin of safety" is an activity that creates the satisfying sense of having eradicated the danger. However, the entire drama is based on illusion. The condition of mutual vulnerability is so robust that whether one side is marginally behind, ahead, or equal, it is still profoundly vulnerable.

Pursuing Victory. A second and perhaps even more important area, in which conventionalized thinking appears, has to do with concepts of winning a war between the two nuclear-armed powers. As discussed, it is no longer viable to have such goals in the event of a war because both sides have unlimited capabilities for escalation. Nevertheless, the notion of achieving such an advantageous termination perseveres in defense thinking. Pentagon officials have spoken about the goal of "prevailing" or "terminating on terms favorable to the United States." In 1982, Marshall Nikolai Ogarkov recognized that "the character and features of today's nuclear war impose heightened demands"; nevertheless he stressed the need "to retain the will to achieve victory over the enemy in any and all conditions." (7)

It should be noted that recently Soviet defense writers have sharply moved away from using such terms as "victory." However this change has not been reflected in a change in force structure of either side. Therefore, some Western observers view this change with a jaundiced eye.

Here again, it is not difficult to understand the psychological attractiveness of the idea of victory. The dramatic imagery of achieving advantage over and subduing would-be aggressors is intrinsically satisfying. And, again, it creates the illusory sense that either side can eradicate the persistent condition of vulnerability.

Higher Order Conventionalization. Although the concept of conventionalization seems to explain much current thinking, on closer analysis the phenomenon is more complex. Many of the same policymakers who at times conventionalize by stressing marginal asymmetries and describing advantageous war outcomes at other times contradict themselves by recognizing the military irrelevance of such asymmetries and the impossibility of winning a nuclear war.

Encountering these inconsistencies, I wondered if there was a way that policymakers resolved such inconsistencies in their own mind. Therefore, I undertook a study in which I reviewed the defense literature and interviewed American defense policymakers and nuclear strategists in the Pentagon, the National Security Council, Congress, and the Rand Corporation. I also interviewed Soviet diplomats, arms control negotiators, academicians, and journalists. In the interviews, when people expressed such inconsistent positions, I would point them out and ask them for an explanation. There were several explanations that recurred frequently.

Accounting for their concern for the balance, many Americans and Soviets used an argument that could be paraphrased as follows: "Well, I know the balance doesn't matter from a military point of view, but other people don't know this. Other people think the nuclear weapons are pretty much the same as conventional weapons. Therefore, it is essential that we have as many nuclear weapons as the other side so that we are not perceived as weaker."

People had different ideas about whose perception is the most critical. In some cases people stressed the importance of appearing strong to Third World countries or allies. Others emphasized the perceptions of domestic audiences. The most frequently cited audience, though, was the other superpower. Both Americans and Soviets expressed concern that key people on the other side believed that an asymmetrical advantage would give them a militarily decisive edge. ("Why else are they spending so much money trying to get it?") To deter such illusions, then, people on both sides argued, it is necessary to maintain equality in our forces. (For a more extensive analysis of how this argument appears in official American defense policy, see my article, "Nuclear Nonsense," *Foreign Policy*, Spring 1985.)

". . . gaining a 'margin of safety' is an activity that creates the satisfying sense of having eradicated the danger."

From my perspective, the most critical element in this kind of thinking is not the argument that there is such a widespread misperception about the relevance of the nuclear balance. Whether or not there is such a misperception, the most critical element is the decision to play along with the misperception as if it were correct. Even though the proponents of this line of thinking do not conventionalize in the sense of misunderstanding the robust nature of mutual vulnerability, they effectively behave as if they do. This can be described as higher order conventionalization. The net effect of such an approach is to confirm the general tendency to conventionalize.

In other cases I asked people to account for the apparent inconsistency between their articulation of the goal of winning a superpower war and their recognition that it was impossible to win such a war. Americans spoke in terms of creating a desired perceptual impact. There was a feeling that the Soviets had gained an edge in the 1960s and 1970s because they were perceived as believing in the possibility of winning a nuclear war. Therefore, so as not to appear lacking "resolve and determination," it is important for the United States to make certain statements and deploy certain capabilities that suggest that the American leadership has such beliefs as well. Here again, the net effect is that policymakers end up acting in a conventionalized fashion.

Both Americans and Soviets interviewed felt it was important for the military to have war-winning goals so as to maintain morale. As one Soviet said: "It is part of their being 'good soldiers.'" An American military officer said that war-winning objectives are psychologically necessary for the military because "that's what the military is for." Other Americans also stressed the need to counteract "defeatism" in the public through "cheerleading."

"Both Americans and Soviets interviewed felt it was important for the military to have war-winning goals so as to maintain morale."

All of these rationales for maintaining conventionalized policies do have a certain logic to them. And there may in fact be some risks involved in firmly recognizing the condition of mutual vulnerability, eschewing efforts to match the other side's arsenal, and unambiguously affirming the impossibility of achieving an advantageous outcome in a war (expressed in force posture as well as rhetoric). There is a viable argument that the other side might interpret such steps as a sign of weakness. If one side comes across as more unambiguously cognizant of the implications of nuclear reality, that side may appear less resolved to retaliate in the event of aggression and therefore deterrence might be weakened. Military morale may suffer.

On the other hand, there are also arguments to be made against such perceptual manipulations. For example, by acting consistently with conventionalized conceptions of military force, each side actually lends credibility to those elements on the other side that conventionalize — elements that one may actually prefer not to strengthen. Both sides naturally take cues from each other as they grope for a meaningful way to respond. There is also the danger that when policymakers strategically express certain beliefs and attitudes they originally did not believe, it may lead them to take on such beliefs or at least to become confused about what they believe. A considerable body of psychological research indicates that just such a phenomenon is likely to occur.

Ultimately, though, I do not think this effort to accommodate misperception and even actively suppress correct perception can be evaluated by speculating about potential costs and benefits. There may indeed be short-term benefits in such manipulations. But considering a more expanded time frame, one is called on to make a more intuitive judgment. In this context, it seems to me, the ultimate need for a more adaptive response becomes particularly compelling.

Adaptation

In contrast to the patterns described above, there are also trends in the Soviet-American relationship that are derived from a conscious recognition and acceptance of the condition of mutual vulnerability. Political leaders on both sides have publicly recognized the annihilating potential of nuclear war and the impossibility of winning one. More importantly, there may be forming what can be described as a security regime in the Soviet-American relationship. A security regime is a set of norms and patterns of state behavior by which states constrain their behavior in a reciprocal fashion. As the regime grows in strength, it gains increasing legitimacy and logically leads to a restructuring of military potential into configurations that are less provocative and threatening. Although it is certainly still in a nascent form, there are indications that such a security regime may be emerging in the Soviet-American relationship.

On several occasions, Soviet and American leaders have made joint statements that explicitly recognize that nuclear weapons have undermined the utility of military force and that call for a cooperative approach to the problem of security. The most outstanding of these is "The Basic Principles of Relations" agreement signed by President Richard Nixon and Secretary Leonid Brezhnev in 1972. It reads that the US and the USSR:

> . . . will proceed from the common determination that in the nuclear age there is no alternative to conducting their mutual relations on the basis of peaceful coexistence . . . They will always exercise restraint in their mutual relations, and will be prepared to negotiate and settle differences by peaceful means. Discussions and negotiations on outstanding issues will be conducted in a spirit of reciprocity, mutual accommodation, and mutual benefit.

> Both sides recognize that efforts to obtain unilateral advantage at the expense of the other, directly or indirectly, are inconsistent with these objectives. The prerequisites for maintaining and strengthening peaceful relations between the US and the USSR are the recognition of the security interests of the Parties based on the principle of equality and the renunciation of the use or threat of force.

Similar principles were signed in the Helsinki Accords and at the Geneva Summit in 1985, when President Reagan and Secretary Gorbachev released a communique saying: " . . . a nuclear war can never be won and must never be fought." (8) Both sides feel compelled to always explain their use of military force in defensive terms.

Such statements have become so common that they tend now to elicit an almost cynical response. Nevertheless, the very fact that such statements have become commonplace, while statements about achieving unilateral advantages are relatively rare, reflects some significant evolution in the normative concepts of state behavior. Such concepts particularly began emerging during World War I as technology greatly extended the destructive effect of war to the general population. The destructive potential of nuclear weapons has further enhanced the emergence of normative concepts that delegitimize the use of military force. Shortly after the development of the first atomic weapons the United States changed the name of the Department of War to the Department of Defense. And in general now, even when states appear to have offensive intentions, they feel compelled to rationalize their behavior in defensive terms.

Furthermore, in the Soviet-American relationship there has, fortunately, been more than the repetition of appealing platitudes. Both sides have also shown significant restraint in their use of force toward the other so that since the end of World War II there have been virtually no shooting confrontations between American and Soviet forces. The unwritten rule that has constrained both sides has been sometimes called the Basic Rule of Prudence. (9) It is widely felt that were it not for this norm of restraint, derived significantly from the recognition of mutual vulnerability, the US and the USSR would very likely have had some major military conflict by now. Both sides still feel free to compete militarily via proxy forces. But even this form of military competition is suffering from declining legitimacy as evidenced by the fact that both sides continually rationalize such behavior as a response to the other side's aggression.

Finally, there are also some rudimentary efforts to restructure military forces into a less provocative form by means of arms control. The results of such efforts have been, at best, mixed. Nevertheless, the fact that arms control continues to be such a major focus of high-level attention is an indicator of the persevering strength of the forces pressing for a Soviet-American security regime.

Needless to say, these are also many features of the Soviet-American relationship that have not accommodated themselves to the demands of such a security regime. Many aspects of American and Soviet policies and force posture continue to be based on the assumption of the utility of military force, the most obvious being the willingness of both sides to use military force directly against established governments close to their borders when they perceive them to be moving in directions contrary to their interests. Both sides have shown minimal interest in mutually reining in the technological developments that contribute to the instability of nuclear arsenals by increasing the incentives for striking first. And, perhaps most significantly, neither side has made any serious move toward deploying their conventional forces in a way that precludes certain offensive options (i.e. "defensive" defense).

Conclusion

In summary, there are two conflicting trends in the Soviet-American relationship. One trend is toward new forms of adaptation to the reality of mutual vulnerability. The other resists such changes by maintaining traditional prenuclear approaches to security. Such traditional approaches are sustained by either suppressing awareness of the changes engendered by nuclear weapons or by actively going along with or promoting others' misperceptions as a means of pursuing political advantage. More adaptive responses involve openly recognizing the reality and significance of nuclear weapons and moving toward the development of a security regime. Such a regime involves reciprocal restraint on the use of force, a gradual delegitimation of the use of force, and corresponding restructuring of arsenals into a less provocative configuration.

> "... *it is attractive to assume that there is a way to make a single political decision that would impel the Soviet-American relationship out of the old and into the new. But it is the Soviet-American relationship itself that must evolve* ..."

Naturally, it is attractive to assume that there is a way to make a single political decision that would impel the Soviet-American relationship out of the old and into the new. But it is the Soviet-American relationship itself that must evolve toward a more adaptive form. This evolution is inherently difficult and will inevitably involve tentative steps forward and righteously indignant steps back. Certainly there is still a significant danger. But at every juncture driving this process forward is the force of awareness of the nuclear reality — a force that does not preordain any outcome but nevertheless grows more powerful as it becomes less encumbered by the influences of self-deception and obfuscation.

The Impact of a US Public Constituency on Arms Control*

Sidney D. Drell

Professor and Deputy Director, Stanford Linear Accelerator Center, Stanford University; Co-Director, Stanford Center for International Security and Arms Control. Dr. Drell is a member of the National Academy of Sciences and past President of the American Physical Society. He has been an arms control advisor to Congress and the White House.

It has often been said that war is too important to be left to the generals and that peace is too vital to be left to the politicians. So, too, are matters of nuclear weapons and policy too important to be left to the nuclear-strategy "experts." In reality, there are no experts on nuclear war. We have never had a nuclear war, and any scientist knows that you must have data before you can become an expert. We do not know how a nuclear war would start, be waged, or finally stopped. No one, including nuclear-strategy "experts," knows what would be left after such a "war."

What this means is that the public must inform and involve itself actively in the formulation of policy on these issues. This requires public outreach, public education, and active dialogue with our public officials. The record we will explore in this article shows that an informed and active public constituency can have a significant effect in shaping sound policy in highly technical areas that determine our very survival.

* Adapted with additions from the Danz Lectures, published in *Facing the Threat of Nuclear Weapons*, University of Washington Press, Seattle, 1983. Reprinted by permission.

The H-Bomb

In the United States, there was no public debate at the time of the fateful decision by President Truman in 1950 to develop the second generation of nuclear weapons, that is, the H-bomb or hydrogen bomb. This was early in the cold war period, and secrecy was applied broadly. As a result, the public played no role in the decision to move ahead to the megaton-scale H-bomb.

". . . nuclear weapons and policy are too important to be left to the nuclear-strategy 'experts.' In reality, there are no experts on nuclear war."

The debate within government on whether, and then how, to proceed with work on the H-bomb in response to the first Soviet A-bomb explosion in late summer of 1949 was carried on almost completely under a thick cloak of secrecy. We have no idea whether in those strained times, an effort to negotiate with the Soviet Union to head off the development of the H-bomb might have succeeded, but we didn't even try. It was nine years later before a serious initiative on peaceful uses of nuclear energy was made in 1958 — but by then it was too late. The genie was out of the bottle and there was no way to deny the basic scientific reality of the hydrogen bomb.

By the early 1960s the design and building of hydrogen bombs had advanced to a mature technology. The scientists in the nuclear weapons laboratories had become what Lord Zuckerman calls "the alchemists of our time, working in secret ways that cannot be divulged, casting spells which embrace us all."

A Powerful Coalition

Testing of H-bombs in the atmosphere continued at a hefty pace through most of the decade of the 1950s, leading to a substantial, worldwide build-up in the level of radioactivity. By 1960, an active and vigorous public constituency around the world had become concerned about this radioactive fallout and its effects on the health of their families and friends. They joined many scientists who understood the weapons in detail to protest continued testing. Scientists could bring a highly informed judgment to bear on the question of how the cessation of nuclear tests in the atmosphere would affect our national security.

This was the first important issue of nuclear weapons in which the public in the US played a major role. Around the same time, some scientists in the USSR, and in particular Andrei Sakharov, were also advocating a ban on testing. In the Western world, concerned citizens by the tens and hundreds of thousands applied strong political leverage while the technical case in support of an atmospheric test ban treaty was presented by concerned scientists. These forces inside and outside of government enhanced one another. Working together, they helped accomplish what may well have been beyond the power of either alone: the Limited Test Ban Treaty signed in 1963 by President Kennedy and General Secretary Khrushchev.

Antiballistic Missiles and Multiple Warheads

By the end of the 1960s, scientists had developed important new weapons technologies which could potentially alter in a fundamental way the nuclear forces of the US and the USSR. One new development was antiballistic missile (ABM) systems, using advanced computers, very high acceleration interceptor missiles, special nuclear warheads, and phased array radars.

The original proposal to deploy ABM systems near large population centers in the United States stirred a major public debate, primarily because many people did not want nuclear-tipped missiles located, figuratively, "in their own backyards." Triggered by these public concerns, the ABM decision became an opportunity for extensive public debate. The halls of Congress and the media became vital educational forums for careful and informed technical analysis of the effectiveness and arms control implications of the proposed ABM system.

Through this unprecedented public debate on a weapons system Congress came to understand that the proposed ABM system was not going to do what was promised. By 1970, it was clear on the basis of technical facts alone, that offensive missiles could respond with relative ease to any practical ABM system. Technical arguments for deployment collapsed and the ABM debate boiled down to its value solely as political leverage for the arms control talks — its value as a bargaining chip for the Strategic Arms Limitation Talks (SALT) negotiations.

The outcome of this was the successful negotiation with the Soviet Union at SALT I of the ABM Treaty severely limiting deployment of ABM systems. That treaty is currently in force. I consider it to be our most important arms control achievement to date.

At the same time as the ABM debate, however, the United States moved ahead rapidly with the development and deployment of Multiple Independently Targetable Reentry Vehicles (MIRVs). The original American justification for MIRVs was that they would penetrate ballistic missile defenses by overwhelming their defensive firepower with an intense rain of many warheads. They were offered as an insurance policy against Soviet ABM deployments which had then begun around Moscow. When, however, the SALT I treaty of 1972 prohibited the deployment of nationwide ABM defenses, American MIRV programs proceeded full tilt. The new rationale for MIRVs became our alleged need for counterforce — the need to threaten a wide repertoire of Soviet military targets, including their retaliatory forces.

MIRVs did not lead to an increase in the visible presence of nuclear weapons. Therefore, in contrast to ABMs, they did not cause a reaction from citizens who wanted no nuclear weapons nearby. In such circumstances we deployed MIRVs with very little public attention or concern, the USSR responded with its own major buildup of MIRV'd forces, and arms control suffered a setback. It is not that there was no opportunity for serious public debate about the pros and cons of MIRVs and their impact on the arms race and our national security. It was simply that there was no specific issue to bring the MIRV decision home to the man in the street and arouse public reaction. Therefore, no US public constituency was created to nurture the cause of arms control in opposition to the MIRV. Moreover, the country was becoming increasingly concerned first with Vietnam and then with Watergate.

". . . Afghanistan mobilized public opinion in the West against arms control, which again demonstrates the essential power of public opinion."

The Failure of SALT II and the Success of the MX Debate

There was also little expressed public interest in the SALT II treaty when it came up for ratification by the US Senate in 1979. The arms control advocates and a few politicians pitched in and argued mightily. However, there was no public outcry as there had been at the time of the ABM debate that set the stage for SALT I. The Senate debate on SALT II dragged on with little public pressure for ratification. Debate was eventually terminated as a result of the Soviet armies entering Afghanistan, and the reaction of the American public to it, making it politically impossible to obtain ratification in the United States. In a reverse way, Afghanistan mobilized public opinion in the West against arms control, which again demonstrates the essential power of public opinion.

The original rationale for the United States developing the MX missile was to respond to the buildup of highly MIRV'd Soviet ICBMs and to decrease the vulnerability of our land-based missile force, thereby improving deterrence. We sought to base the new ICBM so that it could not be attacked and destroyed. However the debate in the United States, which was covered in the media much more thoroughly than the original MIRV decision, revealed deep differences of opinion on counterforce versus deterrence, on the effectiveness of the proposed basing scheme, and on its environmental impact.

The MX basing plan, as it was originally perceived, is no longer with us. Claims of the survivability and effectiveness of "Densepack," "Bigbird," and "Racetrack" — the three schemes with, at one time or another, administration backing — just did not stand up under close technical scrutiny. Today we are deploying only fifty MX missiles, and they have little to do with our security or with deterrence. They are not a major arms control issue.

A Mixed Record with One Conclusion

I see a pattern in this mixed record of the past. The atmospheric test ban treaty and the ABM debate that culminated in SALT I are two major successes in American nuclear weapons policy. Further, the MX program has been restructured and sharply cut back from the original plans. It is notable that these results were achieved with vigorous and constructive public participation and support.

By contrast, the development of the H-bomb and of MIRVs greatly increased the devastating potential and the threat posed by our nuclear weapons. As such, they may be considered failures of our nuclear weapons policy. Although there may have been no feasible alternative to developing the H-bomb, we didn't try to head it off. I find it significant that these technical escalations were undertaken without public involvement or debate, and also without a serious effort at negotiating them away. Another serious setback, after years of negotiating, was the Senate's failure to ratify the SALT II treaty because of a similar lack of an involved public constituency.

The Current Debate: 'Star Wars'

On March 23, 1983, the president of the United States described to the nation his vision of the future in which we are protected against nuclear weapons by a space-age defense, popularly labelled "Star Wars," and no longer have to live in a balance of terror. We are, therefore, encountering once again major decisions that will determine the course of our nuclear weapons policy until the end of the century and beyond. These decisions present challenges and opportunities to our citizens, scientists, and government.

The good news is that this issue is itself not shrouded in secrecy or ignored in the shadows of apathy — to the contrary. In the press, in the churches, in civic organizations, in universities, and in the political arena, a process of education about deterrence has begun in earnest, and nuclear weapons policy is commanding priority attention at this time. There now exists an active and concerned arms control constituency ready to participate in a national debate that we all should welcome — scientists, government, and citizens alike. As a result of this public-inspired debate, Star Wars is still undergoing tough, critical scrutiny, including in particular its technical prospects and its impact on arms control progress. And certainly the president, when he gave his speech in 1983, did not expect to find himself in 1987 with only half the money he wanted to get.

Essential Characteristics of a Public Constituency

The public arms control constituency created during the past few years must continue to grow and prove that it is enduring, informed, constructive, energetic, and has a broad political base.

To endure it must have a clear and understandable goal. This means going beyond a freeze which was an important movement to build a constituency, but was inadequate to sustain it.

"And do not just go talk to friends. It is every bit as important, if not more so, to spend time reasoning with those who hold opposing views."

The public also has to be informed. It has to have a realistic sense that there are no easy, absolute solutions — not in the short term. We have to keep working at the issue to make it become part of the public agenda through public education, public outreach, and meetings with our elected officials. We can make sure that public officials know that this is one of the issues on which they are going to be elected or not elected.

It is effective to choose a few issues and to be very informed on them, so that one does not get caught out or discredited as a result of using shallow overgeneralizations, then stick to those positions like a bulldog. And do not just go talk to friends. It is every bit as important, if not more so, to spend time reasoning with those who hold opposing views.

The public constituency must also be constructive. The attitude has to be one that takes other people's arguments seriously, recognizes that opponents feel deeply about what they believe, and engages in civilized, constructive debate.

The public arms control constituency has to be energetic. Every citizen has his or her talents. Consequently, different people are going to be effective in different ways: in the electoral process, through public outreach, or through active research on the issues.

Finally, one needs to go for a broad political base, that is, not just from the left or the right or the extremes. Support will be required from a broad spectrum of the public.

Public involvement in these issues is not only useful, it is essential. We've had no progress without it. Stimulated by the involvement of the public, we negotiated and ratified SALT I. Without it, we ended up with MIRVs and failed to ratify SALT II.

Restructuring of
Soviet Society

Alexander I. Belchuk

Vice Director of the Institute of the International Labour Movement, USSR
Academy of Sciences; Professor, Doctor of Economy. Author of more than sixty
papers and books, Dr. Belchuk is holder of the State Prize of the USSR for his
work in economics.

The process of change in the Soviet Union is being widely discussed
now.

"Perestroika" (restructuring) and "glasnost" (openness), have become
household words in many languages. The changes first became obvious
following the April 1985 plenary session of the Central Committee of the
Communist Party, gained momentum after the 27th Party Congress held
in February to March 1986, and since the January 1987 plenum of the
Central Committee have been massive.

These changes are revolutionary in their scope, depth, and implications.
They are often compared to the developments of Soviet society after the
20th Party Congress in 1956 which has since become known in the West
as the "de-Stalinization" movement. But to my mind, the present restructuring is by far more radical than that of the late 1950s and early 1960s.

During that earlier period, drastic changes in the political and economic
model were not on the agenda. Now, these basic problems are the focus of
attention.

Restructuring poses many questions, both in this country and abroad.
What areas will be affected by the changes and how deep will they be?
What renewed society will emerge in the Soviet Union as a result of these
developments? Generally speaking, to what extent is Soviet society suscep-
tible at all to change?

229

Could it be that old stereotypes of the Soviet Union as a system which is completely rigid and incapable of transformation will prove correct and some time later, the prophecy "the wind returneth again according to his circuits" will be fulfilled? Many people are thinking back to the experience of the mid-1960s and the gradual rejection of de-Stalinization as well as to the renunciation of any dramatic changes in the economic model.

The concept of Soviet society which is as rigid as, say, some ancient Oriental civilizations, has never been entirely accurate. It was based on the low susceptibility to change of the Soviet political and economic systems which were established in the 1930s and finally worked out in the 1940s and 1950s.

But the political system and economic mechanism, or model, are closely linked. In the long run, both are dependent on the productive forces and the social basis of the society. The gap can't be too wide. And it is the productive forces and social basis of the country that have been affected by sweeping changes since the late 1920s. From a mostly rural and agrarian country, the Soviet Union has developed into an industrial, urban country. In 1928, agriculture employed 75 percent of the working population, and in 1985, only about 20 percent. In 1926, urban population accounted for 18 percent of the overall population, and in the mid-1980s, about 65 percent.

There have been changes in the social structure, the level of education, culture, traditions, customs, values, the system of labor organization, and social psychology as a whole. Historical experience is so very important. Some of the old recipes of the 1930s through the 1970s have proven wrong and unacceptable.

Shifts in spheres of production are widely known and need no comment. The level of production and diversification have increased dramatically: Consumer demand has changed and there are new demands imposed by the scientific and technical revolutions. Life in a modern, very competitive world has evoked dramatic changes. Old political and economic models have become outdated. An urgent need has appeared to replace them. Subjective reasons — that is, reasons which appear to be more related to personality than to the objective forces of history — for some time have delayed introduction of the new models, but now the process of change has started.

While explaining the reasons for, and the driving forces of restructuring, it would be unfair to attribute this development solely to Gorbachev and other Soviet leaders, though the role of subjective factors is considerable. Mechanical determinism — that is the belief that objective material factors will be automatically translated into reality, inherent in much Soviet historical research — is also a dangerous illusion. However, the most important thing is that in Soviet society there appeared an urgent need for deep changes, and Gorbachev finally came on the crest of this wave. Unfortunately, he came after a considerable delay. If only he had come sooner! He said in answer to a question put to him by *L'Unita*, "If there were no Gorbachev there would be someone else. Our society is ready for change; change would make its own way."

Changes in the Political System

Changes in the political sphere have been most conspicuous. A particular role was played by the January 1987 plenary session of the Central Committee and glasnost. A process of deep democratization has therefore preceded all other transformations. It is not an accident that this is so, but to my mind changes in other areas, such as in the economy, were as much needed, or perhaps even more.

"If there were no Gorbachev there would be someone else. Our society is ready for change; change would make its own way."

In any case, democratization has become the main instrument of restructuring; it has become an engine that brings the vessel into motion. It is shaping the general direction of changes and the mechanics of practical decision making.

Democracy is a historically conditioned concept. It is different for different times and societies, as social priorities vary markedly at various stages in historical development. Most important, the instruments ensuring democracy can differ sharply. In the West, this has meant first of all a multiparty system. But such a generalization may not be appropriate.

There were, on the one hand, nondemocratic regimes which have multiparty systems. On the other hand, there are also democratic one-party regimes. It is, rather, the differences in particular programs of politicians and the distribution of functions between legislative, executive, and judicial branches, and the important role of the popular media which also can determine whether democracy really exists.

The purpose of the democratization in the Soviet Union is to ensure a mechanism for expressing opposing views and the coexistence of different social forces within specific Soviet forms. These, as a rule, differ from those existing in other countries. One of them is glasnost which means a new role for popular media. This process should gradually eliminate "zones free from criticism." Already, much more can be said about things which could not be said a year ago, and people are confident that this direction will continue.

Now, top-ranking officials in the party, state, or judicial organs are subjected to sharp criticism. *Pravda*, for example, and other newspapers have started publishing very critical articles condemning abuses in a number of regional and republican party organizations. There was sharp criticism of the first secretaries of Uzbekistan and Kazakstan, two important republics. The leader of the party in Kazakstan, Kunaev, was a full member of the Politburo of the Soviet Union. Rashidov, of Uzbekistan, was a candidate member. Again, in May 1987 another article in *Pravda* "discussed the abuses of power of Shakirov," the first secretary of the party organization in Bashkirya.

The *Literaturnaya Gazeta* and *Izvestia* have several times published material on judicial mistakes and arbitrary rulings of some officials. There was a case in Byelorussia where several people were sentenced to death and later it turned out that they had not committed the crime. Their trial had been carried on by authorities in violation of the procedural codes. There was a great public uproar when all this came to light, and the officials were exposed. Similarly, the newspaper *Izvestia* published in May 1987 an article about an illegal persecution of a religious sect by local authorities in the town of Kazan.

". . . glasnost . . . means a new role for popular media . . . much more can be said about things which could not be said a year ago, and people are confident that this direction will continue."

This list of such publications is far from exhaustive. Much more evidence now appears in our press, which indicates that glasnost and criticism are not only a public campaign in the Soviet Union, but have become integrated into everyday life. Prime Minister Margaret Thatcher and Secretary of State George Shultz, as well as some popular media personalities, have made statements on Soviet television, expressing their views.

Not that this policy enjoys unanimous support in this country. Our newspapers publish angry letters, whose authors argue that such a line is wrong, that it is unfair to give outspoken ideological opponents an opportunity to propagandize their points of view in the Soviet popular media. Our political culture has been shaped through the lives of many generations, and it cannot be changed in a short time.

Of great significance, however, are the changes in political mechanisms. While these represent only initial steps, experiments are going on. Slates of multiple candidates have been introduced in a number of local soviets. Both in state and in party organs, measures have been introduced to ensure control of the execution of power by the people. To ensure the independence of state and social organizations, a process has been started to enlarge the functions of the local soviets, the trade unions, and women's and youth organizations.

As for democratization in economics, at the level of state enterprises attention is being given to labor's increased participation in decision making. A system of elections to some important managerial posts has been introduced. For example, the director of the automobile plant RAF in Latvia was elected from a field of six to seven candidates, by secret ballot of employees. Some of the candidates had chosen themselves to run, that is, had nominated themselves. Direct participation of factory and office workers in decision making in state enterprises is, in principle, very important as it provides additional incentives to increase labor productivity and efficiency.

There is no unemployment in the country, yet many enterprises experience a big labor shortage. In addition, existing labor legislation makes it difficult for administrators to fire even a negligent worker. As a rule, trade unions and judicial organs safeguard workers' rights. This diminishes the effect of "external motivating factors" to raise efficiency and improve quality. In this situation, the role of inner incentives must grow, including enlisting the support of blue- and white-collar workers in decision making about social and production problems in their enterprises. Electing managers all the way up to the director serves the same purpose.

Back in 1983, a law was adopted on labor collectives, which substantially enlarged the rights of employees. But there was a problem with subsequent implementation: At a majority of state enterprises, employees were reluctant to make use of the law. Their wages and salaries were only slightly affected by the profits of the enterprises. Today, that situation must change. In addition to fulfilling the plan targets, as enterprises become increasingly independent, the role of profits has to be significantly increased. These profits can be used to raise income of employees as well as to meet social needs.

Measures are also being taken for developing intraparty democracy. This is particularly important for the Soviet Union and other socialist countries because of the key roles of communist parties in all managerial and ideological processes. Here again, the idea is to strengthen the influence of rank and file party members upon leadership. Party leaders are being subjected to more criticism. In some local party organizations party secretaries are elected directly by secret ballot, without intermediaries.

Changes in Planning and Management Systems

The need for dramatic changes in the system of planning and management has become an objective necessity earlier than in other fields and has been an impetus to the whole process of perestroika. It would be unfair to assume that the centralized planning system the way it was established in the 1930s and 1940s was altogether wrong and deficient. The economic performance of the Soviet Union under this system for five decades is rather impressive. The Soviet Union has become the second industrial power in the world, and when many Western experts say that the "impressive results have been achieved only in military industries," they are in error. To develop a modern military economy without a solid general economic basis is impossible.

Centralized planning has its advantages. It allows for quick mobilization of resources, focuses on key objectives such as industrialization, builds up heavy industry, accelerates development of particular industries, and allows for planning of macroeconomic equilibrium without recessions, avoiding unnecessary strong differences in personal income.

This system also performed another important function: It used strong state power for accelerated transformation of the peasant society into an industrial one. The peasant psychology, the social structure, the ingrained characteristics of labor and its work ethics are, by nature, slow to change. They need decades, if not centuries, to develop naturally.

"A strong state may act as a coachman, whipping up the horses . . . [but] there is a danger that some horses can be whipped to death . . . a strong state should not be a brutal state."

A strong state may act as a coachman, whipping up the horses. True, there is a danger that some horses can be whipped to death, which actually did happen. Such abuses proved, in hindsight, that a strong state should not be a brutal state. If it is, the results can be just the opposite of those intended.

Still, the strong appeal in many developing countries of the Soviet experience in industrialization, in addition to the advantages of centralization, can be explained by the desire to break the vicious cycle of backwardness. This can be done with the help of centralized state power. A market economy suggests a "natural" process, but a slow one, and pressing needs leave developing countries insufficient time, to say nothing about the inevitable excessive social stratification of the society.

In the period of the 1930s and 1940s the state in the Soviet Union acted as an omnipotent transforming power, one that collectivized peasants, turned the major part of them into city dwellers, altered their values and aspirations. Unfortunately, the Soviet Union paid too high a price for this in the Stalin era. Then in the 1950s and 1960s, the shortcomings of an administered economy became quite evident: Many state enterprises had little interest in technical progress or in lowering production costs, or diversification. The quality of goods was inadequate, and a chronic shortage of many products developed, as did absenteeism of workers and employees.

The economic reform of the mid-1960s dwindled and gradually came to naught because it met with resistance from forces who were not interested in its implementation. Besides, the very idea that lay at its basis was neither consistent nor comprehensive, and the old system hadn't yet run out of steam. The Soviet economy was still progressing, but problems began to mount. Late in the 1970s to early 1980s, the resources needed for continued development on the old basis became depleted and radical reform in the economic mechanism became imperative.

The main idea of the reform lies in the transition from an administered, or directive economy, to one based on costs and profits. The full-scale profit-and-loss accounting and "market" economy are not synonymous, though they do have very much in common. In some ways profit-and-loss accounting is a broader term than a market economy. Performance in such a system is judged by comparison of results and expenses even in the stages of production, before the product is yet an actual commodity. Costs and profits can be measured even before sale.

Decisions made at the June 1987 meeting of the Central Committee were very important for our economic reforms. These were aimed at lessening direct control of enterprises from above, giving more independence to state enterprises, shifting to a system of pay as you go and self-financing. The work of the planning system and branch ministries should also be reshaped. Reforms in price formation and the credit system will follow.

It would be premature to say that every detail of the reforms has already been worked out. Many things will have to be done still, many adjustments are still to be made. To my mind, there are still some key problems: for example, the relationship between — and the compatibility of — directive planning and full-scale profit-and-loss accounting of enterprises. And there is still the mechanism of price formation.

The objective difficulty lies in the fact that various parts of the economic mechanism are interdependent, which calls for comprehensive, coherent, and more or less simultaneous transformations. Otherwise, changes in some parts of the mechanism can be blocked by other parts that are still unchanged. The complexity of the economy of such a big country as the Soviet Union makes this task quite a challenge.

Ideological Changes

Public consciousness, especially mass consciousness, is very inert; it doesn't go hand in hand with the development of society. But it is changing, even if it hasn't caught up with changes in the political and economic institutes, especially in this time of such revolutionary and radical reforms. Still, these changes often can't be lasting, or can't be accomplished at all, without the necessary ideological transformation.

The main spheres of ideology directly relevant to the destiny of restructuring are, first, eliminating a dogmatic approach and the aggressive messianism which often accompanies it, that is, the ideology of the export of revolution; and second, making necessary shifts in popular consciousness and in the political culture.

The struggle against dogmatism and with the ideology of aggressive messianism by no means calls for a revision of the entire Marxist philosophy of history with its historical determinism, and the underlying assumption that material conditions determine one's consciousness, or that political and economic structures are dependent upon the level of development of productive forces in the society. On the other hand, Marxist-Leninist theory has always made it clear that it is impossible to export revolution. Revolutionary transformation cannot take place unless favorable conditions exist inside that society. Rejecting the aggressive messianic approach is consistent with this understanding. To go out with aggressive messianic fervor and try with force to impose revolution upon other societies against the will of the people won't work. It does not take into account the timing and development which every society has, which is its own.

"To go out with aggressive messianic fervor and try with force to impose revolution upon other societies against the will of the people won't work."

The socialist movement in Russia began late in the nineteenth century as a contrasting response to attempts of idealistic "narodniks" who used terrorism as an attempt to jump over, or bypass, the inevitable stages in societal development. They tried to bypass the market, or capitalist, stage.

Yet in real life it has been much more complicated. During the period of the October Revolution and subsequent civil war, and even later, many revolutionaries were eager "to march all the way to the English Channel." They naïvely believed that working people in capitalist countries were impatiently waiting for their "brothers in class" to free them from "the oppression of capitalism." Then, when Hitler's Germany attacked the Soviet Union, many Soviet people took it as a hard blow and were disillusioned that German workers and peasants wearing soldiers' uniforms were shooting at their "brothers in class" instead of turning their arms against their commanders.

It is dogmatic, also, to think — as was prevalent — that there is only one "genuine" socialist pattern, the Soviet one, and all others are negative or deviations that should be fought against, for example, the attempts to declare the Yugoslav and Chinese systems as "nonsocialist."

These concepts of the "exclusive" character of the Soviet model began to fade as new deficiencies in the old models continued to emerge and were compared, for example, to the Hungarian pattern in agriculture. The

25th and 26th Congresses in 1976 and 1981 called for "studying the experience" of other socialist countries. The Soviet society has begun to realize that it is not "a bearer of ultimate truth." Recognizing the inevitability and authenticity of the pluralistic concept at the international level simultaneously leads to encouragement of a pluralistic approach at home.

Of great significance has been a critical analysis of certain stages of national history, principally those connected with the Stalin era. Once again, discussions of these problems have become very acute and sharp, both among historians and in wide circles of the population. In addition, shifts in mass consciousness and political education of the population have become an important prerequisite for democratization, and for general restructuring.

In prerevolutionary Russia there was a prolonged period of authoritarian rule under the tsars. Public consciousness and the political culture of the masses had a number of specific features. Vast, scarcely populated lands at the outskirts of the empire permitted the continuous migration of the most active part of the population, those who were not happy with their life in the central part of Russia. They ran to the Southern steppes, ("to the Kozaks"), or the North, or to vast vistas of Siberia. To some extent this eased social tensions in the society. People got accustomed to authoritarian, centralized rule. A period of "bourgeois democracy" as defined by Soviet social science was practically nonexistent.

The prolonged "cult of personality" in the Stalin era didn't contribute to the development of democratic traditions, either.

It is this historical background that explains to a large extent such specific features of mass consciousness of the Soviet population as "administrative thinking," intolerance of opposing ("wrong") views in politics, and "peasant egalitarianism." If market prices are too high, most people will not appeal to increase supply, but rather support an administrative control on prices.

Many people still can't understand why many points of view should be admitted, some of them being utterly wrong ("we do not need many opinions, we need only the right one"). Therefore, it is no accident that newspapers are publishing articles entitled "To Learn Democracy." It is not easy to overcome traditions that have lasted centuries.

Egalitarian moods have always prevailed in the mostly peasant Russian society. To a large extent they have remained intact in the minds of the Soviet people up to this day. That is why high incomes, even if they are earned by efficient work, have often been disapproved of. As a rule, however, such criticism was counterproductive.

Art, and most of all, literature in the Soviet Union play a particular role in politics and ideology. Literature and art, through their best representatives, have always been the "people's consciousness," trumpeters of social and political aspirations of the masses. Russian literature, from the poetry of Pushkin to the novels of Tolstoy and Dostoyevsky, has been on the cutting edge of Russian political consciousness. For example, in the beginning of the twentieth century there was a famous anti-Semitic trial. It was called the Baylis case, and was analogous to the Dreyfus case in France. Baylis was accused of using blood of Christian children for preparing ritual meals. The writer, Korolenko, through his literary work helped to defeat the anti-Semitic attack, and the defendant was acquitted. The case aroused a great deal of public attention in Russia. The members of the art world took a front line position in the fight against anti-Semitism.

There is still an active political role for novelists in the Soviet Union today. There are new novels, like Anatoly Rybakov's *Children of the Arbat,* which tell in detail about the very difficult times under Stalin. Boris Pasternak's *Dr. Zhivago*, critical of all contradictions at the time of the October revolution, will be released soon. The film *Repentance*, which is a crying out against the abuses of a dictator, was released in early 1987, and has been showing to large audiences.

It is a common phenomenon in our history that many novels, films, and poems create a widespread social response, more so than sensational political articles or political books.

The so-called "village prose," which dates from the essays of Ovechkin in the 1950s, is a better source of information on the anatomy of agrarian relations in the Soviet Union, than scientific research on the subject. Art exhibitions very often turn into discussion clubs, etc.

In the renewal of Soviet society that has been ushered in by perestroika, art once again holds a special place. Many new interesting works have appeared. It is becoming increasingly difficult to buy literary magazines, even though the number of copies printed have increased dramatically. During a television discussion sponsored by the literary magazine *Druzhba Narodov* June 1987, one of the Georgian writers said: "We, the writers are mediators between the authorities and the people." In the Soviet Union, such comments are taken quite seriously. And this is again, part of the tradition of Russian literature, dating back to the nineteenth century.

Are there any safeguards for perestroika? This question is being asked repeatedly in the West, and not only in the West. In the multitude of voices of commentators and analysts, one can discern the inevitable skeptical voices, repeating with many a variation that in the long run the prophecy will be fulfilled: "the wind will return again according to his circuits," meaning that the old times will return again, as they have before.

They say that the specific character of the Soviet society and the resistance of those unwilling to cooperate in the restructuring will bar the revolutionary transformations.

I can't accept this point of view, and this is not wishful thinking. The restructuring is being built on a solid foundation. First, the desire for changes and their acceptance of them as inevitable comes both from "above" and from "below." Thus, Gorbachev's policy has a wide social foundation. Second, as an economist, it is vitally important to know that rejecting, or reducing, the present ongoing radical change to something only cosmetic would have most negative implications for the economy. This we can't afford. Third, it is necessary to take into account the laws of development of mass consciousness. In periods of revolutionary shift, once the ghost is let out of the bottle, it is impossible to put it back. As Marx said, "If the masses become possessed with an idea, it becomes a material force." The masses in the Soviet Union have become possessed with the idea of perestroika.

Diffusion of the Idea of Beyond War

Everett M. Rogers

Professor, Annenberg School of Communications, University of Southern
California. Dr. Rogers has written over 19 books and numerous papers. He was a
Fellow of the American Association for the Advancement of Science and the
American Sociology Association and a Fellow and past President of the Interna-
tional Communications Association.

Our purpose here is to explore the diffusion of ideas like beyond war.
There is a huge tradition of research on the diffusion of innovations, over
4,000 studies to date. Almost all of these studies, however, deal with technological innovation, new ideas that have a material referent such as a
product, hardware, or equipment. The present essay deals with the logical
extensions of the diffusion framework to the particular case where the innovation is an idea without a direct material referent.

Diffusion of Innovations Research

Diffusion research began in the United States in about 1940, when a
general theoretical model of diffusion was first formulated. (1) Beginning
about 1960, this diffusion model was applied widely outside of the United
States, especially in many Third World nations, initially without adequate
questioning of how appropriate the model might be in these new con-
texts. For example, only in the 1970s did scholars begin to assess the
distinctiveness of Third World conditions. The diffusion model has been
usefully incorporated into development programs in Latin America, Af-

rica, and Asia. It fits well with the desire of many national governments to convey new ideas in agriculture, health, family planning, and education to their people.

A tremendous body of research has accumulated over the past forty years on the diffusion of innovations. From these investigations have come a series of generalizations about such issues as the characteristics of innovations that influence the rate of adoption and the characteristics of individuals who are likely to adopt an innovation first. (1) We summarize these findings here under the four main elements of the diffusion model: innovation, communication channels, time, and the social system.

Innovation

It should not be assumed, as has sometimes been the case, that all innovations are basically the same. To do so is a gross oversimplification. As illustrated in Figure 1, the rate of adoption of innovations differs widely. The rate of adoption is positively related to several characteristics of the innovation as they are perceived by the members of the system in which the innovation is diffusing:

1. Relative advantage, the degree to which the innovation is perceived to be superior to the idea that it replaces;

2. Compatibility, the degree to which an innovation is perceived as being consistent with the existing values, past experiences, and needs of potential adopters;

3. Complexity, the degree to which an innovation is perceived as difficult to understand and use;

4. Trialability, the degree to which an innovation may be experimented with on a limited basis; and

5. Observability, the degree to which the results of an innovation are visible to others.

These factors help us to understand why most preventive innovations are characterized by a relatively slow rate of adoption: Adopters have difficulty in determining the preventive innovation's relative advantage; preventive innovations often are not very compatible with individuals' values, attitudes, or lifestyles; the cause-and-effect relationships involved are complex; trial is difficult or impossible; and the innovation's results are not very observable since they are delayed. The idea of beyond war is preventive in the sense that it seeks to prevent future armed warfare (beyond war also involves a global vision), and this preventive quality of beyond war may help explain why we would expect its early diffusion to face certain difficulties. An individual must make a decision to adopt a preventive innovation now, in order to prevent a future unwanted event from occurring (which may not occur anyway). We expand on the distinctive qualities of preventive innovations in a later section of this essay.

Communications Channels

A communication channel is the means by which messages get from one individual to another. Mass media channels are more effective in creating knowledge of innovations, while interpersonal channels are more effective in forming and changing attitudes toward an innovation and thus in influencing the individual's decision to adopt or reject the innovation. Most individuals evaluate an innovation, not on the basis of scientific research by experts, but on the basis of the subjective evaluations of near peers who have already adopted the innovation. These peers serve as models whose behavior is imitated by others in the social system. Thus imitation and social modeling are essential elements in the diffusion process. Diffusion is essentially a social process, involving social relationships among individuals in a system.

"Once an innovation is accepted by about 15 to 20 percent of the total population . . . it cannot be stopped."

It is the activation of peer communication networks that leads to the "take-off" in the rate of adoption shown in Figure 1. The most important part of the S-shaped curve is soon after it begins. It stops increasing at a rather slow rate and suddenly begins to increase at an increasing rate. That makes the curve take-off in an S shape. Its shaded area is the point of greatest interest to diffusion scholars. We get very excited at the shaded part of the curve because that is where the mystery gets solved of why diffusion happens. Once an innovation is accepted by about 15 to 20 percent of the total population involved, such as the total population of the US or of the USSR, it cannot be stopped. Then no matter how you try to slow further diffusion, the innovation continues to diffuse. This self-generating quality of the diffusion process has been found in a wide range of conditions, and for a large number of innovations that have been studied.

The first adopters of an innovation, called "innovators," are usually perceived as atypical members of their local community, and their example is not immediately followed by others. The innovators tend to be high in socioeconomic status, have considerable mass media exposure, and travel over a wide area. The next category of individuals to adopt the innovation are called "early adopters." They are people who occupy a key position in the local communication network and are seen to embody the norms of the social system. The early adopters are treated with respect and their behavior is followed by many others in the local system.

Certain individuals in a social system play an especially important role in the interpersonal diffusion of innovations. They are called "opinion leaders." Opinion leadership is the degree to which an individual is able to influence informally other individuals' attitudes or overt behavior. Diffusion programs have often sought to identify the opinion leaders in a community and to obtain their assistance in diffusing innovations to others in the system. Once the rate of adoption for an innovation has reached 15 or 20 percent (that is, when the opinion leaders have adopted it), it is usually impossible to prevent further diffusion of the innovation (as stated previously).

". . . it is usually unrealistic to expect the mass media to persuade individuals to adopt an innovation. At best, the media can bring about behavior change indirectly . . ."

The mass media also have an important role in the diffusion of innovations. The media are unique in being able to quickly reach a mass audience with a standard message. The media can thus create awareness or knowledge of an innovation and may be able to provide "how-to" information. But it is usually unrealistic to expect the mass media to persuade individuals to adopt an innovation. At best, the media can bring about behavior change indirectly, when mass communication influences opinion leaders whose decisions then affect others in the social network.

Time

The element of time is important in several ways: in the innovation decision process by which individuals pass from first awareness to adoption or rejection; in the innovativeness of an individual or other unit of adoption (that is, the relative earliness or lateness with which the person adopts); and in an innovation's rate of adoption (measured as the number of members of a system who adopt an innovation in a given time period).

The Innovation-Decision Process

Now let's look at the adoption of an innovation by an individual, as opposed to a system. We go through stages; the first is "knowledge," which occurs when your consciousness is raised about a problem and you begin to search for some solutions. At the persuasion stage, you form an attitude, a predisposition to action; you change your attitude toward the innovation. The decision stage leads to adoption or rejection of the innovation. The mass media play a major role in creating knowledge of a new idea. They also help set the tone (the agenda) for that topic, making it something that can be discussed, that people could talk about. Discussions in near peer networks, that is, talking about the new idea with someone very much like yourself, is crucial in adoption decisions. Paradoxically, the less technically expert these peers are, the more convincing their experience is to you.

My neighbor across the street is an English literature professor, who adopted a home computer two years ago. His experience made me decide to accept a computer. What convinced me is that my neighbor is not much of an expert on computers, so if he could use a computer to write a book, I could probably do it myself. And indeed, I did.

There are five main steps in the innovation-decision process:

1. Knowledge, which occurs when an individual or some other decision-making unit is exposed to the innovation's existence and gains some understanding of how it functions;

2. Persuasion, which occurs when the individual forms a favorable or unfavorable attitude toward the innovation;

3. Decision, which occurs when the individual engages in activities that lead to a choice to adopt or reject the innovation;

4. Implementation, which occurs when the individual puts the innovation into use; and

5. Confirmation, which occurs when the individual seeks reinforcement of an innovation decision already made (although he or she may reverse this decision if exposed later to different messages about the innovation).

Innovativeness

Innovativeness is the degree to which an individual or other unit of adoption is relatively early in adopting new ideas compared to other members of a social system. Innovativeness is often broken up into five adopter categories: innovators, the first to adopt; early adopters; early majority; late majority; and laggards. Some characteristics of the innovators and early adopters were mentioned previously. The late majority and laggards, in contrast, are low in socioeconomic status and are the most parochial and traditional in their perspectives.

Rate of Adoption

Rate of adoption is the relative speed with which an innovation is adopted by members of a social system. When the cumulative number of individuals adopting a new idea is plotted over time, the resulting distribution is an S-shaped curve (Figure 1). As stated previously, preventive innovations generally have a slower rate of adoption than do other new ideas whose relative advantage is more apparent.

Social System

A social system is a set of interrelated units that are engaged in joint problem solving to accomplish some goal. The structure of a social system affects an innovation's diffusion in several ways.

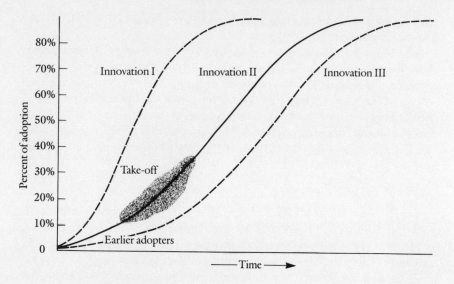

Figure 1. Diffusion of the idea of Beyond War.

Norms are the established behavior patterns of the members of a social system. They define the range of tolerable behavior and serve as a guide or standard. Norms can be a barrier to diffusion, such as religious or cultural norms that affect food habits.

Obviously, an innovation has little effect until it is put into use. Neither researchers nor officials in charge of diffusion campaigns have paid much attention to the consequences of the innovation for the social system; they have usually assumed that it will produce only beneficial results. Often, this has not been so.

Consequences are not unidimensional; they can be classified along at least three dimensions: desirable versus undesirable; direct versus indirect; and anticipated versus unanticipated.

Desirable consequences are the functional effects of an innovation on an individual or social system. Undesirable effects are dysfunctional. Understandably, people want to obtain the functional consequences (like increased effectiveness, efficiency, or convenience) and to avoid dysfunctional effects (such as disruptive changes in social values and institutions). Not all consequences are equally important. Every system has certain qualities that should not be destroyed if the welfare of the system is to be maintained: respect for human life and property, maintenance of individual dignity, and appreciation of others. Many other sociocultural elements can be modified, discontinued, or supplanted with little effect. Most innovations cause both desirable and undesirable consequences.

Consequences may also be classified into those that are direct or indirect. Direct consequences are the changes that occur in immediate response to an innovation. Indirect consequences are the changes that occur as a result of direct consequences.

The indirect consequences of an innovation are often unanticipated. Anticipated consequences are changes due to an innovation that are recognized and intended by the members of the social system. Unanticipated consequences are changes that are neither intended nor expected. A system is like a bowl of marbles; move any one of its elements and the positions of all the others are changed. Usually, the anticipated consequences are also direct and desirable; the unanticipated consequences are usually undesirable and direct.

Diffusion of Beyond War

The concept of beyond war is an ideal case for examination in the context of diffusion theory. Central tenets of the beyond war idea are that war is obsolete, as is nationalism, and that the world is one interconnected, interdependent global system. To date, the Beyond War organization has been relatively successful in launching the diffusion of this idea in the United States. The task ahead is to further diffuse this idea until a critical mass of adopters are reached. Then, diffusion theory predicts that the beyond war idea will continue to spread to a larger population under its own momentum.

However, certain features of this idea pose special difficulties for its diffusion. As stated previously, beyond war is an idea without a direct material referent. Further, beyond war is often perceived as a preventive-type innovation. One tends to focus on the antiwar aspect, at least in the early stages of awareness of this idea. Only a few studies in the diffusion tradition have looked at preventive innovations. Here the individual or organization adopts an innovation now (at time t1) in order to avoid the possibility that an unwanted event will occur at some future time (t2). Examples are smoking cessation to prevent heart disease, energy conservation, and the use of automobile seat belts to reduce the risk of injury. Two distinctive aspects of preventive innovations are that their expected beneficial effects are delayed in time, and difficult to assess because even without the precaution, the harm might never have occurred. A certain degree of uncertainty is always involved in the decision to adopt an innovation, because innovations represent new ideas. The uncertainty is especially great when the innovation is perceived as preventive in nature, as is beyond war.

Several other obstacles usually face the diffusion of prevention innovations.

1. The adoption of preventive innovations is seldom motivated by profit, either by the individuals adopting or by the organizations promoting such adoption (some exceptions are the sale of earthquake insurance, and exercise equipment

for improved cardiac health). Instead, there is usually much greater financial benefit for those opposing the behavior change. An example is the profits made from the sale of arms, cigarettes, and unhealthy foods.

2. The training, rewards, and professional values in many fields discourage prevention. For example, in the medical profession, much greater value has been placed on curing health problems than on preventing disease, even though a preventive approach is much less costly for society.

3. Many people feel that it is impossible for their individual preventive actions to make much difference in affecting important outcomes. Adoption of an innovation like beyond war requires a very high degree of efficacy, a belief that one's actions can determine one's future. I have observed personally that many of the individuals who have adopted the idea of beyond war (by becoming members and/or leaders in this organization) are highly efficacious.

Conclusions

A number of general lessons can be drawn from experiences and research on the diffusion of preventive innovations, which may be applicable to the diffusion of beyond war.

1. Interpersonal communication through peer networks is very important for the adoption of preventive innovations. One of the most important functions of the mass media in prevention campaigns is to activate near peer networks. Most individuals evaluate innovations and decide whether or not to adopt them on the basis of the subjective experiences of their friends and other peers.

2. Changing the context for preventive innovations can sometimes encourage their adoption if program officials capitalize on such change. An illustration is provided by the heightened public interest in personal health and fitness in the United States in recent years, which greatly assists preventive health efforts like smoking cessation and physical exercise.

3. Patriotic appeals by government leaders asking the public to adopt preventive innovations are seldom effective. An example of this point includes energy conservation in the United States. Exhortations from on high do not persuade individuals to change their behavior in most cases.

4. The perceived credibility of the communication source partly determines the success of a prevention diffusion campaign. For instance, electrical power companies and oil companies were not perceived as credible sources of energy conservation information by the American public in the 1970s.

5. Decentralized diffusion systems (with wide sharing of decision-making power) can be effective in diffusing preventive innovations when the changes recommended are of a relatively low-technology nature (as, for example, in the case of solar and other energy conservation measures).

6. The mass media can create awareness/knowledge of preventive innovations and convey useful information about the skills needed for behavior change, but they should not be expected to change strongly held attitudes and behavior.

The diffusion perspective has contributed significantly to the improved effectiveness of a variety of educational programs in past years. Preventive behavior is particularly difficult to bring about, and a considerable potential remains for improving diffusion campaigns for preventive innovations.

Similarity or Diversity?

Vladimir S. Ageev

Doctor of Psychological Sciences, Assistant Professor of Psychology at Moscow State University. Dr. Ageev is the author of the book *Psychology of Intergroup Relations* and a member of the Znanie (Knowledge) Society.

What arouses our interest and draws our attention — that which is new and unusual or that which is known, habitual to us? Who awakens our sympathy — those who are near and similar to us or those who are unlike us, different from us? I am afraid that to these two questions we must give diametrically opposing answers.

When it comes to material objects, what attracts us is novelty. When it comes to the social sphere, that is to say people or cultures, our sympathy is totally on the side of those who are the most like ourselves. These innocent observations have a direct bearing upon the problem of the survival of humankind in the nuclear era and upon the task of developing a new way of thinking "beyond war."

Diversity of Cultures

Our world is infinitely diverse, not only in climate, geography, and nature, but in human cultures. The variety in nature is fully parallel to that in culture, society, and history. Scientists have long debated the causes of such endless variety. Among the explanations that have been advanced, there are some rather curious ones. For example, according to one theory, culture is a mechanism of adaptation with the help of which humankind adapts to external conditions which are changing, often for the worse. When it comes to natural adaptation among animals, there is a tendency for the changes to be physical. But in the case of humankind, which remains physically unchanged, the changes are cultural — methods of economic activity, traditions, customs, beliefs, values, and modes of interpersonal relations. Thus an extraordinary variety of cultures exists on our planet. Now the question is, how do we relate to this diversity?

The history of human civilization is darkened by endless wars, conflicts, confrontation, and enmity of one country or people for another. Prejudice against those who are considered strange or simply different is an extremely widespread phenomena. And there is nothing simpler than to arouse mass enmity and hatred toward the real or imagined enemy. But even in quieter times, mistrust and rejection of anything "foreign" are typical phenomena. Parallel to this there is a prevalent belief in the superiority of one's own culture, way of life, ideas, and values.

To respect the values, to acknowledge and to sympathize with things "foreign" in general (according to some) is against human nature. Perhaps this is put too strongly, but we cannot avoid the fact that such attitudes are indeed widespread. And representatives of technologically well-developed countries are particularly prone to them. There are, of course, good reasons for all this. By dividing the world into "us" and "them," with all the consequences that derive from such a division, we simplify our lives to a considerable extent. We economize our efforts and are able to react without thought in many social situations which would otherwise require judgment, evaluation, and decision making.

Possibly the source of this fundamental division into "us" and "them" lies in the very distant past, when the first humans became aware of themselves as separate from their near but still animal-like ancestors, who became the first "them," the first "foreigners." Perhaps from those earliest times there has existed a faint connotation that "they" are not quite people, not entirely human. Evidence for this is that many peoples' and tribes' names (for example, Navajo) means nothing more than just "people." To overcome this tendency, this powerful psychological barrier, would be to accomplish a true revolution in consciousness. But is such a revolution possible in principle?

A Revolution in Consciousness

Cause for optimism in this respect lies in the fact that there are some such revolutions which have recently or are now occurring right before our eyes. In particular, one took place very recently in the Soviet Union and today we are witnessing the second one.

The first was ecological. Recently in the Soviet Union there has been a truly massive shift in the ecological consciousness of the people. Anthropocentrism in the relations between man and nature has been changed, if I may be permitted to create a new name, to "biocentrism." This change is not unlike that which took place much more slowly from geocentrism to heliocentrism. In recent years, people have become aware of the fact that the world, living nature, the planet Earth were not created merely to answer their own needs. Rather that the biological environment has its own independent value, humankind is part of that environment, and that we depend on nature entirely. We have finally reached the understanding that an approach which seeks to carelessly "use" the environment can be equally lethal for both — for environment and for humanity.

> *"Recently in the Soviet Union there has been a truly massive shift in the ecological consciousness of the people . . . People have become aware of the fact that the world, living nature, the planet Earth were not created merely to answer their own needs."*

This of course does not mean that we are entirely rid of indiscriminant hunters or that there are no longer cases of environmental pollution. What I am stressing is the change in consciousness. The main thing which has been learned by massive numbers of people is the (absolute) value of everything living, of our environment. And this has become immediately obvious in the conduct of people, the atmosphere of our cities, our economic activity. A good example is the refusal to go on with the project for the reversal of the course of the Siberian rivers from north to south. It is also interesting that in television and cinema cartoons for children, wild animals are no longer killed right and left. Even the Big Bad Wolf does not eat Little Red Riding Hood or the Seven Dwarfs, but only holds them for ransom.

The second revolution which also started recently in the Soviet Union is a mass change in attitudes toward alcoholic beverages. This is a very difficult change but one which is already showing hopeful results. I believe that life "beyond alcohol" just as life "beyond smoking," "beyond narcotics," beyond all other dangerous habits is fully possible. But for this as well as for life beyond war, a true revolution in consciousness is necessary.

It is easy to claim the new thinking is possible but much more difficult to formulate, and it is even more complicated to take concrete steps in order to bring about a revolution in mass political thinking. And still it is the role of scientists, it seems to me — taking into account all real circumstances and the nature of man and society — to point out realistic, feasible, and effective means to keep humankind away from a dead end.

The Search for Similarity and the Value of Diversity

In the United States, there is a widely accepted theory which says group conflicts result from incompatible goals, and competition for material, social, and other ends. Competing groups might then be united only by the highest and most general goals which represent extremely desirable outcomes for both sides, but which may be attained only through joint efforts. The following example is often used: Suppose that suddenly there appeared on Earth hostile beings from another planet — then Russians and Americans for sure would very quickly join together in order to fight off the common danger. The existing differences between them would immediately lose their meaning before the new and terrible threat, before which both Russians and Americans as inhabitants of planet Earth would find themselves in an equally difficult position and therefore would recognize each other as near and similar.

And so we return to the beginning of our discussion — in which we stated that mutual understanding, sympathy, and cooperation are possible only when existing conditions permit or enforce feelings of similarity.

It is of course essential to seek a common platform from which various people and states might identify themselves as closer and similar to each other. To acknowledge similarity indeed enhances a climate of trust and sympathy for each other. But it would be utopian to rely only on this path. Such examples (as in the case of people from another planet) are rather artificial. It is not simple to think up concrete, effective "higher goals." By the way, such higher goals as détente, disarmament, and abolition of war have not for some reason brought peoples closer together and eased confrontations between political and military blocks.

An alternative path is not to look for similarities but on the contrary to acknowledge and accept differences. And this is the revolution to which we referred earlier. The essence of this revolution is very simple — we must learn to respect those who are totally different from us, we must value that which is completely different from our ideas and culture.

Moreover, to learn to be proud of the cultural variety of our planet as a common attainment, let us imagine that a certain type of climate or landscape covered the entire world, that there remained only one or two types of animals. In my opinion, we would all lose by this. The losses would be great. The loss of variety would be irreparable. But whereas this loss of ecological variety is commonly recognized to be disastrous, there is a very different situation when we come to the cultural, social, and spiritual variety. Let me once again underline the new way. It consists of respect and recognition of other tribes and peoples not only those like us in some way, but those not like us, because they are different. And this consciousness should not fill us with fear, indignation, and dissatisfaction, but to the contrary, with interest, sympathy, and pride. This is totally atypical of the way things are today. This is why we need a radical change, a thorough restructuring of our consciousness.

One might object, saying that such a way seems to be utopian and unrealistic. But today's ecological ideas, and our understanding of the healthy way of life, are radically different and contradict that which was considered the one and only true way in the very recent past.

". . . the new way . . . consists of respect and recognition of other tribes and peoples because they are different."

But even more important, the first way, the way of looking for similarities at any cost is not without serious dangers. The desire to be alike is very great and this feeling of likeness begins to be exaggerated and even inventive. We begin to take that which we desire for real. And then there is also a danger that we begin to try to create likeness by force, or try to change others so that they would be more like ourselves. But this is against the entire trend of progressive political thought nowadays. So this attractive-at-first-sight path becomes less and less simple and its extreme forms potentially dangerous.

To the contrary, the second path is more desirable because at least it takes for granted the most important cultural and political reality, that is to say the fundamental differences in human society. In the first instance, the attainment of agreement always presupposes some similarity and the removal of some differences. In the ideal there is total similarity and total absence of differences. It is hardly necessary to prove that such a goal is completely unrealistic — not only unrealizable but undesirable, for political and moral reasons.

Interaction of Cultures and the Problem of Preserving Ethnocultural Autonomy

We have now arrived at one of the most difficult problems of modern times. How is it possible to preserve one's ethnocultural autonomy and uniqueness? In our times, which have created conditions of growing interdependence and ever-broadening international contacts, this problem is becoming even more acute, particularly for small and economically backward countries and peoples.

The new thinking cannot ignore this problem as well. The experience of the Soviet Union in nation building may well appear to be useful here. I will touch upon a very small aspect of this problem. In the Soviet Union we have many foreign students among whom there are a number from the developing countries of Africa, Asia, and Latin America. It is a well-known fact that people moving to different cultures face difficulties of adaptation and the necessity to give up many elements of their own background. But where is the optimal dividing line in this psychological restructuring? To what extent will the modification of behavior remain painless and not present a danger to the preservation of the person's ethnocultural identity? Too fast a rate of change and too radical a rejection of traditional cultural values signifies a loss of something very valuable and that is certainly not desirable. Furthermore this might create problems for the young specialists graduating from Soviet universities, as they return to their country of origin and are once more immersed in traditions which they have now rejected. So where is the optimal dividing line between the new and the old? That which is "ours" and that which is "foreign"? And how do direct contacts between people of different nationalities affect this line?

". . . up to very recent times, if something needed changing, it was not our side but the opposing side which should change. Psychologists, however . . . are well aware . . . that resolution can only begin from oneself."

As a member of the faculty of the University of Moscow, I often have to deal with such problems. Recently we carried out a number of investigations of this question: we tried to show the influence on traditional ethnocultural values caused by direct contacts by foreign students with their Soviet counterparts. We compared groups of Vietnamese students with groups of Vietnamese workers of the same age living in our country. The students know the Russian language and can freely communicate with the Soviet people; the workers do not know the Russian language and therefore their contacts with the local population are limited.

We discovered that the students to a considerably greater extent than the workers depart from the traditional norms and standards of behavior. Their personal manners seem to be freer, less constrained, and their behavior seems to be more modern, closer to that of the inhabitants of a large Soviet city. However, at the same time and in spite of our expectations, it was precisely these students and not the workers who turned out to be more oriented toward traditions and their own ethnocultural standards, thinking, and values. Also it is the students more than the workers who feel to a greater degree the differences between the Vietnamese and Soviet culture and who understand their own culture more fully and exactly.

The results of this research give us hope. They show that direct ethnic contacts on one hand modify the behavior of the minority and bring it closer to the behavior of the majority, but on the other hand such contacts help the minority to understand better and to become more conscious of, and to value more, the specifics of their own culture. That is to say we can state that normal, equal, and mutually profitable contacts between two cultures not only are safe from the point of view of destroying the autonomy of the weaker culture but, to the contrary, they permit them both to understand the "foreign" culture, and to become more aware of their own.

I would like to stress the last conclusion with as much emphasis as possible. For an individual or nation, a "foreign" person, nation, or culture becomes a special mirror, looking into which we understand ourselves better. Different cultures may interact among themselves quite successfully without any danger to the autonomy of each. Furthermore, for the purpose of attaining full consciousness of one's uniqueness, intercultural contact appears to be simply indispensable.

So in conclusion, it is all for the better to look for diversity. Whatever is similar between the US and the USSR dilutes tension and creates a good psychological base for détente and a climate of trust. However, from the point of view of a psychologist, this way does not seem to be the only one, and its possibilities are rather limited. Another, more radical way, could be more effective. This is the way of recognizing and accepting differences, that is to say, the acceptance of "them as they are." But, this way demands a full restructuring of our thinking, a true revolution in our consciousness. From a few examples of such revolutions occurring at the present time (although we might also give examples from the past), I have tried to show that in spite of complexities, the inertia of thinking, and conscious and unconscious opposition, such revolutions are in principle possible.

But they of course do not happen by themselves. What can one do in this connection, what practical steps can and must be taken? A major role in this connection could be played by all those who can influence public opinion — politicians, journalists, scientists, and personalities in the arts and culture. We must admit that until very recent times, if something needed changing, it was not our side but the opposing side which should change. Psychologists, however, who are involved in the resolution of interpersonal conflicts are well aware of the fact that this resolution can only begin from oneself. I would like to address this useful advice to all those who have it in their power to exercise influence on the consciousness of broad masses of our planet's population. When it comes to the restructuring in the spirit of peace, of life beyond war, we must start, of course, from ourselves.

New Thinking about Socialism

Fyodor M. Burlatsky

Professor of Philosophy, Vice President of the Soviet Political Science Association. Dr. Burlatsky is a prominent political scientist and observer on the staff of *Literaturnaya Gazeta* in Moscow. He is one of the foremost writers on the issue of new thinking in the Soviet Union.

Two Tendencies

The economic, social, and political reforms that have begun in the Soviet Union are based on new thinking about socialism, its goals and methods, its moral values. This new thinking, which is asserting itself with such force today, has deep roots in the past. In essence, it goes back to the sources of our revolution.

During the 1920s there already existed not only two points of view concerning socialism, but two distinct models which competed with each other in practice.

The first of these models was "war communism" (1918 through 1921). This model was developed under conditions of a cruel civil war. Yet it partially reflected uncertain, half-anarchistic ideas about socialism as a system in which all market mechanisms and money transactions could be abolished, where everything was done on command, where agricultural products were taken directly from the peasant — in a word, through violence.

The second model, the New Economic Policy (NEP) (1921 through 1928), was based on a market economy. Enterprises of various types — state, cooperative, private — competed, and the peasant freely sold his products on the market and bought, in exchange, manufactured goods. A

256

basic ingredient of the NEP was democracy, particularly in the workplace. There was also a struggle between different schools of thought in arts and culture.

This question of the two tendencies was thoroughly studied by Lenin in his speeches and articles at the time of transition from war communism to the NEP. One need only look at such articles by Lenin as "On Significance of Gold at Present and after the Complete Victory of Socialism," "On Cooperation," "How Should We Reorganize the WPIB (Workers-Peasants Inspection Board)," "Better Less, but Better," and others. I think, we should refer again and again to these 1920s documents which, by no accident, are termed "Lenin's political will."

Without going into the question of why and how the NEP was abolished, I will just say that the struggle between the two tendencies, the two approaches or ways of understanding socialism, has been continually in progress over the entire course of our history. Personalities in favor of continuing the NEP, such as N. Bukharin, Y. Rudzutak, A. Rikov, as well as S. Kirov, fell victim to this struggle. They were executed. Following World War II, it was N. Voznesensky who once again brought up the notion of normalization of the economy with the reintroduction of market forces and the principle of cost accounting in production (self-management of factories and collective farms or "kolkhozes"). He too was executed by Stalin.

After Stalin's death, it was N. S. Khrushchev who initiated a "thaw." He contributed enormously to de-Stalinization and set in motion a process of economic and political reforms. This process, however, ran up against hard resistance from conservatives in the country's leadership, as well as the inability of the average citizen to understand the nature of the reforms. Besides, many specific reforms were not properly thought out (for example, the division of the provincial and local party committees and even the Soviet administrative apparatus into two groups: industrial and agricultural). As a result, the reforms bogged down and the country's leadership was taken over by conservatives. This resulted in a slowing of the rate of economic development and in the rate of increase in living standards, and it caused a growing lag in the introduction of new technology.

These problems became particularly acute in the 1970s as a new technological revolution was sweeping the world. We faced a threat of stagnation, social tensions, and even political crisis.

The Beginning of Reform

The April 1985 Plenum of the Central Committee of the Communist Party of the Soviet Union brought to the leadership of the party and the country new forces, headed by M. S. Gorbachev. This move started an intense struggle for revolutionary reform.

International Arena

New thinking and new policy in the international arena are closely bound with problems of war and peace. It seems obvious to everybody that a world nuclear war would not only destroy modern civilization, but all human existence as well. For many decades before and after World War II, both Marxists and anti-Marxists proceeded from the concept that opposition of these two world systems would inevitably lead to a military clash between them, or at least to military competition and confrontation. This has now become a particularly dangerous position from a political point of view. Nuclear weapons have made it clear that this approach is obsolete and that it is time to denounce "cold war" logic.

> *"The quintessential nature of glasnost is that, with its help, an independent public opinion may be born, which may increasingly become a permanent and effective element of our political system."*

To be fair, it is necessary to note that political thought has often been ahead of philosophical thought. Let's recall that as early as the 20th Congress of the Communist Party of the Soviet Union in 1956, the most essential conclusion was stated: War is not predestined or inevitable. The contradictions between socialism and capitalism should be resolved on the basis of peaceful coexistence, economic competition, and ideological struggle.

Thirty years later, it was clear that such an approach was the best means to achieve practical solutions for today's pressing problems of disarmament, as well as for the settlement of regional conflicts in the Middle East, in and around Nicaragua, and in Afghanistan.

Domestic Arena

The intense struggle for revolutionary reform started in April 1985 has not been limited to just the international sphere. On the contrary, it has brought profound forces to bear within the Soviet Union. It has found a firm base of support in new attitudes towards socialism, an orientation toward its humanistic concerns, towards free democratic relationships in economics, as well as in social life and in culture.

The first symptom of this process was "glasnost" (openness). This process is not limited solely to informing society about the activities of the organs of power, nor is it just a demand for truth about all the social problems of our society. It calls for honest information about other countries in the world, about their accomplishments and problems. It provides the right to be critical in the press and television, in every collective, in the party, in the trade unions, and in cooperative organizations. The quintessential nature of glasnost is that, with its help, an independent public opinion may be born, which may increasingly become a permanent and effective element of our political system.

For example: The Soviet government not too long ago decided to reverse the course of Siberian rivers in order to irrigate the Central Asian desert. Such a decision, however, met sharp resistance from Soviet scientists and writers, such as S. Zalygin, V. Rasputin, and V. Astafiev. The press got involved, and the government changed its decision.

Now, thanks to glasnost, the public is able to discuss problems involving our reforms broadly and in depth and to compare alternative solutions. It criticizes bureaucracy, writes of such social diseases as alcoholism, juvenile delinquency, narcotics, and prostitution. Examples include the works *A Sad Detective* by B. Astafiev, *Fire* by V. Rasputin, and *The Executioner's Block* by C. Aitmatov. These novels, and the movie *Repentence* by T. Abuladze deal with acute and deep problems of alcohol abuse, destruction of religion, morality, and the creation of a personality cult within our society.

In my own recently produced television drama "Two Points of View from the Same Office," I tried to show the struggle of opinions within the party itself. I showed two senior party figures, one who supports reform, the other who is in favor of former leadership methods. And in the spring of this year, in my article "Two Points of View on International Journalism" (published in *Sovietskaya Kultura*), I posited the question of correctness of information on the West and the entire contemporary world. That is to say, about the need to develop an informed society in the Soviet Union.

The Essence of 'Perestroika'

So what is the essence of the "perestroika" (structural transformation) which has taken hold of our society? It consists of the task of creating an effective, self-managing economic system, where plans are firmly based on market forces. Also, it seeks to open the road for the introduction of the technological revolution in all spheres of activity — in the economy and its administration, in culture and the mass media. It consists of a qualitative lifting of our people's standard of living to give them enough to eat, a good place to live, and modern industrial consumer goods. Perestroika means that all aspects of our political life must be democratized — our electoral system, our judicial processes, our guarantees of basic human rights. In a word, perestroika must take us into a new socialist society, flourishing, democratic, dynamic, showing rapid progress.

Is it possible to develop self-management and democracy under a one-party system? This is a question one often hears in the West. Yes, it is possible, if democracy is developed within the party itself. The Communist Party of the Soviet Union (CPSU) consists of 20 million people. The victory within the party of the idea of revolutionary reform is the prerequisite for acceptance of the new model of socialism in our society.

Such a sharp turn in the area of politics requires a reevaluation of many stagnant dogmas and stereotypes in our philosophy, in our attitudes towards socialism.

"Perestroika means that all aspects of our political life must be democratized — our electoral system, our judicial processes, our guarantees of basic human rights."

The year 1987 was crucial from the point of view of our attitude toward development programs. In January, the Plenum of the Central Committee set the course for the democratization of the country. Then in June, it set forth a program for the radical reform of our economy. There will be three phases to this economic reform: attaining elementary order and discipline in the economy and in all spheres of its administration; changing working conditions in our agricultural economy and public services, relying on intensive use of family, individual initiative, and volunteer cooperatives; and revamping administrative structures throughout all of industry, based on self-management, self-financing, and cost-accounting practices.

Dynamism and Contradictions

Dynamism has been unleashed in our society by glasnost and perestroika. Before continuing to discuss additional aspects of the revolutionary reforms underway, it is important to understand the context of "contradictions," (i.e. clashes or conflicting approaches) within socialism.

In the 1930s, the significance of contradictions under socialism was exaggerated. Erroneous theoretical political conclusions were even reached, such as the notion that along with the development of a socialist society, the class struggle inevitably intensifies. Also, in China, the concept of "aggravation of contradictions within the nation" became a basis for the devastating "Cultural Revolution." Thus, dramatic excesses evolved in practice.

On the other hand, it would not be an exaggeration to say that over the last twenty to thirty years the contradictions within socialism have been suppressed in Soviet political theory, especially by use of propaganda. Contradictions are essential for the development of socialism, as for the development of any system in the modern world. Conservative thinking tries to deny this fact. The result is stagnation.

In other words, contradictions were viewed as trash which should be discarded as soon as possible or, in a word, "eliminated." Such "elimination" was often reduced to silencing the real problems emerging in our society.

Instead, we need a more profound analysis of the sources of crisis and social tensions in socialist countries, especially those which are in a transitional stage from capitalism to socialism, or in such countries where subjectivism in the policies of the leadership are becoming a factor in slowing down the country's development. It is worthwhile to seek a theoretical interpretation for past crises in a number of socialist countries: Hungary in 1956, Czechoslovakia in 1968, Poland at the end of the 1970s, and the "cultural revolution" in China in the 1960s.

"To assume that socialism is a conflictless society having neither competition nor struggle is not only incorrect, but dangerous."

The main issue when dealing with contradictions in socialism is the realization that they are the most important mechanism of development, an internal engine that supplies dynamics and competitiveness to society. It is an elementary truth for a Marxist that the construction of socialism means overcoming class antagonisms and forming a society of friendly working people of all classes. However, any attempt to disregard contradictions under socialism and any refusal to use them in the interest of developing a flexible policy would mean the stagnation of society. It would also mean weakening the initiative of scientific and technological progress. To assume that socialism is a conflictless society having neither competition nor struggle is not only incorrect, but dangerous. It can result in serious mistakes in economic and social policy. It is perfectly evident that serious transformations in socialistic society are impossible without reforms.

A practical conclusion follows that pluralism, competitiveness, and honest struggle are important stimuli of the acceleration of our development. Workers, peasants, writers, actors, artists, doctors, and waiters are all competing in the process of creating material and spiritual values and examples of the highest quality work. And who are the judges? They are the readers, viewers, and consumers of these values, in short, the people. And people judge in the simplest way: They either read or do not read a book; they go or do not go to a play, a movie, or an exhibit; they either buy or do not buy goods; they go or do not go to a particular restaurant, and so on. And there should not be any administrative or authoritative privileges for those who create these values, regardless of their positions and titles. There should be no artificially created bottlenecks in order to enforce a product upon people. The game should be played honestly with the public.

This is how Lenin thought in the 1920s when competitiveness was encouraged in the economy, culture, literature, and the arts. None of these areas had the authority or possibility to "liquidate" its opponents, to establish a monopoly. Everybody faced the necessity to work hard, to learn, and to develop their talents.

Revolutionary Reforms

So competitiveness and contention are very much a part of a healthy socialist system. In addition to aspects already discussed, further reforms are essential and are underway. This will require reexamining public property in order to put the actual producer — worker, peasant, working intellectual — under conditions which will stimulate high-quality labor, a deep interest in using the latest achievements of science, machinery, and technology, and further improvement of professional skills. The point is we need a more consistent application of the core principle of social justice that rules our society: "From everyone according to his ability, to everyone according to his work."

Therefore, it is not accidental that the question of socialist property has now assumed an important place in our theory and practice. An idea of some lower and higher forms of property has been dropped. Underestimation of the importance of private (cooperative) and other forms of corporate and group property, and of the possibilities of using individual family contracts on a broad scale are being overcome. The new approach is being manifested in many recent resolutions and legislative procedures.

The use of family contracts in China has provided for a rapid increase in agricultural output and in the standard of living. The development of individual forms of labor and cooperatives in towns and villages may have a significant impact.

The Question of Democracy

Socialism cannot exist without consistent development of democracy. Perhaps only now do we understand the importance of this principle for the acceleration of our socioeconomic development and for use of the latest achievements of the technological revolution for the entire spiritual and moral renovation of society.

Some resolutions planned by the party are not being carried out as quickly as they should be. Management who think conservatively and lack the democratic and legal substantiation of the reforms appear to be "spinning their wheels" in resistance to change. Another reason for slowness of reforms is passive attitudes on the part of the people. As more and more individuals participate, public opinion in turn will become one of the most significant vehicles of the political system, part of decision making, and a control for the prompt and steady fulfillment of goals. This will take place through the election of individuals to office, public debate, and constructive criticism of party and enterprise leadership.

". . . public opinion in turn will become one of the most significant vehicles of the political system, part of the decision making . . ."

Procedures for electing leaders of enterprises and collective farms are being developed. Changes are also being introduced into our political election system. For instance, the nomination of several candidates is becoming a rule for the election of top party organs. Similar practices are being introduced into the election system of our representative organs, the "soviets," and potentially into the election of the Supreme Soviets of national republics and our Soviet parliament, the Supreme Soviet of the USSR.

Having said that, the nomination of several candidates for the same position at elections to the soviets creates some problems since all the candidates represent a united block of communists and nonparty members. In such a case, emphasis will not be on the comparison of their programs, but rather on the candidates' personal qualities.

In short, democracy is one of the most important values for every person: the right and opportunity to participate in the administration of state and social affairs guaranteeing protection of one's legitimate interests. Finally, we need democratization for overcoming red tape, corruption, bribery, and other abuses which are unfortunately still taking place in our society.

Socialism and Humanism

New thinking and contemporary social practices have as an ultimate goal the stimulation of a new approach to understanding socialism as a whole, its humanity, and its moral-ethical criteria. As General Secretary M. S. Gorbachev said in one of his presentations: "No system has the right to exist unless it properly serves a human being."

It is common knowledge that the gains of modern socialism have been accompanied by negative phenomena. Some of these were directed at the people it was serving. One need not mention the development of phenomena such as a personality cult, unjustified repression, and an exaggerated role of violence, which have badly damaged socialism and its image in the eyes of world public opinion.

No one should be frightened by the concept of ethical socialism as an important component of scientific socialism. Socialism has a simple and obvious goal: the welfare and culture of a working person. All the rest — for example, the nationalization of industry — are a means for realization of this goal. Engels, after Marx's death, once made the penetrating remark that if Marx had the opportunity to know some of his followers, he would retort: "I am not a Marxist."

"Engels, after Marx's death, once made the penetrating remark that if Marx had the opportunity to know some of his followers, he would retort: 'I am not a Marxist.'"

Marx and Engels not only did not ignore the ethical principles of socialism, but on the contrary strongly criticized those pseudo-communists who denied culture and civilization. This is what Marx wrote about brutal, "barracks"-type communism, a "morbid shadow" of truly scientific communism:

> This communism, denying everywhere the personality of a human being, is only a consistent expression of private property . . . Any man with private property, as such, experiences, at least toward a wealthier man with private property, envy and thirst for parity . . . Brutal communism, proceeding from an idea of some minimum for everybody, is an implementation of this envy and parity. This form of communism is limited. One can see that this manner of liquidating private property is not a true assimilation. It groundlessly denies the whole realm of culture and civilization and signifies the return to the unnatural simplicity of a poor and crude man who did not rise above or understand the concept of private property.

These are some of the trends of transformation that are vigorously unfolding in our country.

Questions of Westerners

Representatives of the Western world quite often ask questions and express their doubts about the efficiency of our changes. The most frequent question is: What is the guarantee that the transformation process in the Soviet Union is irreversible? Will it not happen again, as in the early 1960s, when new serious political and economical reforms began but produced no results?

This is an important question. The leaders of our country and our party must not only think about this question, but also do whatever is possible to carry out the transformation at all levels. There are at least two factors pointing towards the guarantee of success in our reforms.

The first is the political will of our party and its leadership who have seriously embarked on restructuring. There is no turning back. We understand and are deeply convinced that there is no other road available. We cannot impede this path. There is no other alternative for accelerating the development of our country than by using the modern achievements of the technological revolution — none.

Another perhaps even more important point of guarantee of transformation will be the growing involvement of all our people, of every Soviet citizen in this process. Of course, people do not get involved only because appropriate publicity and encouragement are provided. When practical results are observed, their conviction in the necessity of transformation strengthens. The development of cooperatives and their operation on a self-supporting basis, together with the emergence of new standards of labor and life, are leverages used in involving every person in the transformation, resulting in efficiency and professionalism. In a word, democratization is, in the final analysis, the best guarantee of the success of our revolutionary cause.

The second question often asked by foreigners is: Where is the resistance to the transformation coming from? They look for the sources of resistance in different layers of society, in social groups, especially in spheres of management termed bureaucracy in the West. In fact, resistance has not emerged from a certain group or organized opposition. There is no political opposition to the transformation in our country. The major opponent of perestroika is tradition, traditionalism, conservative thinking, and the habits and behavioral stereotypes of both the bosses and the masses.

Therefore, the resistance exists on a "vertical" rather than a "horizontal" plane. On all levels of society we meet people who find themselves involved with great enthusiasm in transformation. Undoubtedly, they constitute the majority and are the vast social basis of our revolutionary transformations. But at the same time, on all levels we find people who have doubts about transformation, and the necessity of its deep, radical structural changes. It is these latter individuals who fear the loss of their positions and material privileges.

Sometimes the third question we are asked by Westerners is whether today's transformations mean some stepping back from socialism and using capitalist methods. Such questions can be explained either by their misunderstanding or dogmatic interpretation of socialism, or by their failure to understand the true nature of it.

I would remind everybody that our transformation is bound in the slogan: "More socialism!" For example, "more socialism" means a proper use of commodity-money relations. It is a serious misconception that commodity relations originate from capitalism. It is a known fact that commodities and money existed long before the emergence of capitalism. They existed both under slave-owning and feudal systems. These relations cannot disappear under socialism. Money remains a basic measurement of expense and exchange. In other words, we come back to the Leninist interpretation where the socialist plan goes side-by-side with the market-place; where democratization represents the most essential and important aspect of socialism.

Finally, we are asked about the relationship between the internal reforms and foreign policy of the Soviet Union. Some claim that our efforts in the area of disarmament can be explained by the economic difficulties that exist in our country and by an exclusive intention to reduce the military budget for the sake of development of a civilian industry. This is your target, they tell us. It is true that there is a tie between our domestic and international policies. But it is not governed by those motives.

Of course, we want to reduce our military budget. Understandably, we want to employ the reserved funds for peaceful branches of our economy. But don't other countries, including the leading Western powers, need the same thing? This is a common problem.

New thinking about the question of global survival, including our own, is what governs the policy of the Soviet Union in the world arena: This is what motivates us in the struggle for disarmament, for the gradual elimination of nuclear weapons, for banning the biological and chemical weapons, and the limitation of conventional weapons,

Besides, the release of resources now spent by mankind for military purposes will open broad possibilities for providing assistance to developing countries. This would greatly contribute to the resolution of the North-South problem and other current global problems.

April 1987 meeting, Ben Lomond, California.

Bottom row, left to right: Alexander Nikitin, Ross Lavroff, Martin Hellman, Elena Loshchenkova, Anatoly Gromyko, Kenneth Boulding, Sergei Kapitza.

Second row: William Busse, Linn Sennott, Harold Sandler, John Richardson, Steven Kull.

Third row: Theodore Taylor, Donald Fitton, Andrei Melville, William McGlashan, Jerome Frank, Richard Lagerstrom, Craig Barnes.

Writing This Book

Elena Loshchenkova

Physicist, Senior Research Staff of the Space Research Institute, Soviet
Academy of Sciences, Moscow. Dr. Loshchenkova is Executive Secretary
of the Committee of Soviet Scientists for Peace against the Nuclear
Threat.

Craig S. Barnes

Director, Editorial Board, Beyond War Foundation, Palo Alto, California.
Attorney at Law. A political analyst, essayist, and columnist since 1971,
Mr. Barnes has published numerous articles and commentaries in newspa-
pers and magazines.

*The process of creating this book began in October 1985 following months of
concept discussions, by telex and in face-to-face meetings. These were followed by far-flung contacts with prospective authors to discuss the format of
the book and the underlying principles which would guide the text. When
manuscripts began to come in, there were concept discussions with nearly
all of the authors, both in the USSR and the US. Discussions were followed
by revisions, more discussions with the authors, and more revisions, all of
which were tracked through two languages. During the last year of the
work, there were a total of eight weeks of face-to-face discussions between
Soviet and American editors and authors. By the end of the preparation,
during one seventeen-day session in Moscow, counting the two languages,
there were sixty manuscripts in circulation being revised, translated, revised, and retranslated in an ongoing process until consensus was reached
on final content.*

Toward the close of the work on this project, some of the Soviet
and American editors were sitting together, asking how it was that

we had gotten this far. Why had this project succeeded when so many others had ended on the rocks? What was different?

The project started simply enough, when some representatives from Beyond War* came to a committee of Soviet scientists† to see if we could agree on principles which could move our two nations beyond war. The Soviet reply was, more or less, that statements of principle are easy, how could we take some action?

One thing led to another, and at first we planned to do a conference together, asking scientists from all over the world to participate. Later, a book was proposed, and working on that book has been the experience of a lifetime for all of us.

There have been some difficult times. We have had passionate conversations about fear, and about military power and wars of liberation, and popular participation in government. And we have not yet resolved all those differences. So we didn't get to where we are because we solved all our disagreements.

That was probably the first thing we learned. We could go forward and work together for a common goal even if we didn't agree on many things. It is as if we learned by experience the point about diversity that is made by some of the writers in this book. Soviets and Americans come to the table bringing with them totally different backgrounds, vocabularies, and national ideologies. We had to learn that we would have to be not only tolerant of each other, but sensitive in the best sense to what makes the other person uncomfortable, nervous, or even wary of the opinion of his peers. And this is a problem which definitely goes both ways. *We had to imagine what it would be like to live in the other culture and have the career obstacles, the public attitude, and the governmental leader-*

---

* Beyond War is a non-partisan educational movement whose goal is to bring about an end to war as a means of resolving conflict. It is comprised of hundreds of full-time and thousands of part-time volunteers in the United States and abroad. The volunteers are from all walks of life, including business, the professions, agriculture, the arts, as well as the scientific and academic communities. The Beyond War National Office, located in Palo Alto, California, serves as a communication and resource center for the activities of the movement.

† The Committee of Soviet Scientists for Peace against the Nuclear Threat is a nongovernmental group of professionals, including physicists, chemists, biologists, and political scientists and other scholars who do most of their work in the area of arms control and disarmament. The Chairman of the Committee is Academician Evgeni Velikhov, and the three deputy chairmen, who were very helpful in supporting this project are Academician Roald Sagdeev, Prof. Andrei Kokoshin, and Prof. Sergei Kapitza. The latter is a contributor to this volume.

ship of the other side. And doing that made a difference in how we treated each other.

Sometimes we had the experience of being absolutely sure of what we knew and thinking that someone on the other side was completely wrong. But even when one person thought another might have the most profound misperception, we found we had to stay open to the fact that each of us has only a narrow, highly conditioned frame of reference through which we view the world. We are all novices when it comes to building a world beyond war. So we had to stay open to the possibility that it could be we, not they, who were misperceiving.

That attitude made a difference. We argued and we came to road blocks. And in the end we asked each other, how was it that we got around those road blocks? The answer seemed to be that different people with a common goal can find a way to work irrespective of all the differences in background and difficulties in communication.

The goal was survival. But survival doesn't convey all the right meaning. It isn't just the negative threat of extinction which drove us. There was a sort of inextinguishable desire to describe something about the future which was new and good. We were pulled by that, and pushed, at the same time, by the nuclear imperative.

And then, toward the end, we found ourselves on a slippery slope of a new kind. We could end up with a lofty statement about war, and the obsolescence of war, and the whole thing could be at such a high level of principle and abstraction that it could have practically no meaning. We didn't need just another statement of principle. There had to be an application of the principle. If, as the writers of the papers had convincingly persuaded us, a nuclear war is inevitable on our present course, then where does change begin? What is the action?

We had successfully avoided trying to identify all the bad American movies and Soviet posters, and we stayed away from the historical analyses of who started what in 1917, 1939, 1950, 1962, and 1979. But we had also to make clear that general statements of principle about ending war are not sufficient. The superpower relationship, and the arms buildup, and dependence upon force worldwide must be stopped if civilization is to survive. We are not only talking about the future. There are present discrepancies. By drawing attention to them it is our hope that they can be attended and eliminated.

So that had to be said, too. But it had to be said in a way which could be heard; a way that would not so alienate that it would fall on deaf ears. We were engaged constantly in an effort to discover a vocabulary that could be understood in common rather than emphasizing things that separate us.

In English, for example, there is a word "constituency" which does not exist in Russian. In Russian there is a word "mechanism" which has no English equivalent. Both words are important in the way they are used in articles in this book. How could it be that something of so much importance to one side did not even have a word to describe it in the other? We discovered that when they did not have our word it would be very easy to think of that as a defect, but that when we did not have their word, it could seem that their word was really not very important. So, again, we lived the experience of the articles in the book, this time on images of the enemy.

In presenting the reader with the results of this effort, we understand its limitations. On the one hand, many concepts and phenomena of contemporary life are not examined. For example, we have not explicitly mentioned the American military-industrial complex or its Soviet counterpart. On the other hand, a multi-authored volume necessarily leads to some repetition. While aware of these limitations, we hope the reader will find that the advantages of avoiding blame and of drawing on the wisdom of many viewpoints outweigh these limitations.

The experience of doing the project was a validation of the things that the authors were telling us should be true. A common goal, basic goodwill, openness of mind, and a willingness to hear the other person out, were the things that brought the book to completion. For all of us it was a real exercise in new thinking.

In the process of working with each other, we had a fantastic cross-cultural experience. We became colleagues, genuinely able to agree and disagree, forcefully, but also kindly and with humor. We became even more than friends.

References

"Preface: A Message to the Scientific Community"

1. International Institute for Environment and Development and World Resources Institute, *World Resources 1986* (New York: Basic Books, 1986).

2 I. T. Frolov, ed., *The Earth and Mankind: Global Problems*, in Russian (Moscow: MYSL, 1985).

3. Richard Rhodes, *The Making of the Atomic Bomb* (New York: Simon and Schuster, 1986).

Editors, "The Challenge to Change"

1. Theodore B. Taylor, "Proliferation of Nuclear Weapons." In this Challenge to Change section, references refer to articles appearing in this book.

2. Paul Bracken, "Instabilities in the Control of Nuclear Forces."

3. Boris V. Raushenbakh, "Computer War."

4. Linn I. Sennott, "Overlapping False Alarms: Reason for Concern?"

5. Sennott.

6. Alan Borning, "Computer System Reliability and Nuclear War."

7. Marianne Frankenhaeuser, "To Err Is Human: Nuclear War by Mistake?"

8. Einar Kringlen, "The Myth of Rationality in Situations of Crisis."

9. Frankenhaeuser, and Natalia P. Bekhtereva, "Dangers and Opportunities for Change from a Physiologist's Point of View."

10. Kringlen.

11. Martin E. Hellman, "Nuclear War: Inevitable or Preventable?"

12. Anatoly A. Gromyko, "Security for All in the Nuclear Age."

13. John M. Richardson, Jr., "Messages from Global Modeling about an Interdependent World."

14. Beyond War, Richard T. Roney, ed., "Beyond War."

15. Soviet cosmonaut Yuri Gagarin. (Also see "Beyond War" article in this book for a complete quote.)

16. Apollo 9 astronaut Russell Schweickart. (Also see "Beyond War" article in this book for a complete quote.)

17. Richardson, and Beyond War.

18. Ales Adamovich, "Problems with the New Way of Thinking," and Gromyko.

19. Andrei V. Kortunov, "Realism and Morality in Politics."

20. Adamovich.

21. Jerome D. Frank and Andrei Y. Melville, "The Image of the Enemy and the Process of Change."

22. Frank and Melville.

23. Beyond War.

24. Kortunov.

25. Kenneth E. Boulding, "Moving from Unstable to Stable Peace."

26. Vladimir S. Ageev, "Similarity or Diversity?"

27. Fyodor M. Burlatsky, "New Thinking about Socialism," and Gromyko.

28. Robert Axelrod, "The Evolution of Cooperation."

29. Beyond War.

30. Richardson.

31. Beyond War.

32. Alexander I. Nikitin, "The Concept of Universal Security: A Revolution in Thinking and Policy in the Nuclear Age."

33. Nikitin.

34. Alexander I. Belchuk, "Restructuring of Soviet Society."

35. Kortunov.

36. Gromyko.

37. Stanislav K. Roshchin and Tatiana S. Kabachenko, "Young People and Nuclear War."

38. Everett M. Rogers, "Diffusion of the Idea of Beyond War."

39. Burlatsky.

40. Rogers.

41. Burlatsky and Belchuk.

42. Burlatsky and Belchuk.

43. Burlatsky and Belchuk.

44. Rogers.

45. Sidney Drell, "The Impact of a US Public Constituency on Arms Control."

46. Drell, Rogers, Burlatsky, Belchuk, Adamovich.

47. Bekhtereva.

48. Bekhtereva.

49. Rogers.

50. Bekhtereva.

51. Bekhtereva.

52. Boulding.

53. Beyond War.

54. Kortunov.

55. Bekhtereva.

56. Rogers.

57. Frank and Melville.

58. Roshchin and Kabachenko.

59. Adamovich and Gromyko.

60. Ageev and Burlatsky.

61. Andrei Y. Melville, "Nuclear Revolution and the New Way of Thinking."
62. Gromyko and Nikitin.
63. Steven Kull, "Nuclear Reality: Resistance and Adaptation."
64. Zamoshkin, "Nuclear Disarmament: Ideal and Reality."
65. Adamovich and Beyond War.
66. Drell.
67. Belchuk.

Inevitability: Collision Course with Disaster

Alan Borning, "Computer System Reliability and Nuclear War"

1. Barry Goldwater and Gary Hart, *Recent False Alerts from the Nation's Missile Attack Warning System,* Report to the Committee on Armed Services, United States Senate (Washington, D.C.: Government Printing Office, 1980).

2. William M. Arkin, "Nuclear Weapon Command, Control, and Communications," in *World Armaments and Disarmament: SIPRI Yearbook 1984* (London and Philadelphia: Taylor & Francis, 1984), pp. 455–516.

3. Bruce G. Blair, *Strategic Command and Control* (Washington, D.C.: Brookings Institution, 1985).

4. Paul Bracken, *The Command and Control of Nuclear Force* (New Haven: Yale University Press, 1983).

5. W. Richards Adrion, Martha A. Branstad, and John C. Cherniavsky, "Validation, Verification, and Testing of Computer Software," *ACM Computing Surveys,* Vol. 14 No. 2 (June 1982), pp. 159–192.

6. N. G. Leveson, "Software Safety: Why, What, and How," *ACM Computing Surveys,* Vol. 18 No. 2 (June 1986), pp. 125–163.

7. Charles C. Perrow, *Normal Accidents: Living with High Risk Technologies* (New York: Basic Books, 1984).

8. Lloyd J. Dumas, "Human Fallibility and Weapons," *Bulletin of the Atomic Scientists,* Vol. 36 No. 9 (November 1980), pp. 15–20.

9. David L. Parnas, "Software Aspects of Strategic Defense Systems," *American Scientist,* Vol. 73 No. 5 (September–October, 1985), pp. 432–440.

Linn I. Sennott, "Overlapping False Alarms: Reason for Concern?"

1. The Center for Defense Information, "Accidental Nuclear War: A Rising Risk?" *The Defense Monitor,* Vol. 15 No. 7 (1986).

2. Linn I. Sennott, "Distributions Arising in False Alarm Analysis of Defense Surveillance Systems," conference on The Risk of Accidental Nuclear War, Vancouver, May 26–30, 1986. (Conference proceedings to appear 1988.)

3. Michael Wallace, Brian Crissey, and Linn Sennott, "Accidental Nuclear War: A Risk Assessment," *J. Peace Research,* Vol. 23 No. 1 (1986), pp. 9–27.

4. D. McLane, "North American Security Rests on NORAD Mission," *Defense Systems Review,* January 1984.

5. John Steinbruner, "Nuclear Decapitation," *Foreign Policy,* Vol. 45 (Winter 1981–1982), pp. 16–18.

6. Bruce G. Blair and Robert McNamara, "Science and the Citizen," *Scientific American,* Vol. 255 No. 4 (October 1986), pp. 74, 76.

7. Dusko Doder, "Kremlin Defense Official Warns of Policy Shift to Quicken Nuclear Response," *Washington Post,* July 13, 1982, p. A–1a.

Boris V. Raushenbakh, "Computer War"

1. Gene F. Franklin, J. David Powell, and Abbas Emami-Naeini, *Feedback Control of Dynamic Systems* (Reading, Massachusetts: Addison-Wesley, 1986).

Marianne Frankenhaeuser, "To Err Is Human: Nuclear War by Mistake?"

1. David A. Hamburg, "The World Transformed: Critical Issues in Contemporary Human Adaptation," *Mack Lipkin Man and Nature Lectures* (New York: American Museum of Natural History, 1987).

2. Lloyd J. Dumas, "Human Fallibility and Weapons," *Bulletin of the Atomic Scientists,* Vol. 36 No. 9 (November 1980), pp. 15–20.

3. Marianne Frankenhaeuser and Gunn Johansson, "On the Psycho-Physiological Consequences of Understimulation and Overstimulation," in L. Levi, ed., *Society, Stress and Disease, Vol. IV: Working Life* (London and New York: Oxford University Press, 1981) pp. 82–89.

4. Donald E. Broadbent, *Decision and Stress* (London and New York: Academic Press, 1971).

5. Marianne Frankenhaeuser, "To Err Is Human — Psychological and Biological Aspects of Human Functioning," in *Nuclear War by Mistake — Inevitable or Preventable?* Report from an International Conference in Stockholm, February 15-16, 1985.

6. Irving Janis, *Victims of Groupthink* (Boston: Houghton Mifflin, 1972).

Einar Kringlen, "The Myth of Rationality in Situations of Crisis"

1. Irving Janis, *Victims of Groupthink* (Boston: Houghton Mifflin, 1972).

2. I. Longstreth and H. Scoville, Transcript of Robert McNamara Press Briefing, at the Arms Control Association, Washington, D.C., September 14, 1983.

3. "Nuclear Arms Reduction Proposals," Hearings before the Committee on Foreign Relations, US Senate, 97th Congress, Second Session, April–May, 1982 (Washington, D.C.: Government Printing Office, 1982).

4. Marvin R. Burt, Mark M. Biegel, Yukio Carnes, and Edward C. Farley, *World-wide Survey of Nonmedical Drug Use and Alcohol Use among Military Personnel: 1980, Final Report* (Bethesda, Maryland: Burt Assoc., Inc., Contract No. MDA 903-79-C-0667, November 14, 1980).

5. Hearings on Military Construction, Appropriations for 1979, House Committee on Appropriations, Subcommittee on Military Construction, 95th Congress of the US, Second Session (Washington, D.C.: Government Printing Office, 1978).

Stanislav K. Roshchin and Tatiana S. Kabachenko, "Young People and Nuclear War"

1. Milton Schwebel, ed., *Behavioral Science and Human Survival* (Palo Alto, California: Behavioral Science Press, 1965).

2. Sibylle K. Escalona, "Children and the Threat of Nuclear War," in Schwebel.

3. John E. Mack, "But What about the Russians?" *Harvard Magazine,* Vol. 84 No. 4 (March–April, 1982), pp. 21–24, 53–54.

4. John E. Mack, "The Perception of U.S.-Soviet Intentions and Other Psychological Dimensions of the Nuclear Arms Race," *American Journal of Orthopsychiatry,* Vol. 52 No. 4 (1982), pp. 590–599.

5. *Newsweek,* October 11, 1982.

Theodore B. Taylor, "Proliferation of Nuclear Weapons"

1. J. Carson Mark, Theodore Taylor, Eugene Eyster, William Maraman, and Jacob Wechsler, "Can Terrorists Build Nuclear Weapons?" in Paul Leventhal and Yonah Alexander, eds., *Preventing Nuclear Terrorism,* Report of the International Task Force on Prevention of Nuclear Terrorism (Lexington, Massachusetts: Lexington Books, 1987), pp. 55–66.

2. David Albright, "Civilian Inventories of Plutonium and Highly Enriched Uranium," in Leventhal and Alexander, pp. 263–297.

3. John R. Lamarsh, "Dedicated Facilities for the Production of Nuclear Weapons in Small and/or Developing Nations," Appendix VI-A, in *Nuclear Proliferation and Safeguards, Appendix Volume II, Part Two,* Office of Technology Assessment, Congress of the United States (Washington, D.C.: Government Printing Office, June 1977), pp. VI-35–42.

4. Warren Donnelly, et al., Updated "Issue Briefs" on Foreign Nuclear Programs, Environment and Natural Resources Policy Division, Congressional Research Service (Washington, D.C.: US Library of Congress, 1987).

5. *Sunday Times* (London), October 5, 1986, pp. 1–3.

6. Tom Gervasi, *America's War Machine: The Pursuit of Global Dominance* (New York: Grove Press, 1985), pp. 85, 88.

7. *Bulletin of the Atomic Scientists,* Vol. 43 No. 4 (May 1987), p. 57.

Martin E. Hellman, "Nuclear War: Inevitable or Preventable?"

1. "Theory of Probability," *Encyclopædia Britannica,* 1984 Ed., Vol. 14 (Chicago and London), p. 1105.

2. Richard A. Epstein, *The Theory of Gambling and Statistical Logic* (New York: Academic Press, 1977), p. 54.

3. Patrick Billingsley, *Probability and Measure,* 2nd Ed. (New York: Wiley Interscience, 1986), p. 485.

4. Robert F. Kennedy, *Thirteen Days: A Memoir of the Cuban Missile Crisis* (New York: Signet New American Library, 1969).

5. William L. Ury, *Beyond the Hotline* (Boston: Houghton Mifflin, 1985).

6. Jack Dennis, ed., *The Nuclear Almanac: Confronting the Atom in War and Peace* (Reading, Massachusetts: Addison-Wesley, 1984).

7. James McCartney, "Why Military Balks at Plans for War," *San Jose Mercury News* (San Jose, California), April 13, 1986, pp. 1, 7A.

8. Theodore Taylor, "Proliferation of Nuclear Weapons," article in this volume.

Global Thinking: Vision for the Future

Richard T. Roney, ed., "Beyond War: A New Way of Thinking"

1. Arnold J. Toynbee, *Mankind and Mother Earth* (Oxford: Oxford University Press, 1976).
2. Lester R. Brown, *State of the World 1987. A Worldwatch Report on Progress toward a Sustainable Society* (New York: W. W. Norton, 1987).
3. Bernard Lovell, *Emerging Cosmology* (New York: Columbia University Press, 1981).
4. Richard E. Leakey and Roger Lewin, *Origins: What New Discoveries Reveal about the Emergence of Our Species and Its Possible Future* (New York: E. P. Dutton, 1977).
5. Jacob Bronowski, *The Ascent of Man* (Boston: Little, Brown and Co., 1973).
6. Paul R. Ehrlich, *Extinctions: The Crisis and the Consequences of the Disappearances of Species* (New York: Random House, 1981).
7. *Yuri Gagarin* (Moscow: Novisti Press, 1977), pp. 14 and 17.
8. Russell Schweickart, "No Frames, No Boundaries," in *Island in Space: Prospectus for a New Idea*, United Nations Association (Canada: Agency Press, 1986), p. 10.
9. Abraham H. Maslow, *Toward a Psychology of Being* (New York: Van Nostrand Reinhold, 1968).
10. Jonas Salk, *Anatomy of Reality: Merging of Intuition and Reason* (New York: Columbia University Press, 1983).
11. Charles McC. Mathias, Jr., "Habitual Hatred — Unsound Policy," *Foreign Affairs,* Vol. 61 No. 5 (1983), pp. 1017–1030.
12. Sam Keen, *Faces of the Enemy: Reflections of the Hostile Imagination* (San Francisco: Harper and Row, 1986), pp. 20–85.

John M. Richardson, Jr., "Messages from Global Models about an Interdependent World"

1. Donella H. Meadows, John M. Richardson, Jr., and Gerhart Bruckmann, *Groping in the Dark: The First Decade of Global Modeling* (Chichester: John Wiley & Sons, 1982).
2. Aurelio Peccei, *The Human Quality* (Oxford: Pergamon, 1977).
3. Donella H. Meadows, "Lessons from Global Modeling and Modelers," *Futures,* Vol. 14 No. 2 (1982), pp. 113–114.
4. *The Global 2000 Report to the President* (Washington, D.C.: Government Printing Office, 1979).
5. Charles L. Hamrin, "The Impact of the China 2000 Study," *Global Perspective Quarterly* (Washington, D.C.: Global Studies Center, Winter 1987).
6. Gro H. Brundtland, "Norway's Prime Minister Believes New Approaches to Development Are Possible," *Tribute,* Vol. 1 No. 3 (1987), pp. 386–387.
7. The Hunger Project, *Ending Hunger: An Idea Whose Time Has Come* (New York: Praeger, 1985).
8. Donella H. Meadows, "Whole Earth Models and Systems," *Coevolution Quarterly,* Vol. 34 (Summer 1982), pp. 20–30.

9. Ruth Sivard, *World Military and Social Expenditures* (Washington, D.C.: World Priorities, 1986).

Anatoly A. Gromyko, "Security for All in the Nuclear Age"

1. Leo N. Tolstoy, *The Teachings of Jesus, Complete Works,* Paul I. Biryukov, ed., Vol. 15 (Moscow: Prosrednika, 1912).
2. Günter Kunz, *The Environment: Industry and the Environment — Friends Forever, Discussions,* in German (Munich: Deutscher Taschenbuch Verlag, 1983), p. 161.
3. Kunz, p. 164.
4. Kunz, pp. 26–27.
5. Kunz, pp. 46–47.

Ales Adamovich, "Problems with the New Way of Thinking"

1. *Friendship of Peoples,* No. 10 (1984), p. 174.
2. *Literaturnaya Gazeta,* November 5, 1986.
3. Interview in the journal *Problems of Philosophy,* No. 4, (1986).

Process of Change: Individual Action and Collective Transformation

I. Survival as the Superordinate Goal

Kenneth E. Boulding, "Moving from Unstable to Stable Peace"

1. Adam Smith, *The Wealth of Nations* (New York: Modern Library, 1939), pp. 657–658.
2. Kenneth E. Boulding, *Stable Peace* (Austin: University of Texas Press, 1978).
3. Karl Deutsch, et al., *Political Community and the North Atlantic Area* (Princeton, N.J.: Princeton University Press, 1957), pp. 5–7.

Alexander I. Nikitin, "The Concept of Universal Security: A Revolution of Thinking and Policy in the Nuclear Age"

1. Yevgeni I. Chazov, Leonid A. Ilyin, and Angelina K. Guskova, *Nuclear War: The Medical and Biological Consequences, Soviet Physicians' Viewpoint,* English text edited by Boris Lunkov (Moscow: Novosti Press, 1984).
2. Yevgeni Velikhov, ed., *The Night After: Climatic and Biological Consequences of Nuclear War,* Prepared by the Soviet Scientists' Committee for the Defense of Peace against the Nuclear Threat, translated into English by Anatoli Rosenzweig (Moscow: Mir Publishers, 1985).
3. *Common Security: A Program of Disarmament,* Report of the International Commission on Disarmament and Security Issues, under the chairmanship of Olof Palme (Moscow: Progress Publishers, 1982).
4. *Common Security,* p. 190.
5. *Common Security,* p. 205.
6. Jimmy Carter, *Keeping Faith* (London: Collins, 1982), p. 249.

Andrei Y. Melville, "Nuclear Revolution and the New Way of Thinking"

1. Georgi Shakhnazarov, "The Logic of the Nuclear Era," *XXth Century and Peace,* April 1984.
2. Ralph White, *Fearful Warriors: A Psychological Profile of U.S.-Soviet Relations* (New York: Free Press, 1984).
3. Robert Jervis, *The Illogic of American Nuclear Strategy* (Ithaca and London: Cornell University Press, 1984).
4. Robert Lifton, *The Future of Immortality* (New York: Basic Books, 1987).
5. Jerome Frank, *Sanity and Survival: Psychological Aspects of War and Peace* (New York: Random House, 1982).
6. John Mack, "Resistance to Knowing in the Nuclear Age," *Harvard Educational Review,* August 4, 1984.
7. Hans Morgenthau, "The Fallacy of Thinking Conventionally about Nuclear Weapons," in David Carlton and Carlo Schaerf, eds., *Arms Control and Technological Innovation* (New York: International School on Disarmament and Research on Conflicts, 1976).
8. Steven Kull, "Nuclear Nonsense," *Foreign Policy,* Vol. 58 (Spring 1985), pp. 28–52.

Robert Axelrod, "The Evolution of Cooperation"

1. Ian Hay, *The First Hundred Thousand* (London: Wm. Blackwood, 1916).
2. John H. Morgan, *Leaves from a Field Note-Book* (London: Macmillan, 1916).
3. Robert Gilpin, *War and Change in World Politics* (Cambridge: Cambridge University Press, 1981).

II. Resistance to Change

Natalia P. Bekhtereva, "Dangers and Opportunities for Change from a Physiologist's Point of View"

1. Natalia P. Bekhtereva and D. K. Kambarova, "SMPF — Key to Understanding Emotions," *Science and Mankind,* Annual International Edition, 1985, pp. 41–49.
2. Natalia P. Bekhtereva and D. K. Kambarova, "Neurophysiology of Emotions, and Some General Brain Mechanisms," in *Individual Differences in Movement,* a collection by Bruce Kirkcaldy, ed. (Lancaster and Boston, The Haage Dordressht: MTP Press, Ltd., 1985), pp. 169–192.
3. Natalia P. Bekhtereva, *The Healthy and Unhealthy Human Brain* (Leningrad: Press House Nauka, 1980).
4. Natalia P. Bekhtereva, *The Neurophysiological Aspect of Human Mental Activity,* 2nd Ed. (New York: Oxford University Press, 1978).
5. Natalia P. Bekhtereva, Iuri L. Golitzin, Iuri D. Kropotov, and Medvedev, *Neurophysiological Mechanisms of Thinking* (Leningrad: Press House Nauka, 1985).

Jerome D. Frank and Andrei Y. Melville, "The Image of the Enemy and the Process of Change"

1. Sam Keen, *Faces of the Enemy: Reflections of the Hostile Imagination* (San Francisco: Harper and Row, 1986).

2. *Gallup Poll: Public Opinion, 1959–1971, Vol. III* (New York: Random House, 1972), p. 2015.

3. Jamie Kalven, "A Talk with Louis Harris," *Bulletin of the Atomic Scientists,* Vol. 38 No. 7 (September 1982), pp. 3–5.

4. I. Ahmad and J. Hasmi, *World Peace through Improved Perception and Understanding.* Proceedings of the Thirty-Second Pugwash Conference on Science and World Affairs. Warsaw, Poland, August 26–31, 1982 (Basingstoke, England: Taylor & Francis, 1982).

5. Herbert C. Kelman, ed., *International Behavior. A Socio-psychological Analysis* (New York: Holt, Rinehart & Winston, 1965).

6. Muzafer Sherif and Carolyn W. Sherif, *In Common Predicament: Social Psychology of Intergroup Conflict and Cooperation* (Boston: Houghton Mifflin, 1966).

7. Deborah Shapley, "Pax Antarctica," *Bulletin of the Atomic Scientists,* Vol. 40 No. 6 (June–July 1984), pp. 30–33.

Steven Kull, "Nuclear Reality: Resistance and Adaptation"

1. Hans Morgenthau, "The Fallacy of Thinking Conventionally about Nuclear Weapons," in David Carlton and Carlo Schaerf, eds., *Arms Control and Technological Innovation* (New York: Wiley, 1976) pp. 256–264.

2. Robert Jervis, *The Illogic of American Nuclear Strategy* (Ithaca, New York: Cornell University Press, 1984).

3. "Prepared Text of Reagan's Speech on Central America," *New York Times,* May 10, 1984.

4. Casper Weinberger, *DOD Annual Report FY 1984* (Washington, D.C.: Government Printing Office, 1983) p. 19.

5. Quoted in Strobe Talbott, *Deadly Gambits* (New York: Alfred A. Knopf, 1984) p. 28.

6. Quoted in John Lewis Gaddis, *Strategies of Containment* (Oxford: Oxford University Press, 1982) p. 321.

7. Nikolai V. Ogarkov, *Always in Readiness to Defend the Homeland* (Moscow: Voenizdat, 1982), translated in Soviet Press Selected Translations, November–December, 1982 (US Air Force Publications), p. 323.

8. *Department of State Bulletin,* Vol. 86 No. 2106 (January 1986), p. 8.

9. Alexander L. George, "Crisis Management: International Political and Military Considerations," *Survival,* Vol. 26 No. 5 (1984), pp. 223–234.

III. Bringing New Thinking to Life: Building Public Support

Everett M. Rogers, "Diffusion of the Idea of Beyond War"

1. Everett M. Rogers, *Diffusion of Innovations* (New York: Free Press, 1983).

DATE DUE

Demco, Inc. 38-293